*Amidst the hysteria surrounding cyberbullying and sexting, Hinduja and Patchin represent a sane, sensible voice that helps us all better understand these phenomena and what is really happening here. This book is filled with useful information and practical tips for those who seek to create positive school climates where bullying of all kinds is minimized. Every educator should buy it and read it.*

—Kevin Jennings
Former Assistant Deputy Secretary of Education

*Working with schools around the country, I know firsthand how much pressure there is to find an "answer" to bullying in schools, whether because of recent laws mandating programs and training or the community demanding answers. It's hard to know what resource is best. It's especially confusing because a bullying-prevention industry has bloomed to take advantage of this need but so many of these programs lack content based on a realistic analysis. I'm not at all surprised that Justin Patchin and Sameer Hinduja have created the resource all schools should use in* School Climate 2.0, *either to meet the new legal requirements or truly do the hard and comprehensive work of creating a culture of dignity in a school. From understanding the true dynamics of cyberbullying, to outlining a common-sense strategic plan for educators that will work with their individual community,* School Climate 2.0 *to my mind is really the most important resource currently available. I will more than strongly advise every school I work with to use this book. Say it this way: if I could make* School Climate 2.0 *mandatory reading for every school administrator in the country, I would.*

—Rosalind Wiseman
Author, *Queen Bees and Wannabes*

*Blaming technology is easy. Addressing the socio-cultural dynamics that shape young people's lives is hard. Yet, to address hard problems like bullying and sexting, this is precisely what we need to do. In* School Climate 2.0 *Sameer Hinduja and Justin W. Patchin flesh out the relationship between technologically mediated issues and school climate before offering valuable strategies for educators and community members to address problems in their schools. Both grounded and practical, this is a must-read for all who are scratching their heads about how to prevent bullying and sexting.*

—danah boyd, PhD
Senior Researcher, Microsoft Research

*By cutting through all the media hype and speculation, Hinduja and Patchin present an accurate and helpful analysis of issues related to young people's use of technology. By pointing out that the vast majority of youth are using technology safely and responsibly, they're able to focus on the real issues, the real problems, and the kids who need our help. By basing their advice on rigorous research, they are able to come up with strategies that are effective and appropriate. I'm especially pleased that the authors focus on social norms and school climate by sharing insights into how the overall climate of a school affects the behavior of everyone in it.*

—Larry Magid
Technology Journalist and Internet Safety Advocate

*This is an immensely helpful and well-sourced book. It gives a thorough introduction to adolescents' use of new technologies and sexting and cyberbullying. It makes a strong case that school climate is a vital factor in regulating these abuses. There are excellent chapters on how practical intervention strategies can be implemented in schools. It will be a great resource for teachers, educators, and parents.*

—Peter K. Smith
Emeritus Professor, Unit for School and Family Studies
Goldsmiths, University of London, UK

*A rarely seen compendium of school strategies that have worked,* School Climate 2.0 *moves past the headlines to offer a textured discussion of what we really need to strengthen school culture and improve teens' and schools' relationships to social media.*

—Rachel Simmons
Author, *Odd Girl Out*

*Sameer Hinduja and Justin Patchin remind us early on that, contrary to most media hype, most young people use their ubiquitous technologies safely and responsibly the majority of the time. Then, they discuss how a positive school climate is fundamental for all of learning and teaching. They share innovative, pragmatic strategies to enhance climate and thereby foster a better social environment— which will reduce behavioral problems offline and online among youth. This very readable, very user-friendly book should be considered mandatory for all preservice teacher education programs and be used as a guide for planning ongoing inservice training as schools prepare to better meet the needs of their 21st century students.*

—Mike Donlin
Cyberbullying and Digital Safety Consultant

*While Sameer Hinduja and Justin Patchin have a history of providing leadership in solid research and effective outreach on issues of youth risk in a digital age, in this book they have massively out-done their past excellence. Grounded in the understanding that the majority of young people make good choices online and effectively handle the negative situations that do occur, but that a minority of young people are at higher risk, Hinduja and Patchin craft recommendations for a positive school climate approach to help all young people learn to make good choices and assist their peers.*

—Nancy Willard
Director, Center for Safe and Responsible Internet Use

*Finally, a book that takes a holistic approach to the cyberbullying problem! There is no dividing line between school and home when it comes to the ways members of this generation relate to one another. A positive school climate can only help create a more positive home environment, and vice versa. This book gives readers specific guidance regarding how to prevent cyberbullying, sexting, and other problematic online behaviors.*

—John Halligan
Motivational Speaker, Ryan's Story Presentation LTD

*"This book will help administrators lead their schools to form and keep policies that reduce or elimi-nate cyberbullying."*

—Brigitte Tennis,
Headmistress, Stella Schola Middle School, Redmond, WA

SAMEER HINDUJA | JUSTIN W. PATCHIN

# SCHOOL CLIMATE 2.0

Preventing
**CYBERBULLYING**
and
**SEXTING**
One Classroom
at a Time

**CORWIN**
A SAGE Company

## CORWIN
A SAGE Company

FOR INFORMATION

Corwin
A SAGE Company
2455 Teller Road
Thousand Oaks, California 91320
(800) 233-9936
www.corwin.com

SAGE Publications Ltd.
1 Oliver's Yard
55 City Road
London, EC1Y 1SP
United Kingdom

SAGE Publications India Pvt. Ltd.
B 1/I 1 Mohan Cooperative Industrial Area
Mathura Road, New Delhi
India 110 044

SAGE Publications Asia-Pacific Pte. Ltd.
3 Church Street
#10-04 Samsung Hub
Singapore 049483

Acquisitions Editor: Debra Stollenwerk
Associate Editor: Desirée A. Bartlett and
                  Joanna Coelho
Editorial Assistant: Kimberly Greenberg
Project Editor: Veronica Stapleton
Copy Editor: Paula L. Fleming
Typesetter: Hurix Systems Pvt. Ltd.
Proofreader: Kristin Bergstad
Indexer: Molly Hall
Cover Designer: Rose Storey
Permissions Editor: Adele Hutchinson

Printed in the United States of America

*Library of Congress Cataloging-in-Publication Data*

Hinduja, Sameer, 1978-
School climate 2.0 : preventing cyberbullying and sexting one classroom at a time / Sameer Hinduja, Justin W. Patchin.

p. cm.

Includes bibliographical references and index.

ISBN 978-1-4129-9783-6 (pbk.)

1. Bullying in schools—Prevention.
2. Cyberbullying—Prevention. 3. Classroom environment. I. Patchin, Justin W., 1977- II. Title.

LB3013.3.H568 2012

371.5'8—dc23

2011052601

This book is printed on acid-free paper.

SUSTAINABLE FORESTRY INITIATIVE
Certified Chain of Custody
Promoting Sustainable Forestry
www.sfiprogram.org
SFI-01268
SFI label applies to text stock

13  14  15  16  10 9 8 7 6 5 4 3 2

# Contents

Additional materials and resources related to *School Climate 2.0: Preventing Cyberbullying and Sexting One Classroom at a Time* can be found at http://www.schoolclimate20.com

# *Preface*

*Many schools are buying expensive antibullying curriculum packages, big glossy binders that look reassuring on the bookshelf and technically place schools closer to compliance with the new laws. But our research on child development makes it clear that there is only one way to truly combat bullying. As an essential part of the school curriculum, we have to teach children how to be good to one another, how to cooperate, how to defend someone who is being picked on, and how to stand up for what is right.*

—Senior Lecturer Susan Engel and Professor Marlene Sandstrom, psychology, Williams College, Massachusetts

For the last ten years, we have been exploring the online lives of adolescents: the good, the bad, and everything in between. Advances in technology have revolutionized the way teens communicate, learn, and interact. Our research has taught us that, despite what the media might have us believe, most of what teens are doing online is very positive. The vast majority of adolescents use technology safely and responsibly the vast majority of the time. However, some do make mistakes or use technology in ways that create significant problems for themselves or others. Cyberbullying and sexting are examples of two such problems that receive a significant amount of media attention. As you will learn in this book, these behaviors are not at epidemic levels, but at the same time they should not be ignored. So what can you do?

This book seeks to explain and promote the importance of school climate in preventing teen technology misuse. Most of books and articles in print today simply describe the nature of cyberbullying or sexting (e.g., what it looks like, how much of it is occurring, and among whom). While this is an important first step, we seek to meaningfully build on the knowledge base and more explicitly connect the high-tech behaviors of teens to the school environment.

Much of what you will read is based on information we have learned through our decade-long exploration of the ways teens are using and misusing technology. We have completed seven formal independent studies involving over 12,000 students from over 80 middle and high schools from different regions of the United States. To guide the discussion, this book specifically features information from our most recent study, a random sample of over 4,400 middle and high school students (11 to 18 years old) from one of the largest school districts in the United States. Surveys were administered to students in 2010, and the information gathered represents some of the most recent and comprehensive data on these topics. We will also refer to the work of many others who have labored to better understand how adolescents use, misuse, and abuse these technologies.

In addition to the quantitative data collected, we have also informally spoken to thousands of teens, parents, educators, law enforcement officers, and countless other adults who work directly with youth. Our observations are essentially a reflection of their experiences. During these interactions, we have been fortunate to learn from those on the front lines about what they are dealing with, what is working, and what problems they are running into. The stories we hear are largely consistent with the data we and others have collected that will be presented throughout this text. We also receive numerous emails and phone calls on a weekly basis from educators, mental health professionals, parents, and other youth-serving adults looking for help with specific issues. These conversations help us to understand and consider the problem from a variety of angles and perspectives. All of the stories included in this book are real. In some cases the language has been modified slightly to fix spelling and grammar mistakes and improve readability, but the overall messages have not been changed.

## IMPORTANT FEATURES OF THE BOOK

This book not only concisely boils down the latest available research on cyberbullying and sexting in a manner relevant and accessible to you, but—more importantly—strives to provide you with a road map for developing a positive climate at your school to reduce teen technology misuse. To reinforce the key concepts, there are a number of valuable in-text features, including the following:

- Breakout boxes with important concepts explained in detail
- Illustrations to help illuminate specific strategies
- Views from educators who understand the power of a positive school climate
- Discussion questions after each chapter

- "Prevention Points" in each chapter that highlight significant points
- Chapter summaries
- Index

In addition to these valuable resources, we also have put a number of extras on the companion website at www.schoolclimate20.com. These include the following:

- Online quizzes for each chapter
- A Twitter feed and Facebook Fan Page with new Prevention Points you can put into action at your school
- Success stories from those on the front lines
- Emerging best practices in school climate research and evaluation
- New downloadable activities and worksheets
- Supplemental staff development questions
- Questions to facilitate further discussion and follow-up among your students
- Featured case studies

Resources will be added and continuously updated on the site, so visit often!

## BREAKDOWN OF CHAPTERS

Before we can dive into the details of *School Climate 2.0*, it is essential to build a solid foundation of understanding the online behaviors of adolescents. In Chapter 1 we begin the discussion by focusing on the intersection of teens and technology and how the inseparability of adolescents from their high-tech devices affects, and is influenced by, what is going on at school. In Chapter 2, we outline the characteristics of a positive school climate along with some of the beneficial outcomes associated with such an environment.

In Chapter 3 we detail the nature of bullying in the 21st century. In many ways the bullying of today is very similar to the way it was when we were growing up. But technology has enabled would-be bullies to extend their reach, resulting in many significant challenges for educators, parents, and others who are working to resolve relationship problems. *Cyberbullying*, which we define as *willful and repeated harm inflicted through the use of computers, cell phones, and other electronic devices*, typically refers to incidents in which students threaten, humiliate, or otherwise hassle their peers through malicious text messages, web pages, or postings on Facebook or YouTube. It is clear that peer harassment that occurs on school grounds is a significant threat to a positive school climate. That said, *online* bullying also disrupts the ability of students to feel safe and secure at school. The vast majority of the time, targets of cyberbullying know the person doing the bullying (85 percent of the time in our research), and most of the time the bully is someone from their school. If students regularly post hurtful, embarrassing, or threatening messages to a fellow classmate's Facebook page, for example, it unquestionably affects that student's ability to feel comfortable, free, and safe to focus on learning at school.

Chapter 4 describes *sexting*, which we define as *the sending or receiving of sexually explicit or sexually suggestive nude or seminude images or video* that generally occurs via cell phone (although it can also occur via the Web). Some have described this problem in dismissive ways, calling it this generation's way of "flirting" or characterizing it as a safer way to experiment sexually and come to terms with one's own sexuality. While this may be true in part, engaging in sexting can lead to some significant social and legal consequences.

We begin to tie everything together in Chapter 5, where we explicitly link school climate to online misbehaviors. Here again we argue that schools with better climates will see fewer cyberbullying, sexting, or other online problems among students. Ancillary benefits for educators who harness the power of a positive climate at school may include better attendance, higher school achievement, and more cooperative attitudes across the student body and among staff. A school with a positive climate is definitely more enjoyable to work and learn in, and can therefore lead to many other beneficial outcomes for students and staff alike. The remaining chapters of the book focus on providing you with strategies to establish and maintain a positive climate (Chapter 6) through peer mentoring and social norming (Chapter 7), assessment (Chapter 8), and appropriate response strategies (Chapter 9).

# *Acknowledgments*

We are particularly proud of this book and hope that it conveys knowledge and strategies that can make a meaningful difference in improving schools. That is what we are all about; we believe that you picked this up because you feel the same. Just as you need the assistance of others at your school to promote a positive climate, we have needed the assistance of a number of important individuals in our personal and professional lives to move the ideas from our heads onto these pages.

We are first and foremost very grateful to have supportive families who have nurtured and inspired us over the years. We would also like to convey appreciation to our professional colleagues who stand alongside us on the front lines of online safety issues among youth. In particular, we thank those who contributed their insights and experiences to this volume. They include Lissa Albert, Steve Bollar, Alan Chmiel, Alison Trachtman Hill, Nathan Jeffrey, Barry Kamrath, Amanda Lenhart, Kim Mazauskas, Gary McDaniel, Allyson Pereira, Mark Trachtenbroit, and Derek Waterstreet. We also thank Charley Nelson and the Jostens Renaissance program for showing us what a good school climate can look like.

In addition, the Office of Research and Sponsored Programs at the University of Wisconsin–Eau Claire and the Division of Research at Florida Atlantic University provided valuable financial assistance to our research efforts, which allows our ideas to be substantiated in part by data. We would also like to thank the staff at Corwin and SAGE Publications for working with us to produce a book that will help educators tackle some of the challenging problems created by the misuse of technology.

Finally, we would like to thank God for giving us the opportunities and abilities to make a positive difference in the lives of adolescents. We are very blessed to truly love what we do.

# PUBLISHER'S ACKNOWLEDGMENTS

Corwin would like to thank the following individuals for taking the time to provide their editorial insight:

Carol S. Cash, Assistant Professor
Virginia Polytechnic Institute and State University
Blacksburg, VA

Ann Dargon, Superintendent
Ashland
Wareham, MA

Tonia Guidry, Teacher
Golden Meadow Middle School
Golden Meadow, LA

Brigitte Tennis, Headmistress
Stella Schola Middle School
Redmond, WA

# *About the Authors*

**Sameer Hinduja,** PhD, is an Associate Professor in the School of Criminology and Criminal Justice at Florida Atlantic University (FAU). He is recognized internationally for his groundbreaking work on the subjects of cyberbullying and safe social networking. He works with the US Department of Education and many state departments of education to improve their policies and programming related to teen technology misuse. He has written four books, and his interdisciplinary research is widely published in a number of peer-reviewed academic journals. Dr. Hinduja received his PhD from Michigan State University. At FAU, he has been named both Researcher of the Year and Teacher of the Year, the two highest honors across the university.

**Justin W. Patchin,** PhD, is an Associate Professor of Criminal Justice at the University of Wisconsin, Eau Claire. He received his PhD from Michigan State University. For over ten years he has been exploring the intersection of teens and technology, with particular focus on cyberbullying, social networking, and sexting. He travels around the country training educators, counselors, law enforcement officers, parents, and youth on how to prevent and address the consequences of cyberbullying. Dr. Patchin has written four books and numerous articles on adolescent behaviors online. He has presented at the White House and the FBI Academy and has appeared on CNN, on NPR, and in the *New York Times* to discuss issues related to teens' use and misuse of technology.

Dr. Hinduja and Dr. Patchin co-direct the Cyberbullying Research Center (www.cyberbullying.us) and authored *Bullying Beyond the Schoolyard: Preventing and Responding to Cyberbullying* (also with Corwin), which was named Educator Book of the Year by ForeWord Reviews.

# 1

## Teens, Technology, and Trouble

*Our students are always online and always on their phones, and some of them are misusing technology in pretty bad ways. And it's affecting what we're trying to accomplish at our school. We've set numerous rules, and outlined a number of sanctions—some of which are severe. We've implemented blocks and filters. But I feel these strategies are piecemeal. There has got to be a better approach. There has got to be something else we can do.*

—educator from Florida

### THE STORY OF SAM

Awkward-looking, skinny, tremendously introverted, and simply not popular, Sam found growing up difficult. He couldn't hold eye contact with anyone; he couldn't talk to girls; and he spent a great deal of his time outside of school reading, studying, and playing with computers. He was the quintessential nerd. But don't be misled. Sam wanted to be popular. He wanted to wear the cool clothes; attract the attention of the cute cheerleaders; be strong and tough and confident; and display charm, wit, and humor at all times. But it didn't happen. And so Sam muddled his way through elementary and junior high school, often the victim of both benign and malicious bullying, and just did his best to keep growing up. One particular instance vividly stands out in his mind.

The year was 1991. Sam was in eighth grade and was excited about wrapping up the school year and moving on to high school, where things might open up for him in terms of a social life and popularity. It could definitely happen, he thought to himself! In his physical education (PE) class, he was finally beginning to gain a little more confidence in himself, and he enjoyed casually chatting with one of the prettiest girls in the school—also an eighth grader. Well, it turned out that one of the sixth-grade guys who was also in that PE class had over the course of the quarter developed a crush on her . . . and had actually asked her "out"—and she had accepted. So, they were together. Sam didn't think to modify his casual chatting behavior with the girl, which—in the sixth grader's eyes—apparently was a threat to his blossoming romantic relationship. And so Sam was made fun of, and called names, and threatened, and disrespected, and embarrassed, and mistreated by the sixth grader and his friends—all classic forms of bullying.

Sam did his best to shrug off the verbal assault when it came and thought that the sixth grader would soon tire and move on to someone else. But he didn't. Instead—straight out of a Saturday morning movie—the other boy challenged Sam to a fight at the flagpole after school. Sam had to show up—he was attempting to embrace a new image as he transitioned into high school, and it was necessary to leave behind any semblance of being a wimp. In addition, almost everyone in his PE class had heard about the challenge, and he could not lose face. The challenger was a sixth grader, for crying out loud! Even though the other boy was two years younger, he was physically bigger and stronger, so Sam steeled his nerves and tried to chase away the fear by psyching himself up. He could do this. And so he did—he met the sixth grader at the flagpole after the final school bell had rung that afternoon.

And Sam got the living crap beat out of him.

For many reasons, it was an instructive incident for Sam—who, by the way, is actually Sameer, one of the authors of this book. It was the last major experience with bullying that he had—partly due to his growing self-confidence, and partly due to a more mature high school culture where everyone was pretty much doing their own thing. He was lucky. Some adolescents continue to experience bullying into high school and beyond. Or even worse, some don't make it that far.

## WHAT WOULD HAPPEN TO SAM TODAY?

As we began to write this book, we thought a lot about what might have transpired between the sixth grader and Sameer had computers and cell phones had been as ubiquitous as they are today. We wondered how he might have been cyberbullied given the very same circumstances. It is possible that the sixth grader would have circulated malicious statements via text messaging about Sameer's race, the way he physically looked, the clothes and shoes and length of socks he wore, his "nerdiness," and his "wimpiness." In addition, many students frequented a Facebook "Fan Page" devoted to his junior high school; the sixth grader could have posted comments viciously insulting him and his motives. Using his smartphone, he could have taken a picture of Sameer in the locker room wearing only his underwear and then sent it via Twitter to the rest of the student body.

These behaviors would likely have occurred right alongside the bullying that was going on at school. That's because what happens online is often happening at school; research has shown that most cyberbullies are generally not strangers but peers from school.[1] So all of this begs the question: Why *did* it happen, and why *does* it happen? One of the big-picture reasons we keep coming back to has to do with the environment in which students learn, interact, and simply exist at school.

If you'll travel back in time with us, you'll recall that you did better in classes, grades, and schools where you felt safe, secure, noticed, supported, cared for, encouraged, caught up in school spirit, and a part of something bigger and grander than yourself—a "community" to which you really belonged. Sameer didn't have that growing up in middle school. When he was targeted, he didn't know what to do. He didn't know where to go for help. And his school environment was one in which bullying seemed commonplace, and the potential for being victimized in some way or another was in the back of his mind every day. It wasn't encouraged or condoned by administration, but no meaningful efforts were made to build an atmosphere where peer respect was extremely cool and peer harassment was deemed completely uncool. No attempts were made to intentionally create a social movement to get everyone (administrators, educators, staff, students, and even parents) on board to share the load of promoting positive interactions and heart-level acceptance of each other. It just wasn't happening, perhaps because it wasn't a priority and perhaps because other tasks were deemed more important.

> **Prevention Point**: Technology is a double-edged sword that should not be wielded carelessly.

Sameer's experience was not unique back then, nor is it out of the ordinary to see in schools today. However, a lot has changed in just one generation in terms of how students learn and communicate with friends and teachers. Technological interaction has become as ubiquitous today as Teenage Mutant Ninja Turtles lunch boxes were when we were growing up. For the most part, this is a good thing. The Internet and cell phones allow students to connect and interact with people and content in ways previously unimaginable. But technology is a double-edged sword that should not be wielded carelessly. Cyberbullying and sexting are just two examples of ways some teens misuse technology. Before detailing these problems, it is important to better understand the full extent to which students have embraced high-tech devices.

## TEENS AND TECHNOLOGY

More teenagers in the United States are going online than ever before. Data from the Pew Internet & American Life Project show that 95 percent of those aged 12 to 17 use the Internet.[2] Over 11 million youth go online every single day. Almost three-fourths of teens have a desktop computer, and 18 percent have a laptop. The vast majority (93 percent) go online with their desktop or laptop computer, though an increasing number are accessing the Internet with their cell phones, gaming consoles, and portable gaming devices. Over three-quarters of teenagers have a broadband (high-speed) connection to the Internet at home.[3] As of spring 2011, 76 percent of all teens between the ages of 12 and 17 used online social networking sites, an increase from 58 percent in 2007.[4]

Cell phones, too, have become an efficient way for teens to communicate, surf, and contribute to discussions while on the go. The combination of mobility, the ability to initiate communication at any time (e.g., during periods of emergency or boredom), the decreasing cost of ownership, and continual (and remarkable) improvements in technological capabilities have made cell phones "must-have" devices for teens and adults alike. The most fundamental benefit is that individuals can make or receive calls from almost any location to almost any other location. According to the Pew report, approximately 77 percent of teens owned cell phones in spring 2011.[5]

Of course most cell phones today can do much more than make simple voice calls. They can be used to send and receive text messages (also known as short-message service [SMS] or "texts"). Among teens who own a cell phone, 88 percent say they have sent a text message to another's phone, and 54 percent do it daily.[6] In fact, two-thirds of teens who text say they are more likely to reach out to friends in that manner, rather than talking to them via a voice call. Many teens text others quite regularly: 28 percent send 11–50 texts a day, 16 percent send 51–100, and 31 percent send 100 or more texts every single day—more than 3,400 texts per month in 2011. Girls send and receive about 132 texts per day, while boys send and receive around 94.[7]

In addition to allowing calling and texting, many cell phones can serve as personal digital assistants and provide a host of services such as Internet and email connectivity; games; digital camera functionality; contact information storage; digital music and video player; two-way walkie-talkie; calculator; calendar; appointment reminders; to-do lists;

alarms; integration with home security systems, appliances, and vehicles; and pretty much anything else you can imagine (there's an app for that!). Teens seem to be very interested in taking full advantage of all of the features that their mobile devices offer. According to Pew,[8]

- 83 percent have taken pictures;
- 64 percent have exchanged pictures;
- 54 percent have recorded video;
- 32 percent have exchanged video;
- 31 percent have used instant messaging;
- 27 percent have used the Internet;
- 23 percent have used use social networking sites; and
- 21 percent have sent email.

It is clear that many adolescents are no longer dependent on a desktop or laptop computer as their mobile phones can do many of the same things. Regardless of whether an individual takes advantage of one, some, or all of their capabilities, cell phones have become the most ubiquitous device of the 21st century thus far.

Internet-enabled devices like computers and cell phones allow adolescents to engage in a host of positive activities. For example, they can conduct research for schoolwork online, communicate with friends in real time, play games, and engage in a number of other pro-social activities. These benefits have in part contributed to their proficiency and comfort with these devices and are an integral part of almost all of their day-to-day activities. If you are raising a teen, you know he or she seems surgically attached to the phone and is pretty much always checking, sending, and posting messages, comments, pictures, and the like—for the primary purpose of socializing and keeping up to date with all that is going on.

Technology puts access to unlimited amounts of information, the ability to entertain yourself, and the ability to quickly and easily communicate with others at your fingertips. Online participation also teaches youth various social and emotional skills that are essential to successfully navigate life. For example, cyberspace provides a venue for identity formation and exploration, opportunities to be introduced to new and different worldviews and opinions, and moments to refine critical-thinking and decision-making skills. Directly and indirectly, youth are reaping a number of extremely important educational, affective, developmental, and relational benefits by embracing and exploiting all that technology has to offer.

## TECHNOLOGY IN SCHOOLS

Computers have long been a fixture in many American schools. Indeed, we had computers in our middle schools in the late 1980s. And when we visit schools today—large and small, rural and urban—they (of course) all have computers. Many schools have computer labs or general-access machines in libraries or other common areas. In addition, many classrooms have their own computer(s), and teachers regularly use various technologies to deliver educational content or enhance instruction. Some schools have even provided laptops to each individual student ("one-to-one" schools). While there is some debate about whether these programs are worth the money, it is clear that technology is a big part of education.[9]

Despite the close connection between schools and technology, many districts have balked at allowing students to bring in their own devices. Many schools prohibit the use, or even display, of mobile devices (especially cell phones) during school hours, while some allow use during specified periods (e.g., during lunch or between classes). We have received many phone calls from administrators who are considering opening up their schools to student-owned mobile devices because of the headaches associated with attempting to keep them out and the positives that may accompany using them to help kids learn. According to a report published by Walden University, "Teachers who use technology frequently . . . report greater benefits to student learning, engagement and skills from technology than teachers who spend less time using technology to support learning."[10]

To be sure, allowing students to bring their devices to school holds much promise for furthering their education. Most schools do not have enough resources to provide a laptop or tablet for each student, and since many students already have a cell phone, tablet, or other portable device, few additional expenditures are required (e.g., the school can lend devices to the handful who don't own one). Once equipped, teachers can ask students to research particular questions using their devices. They can use audience response systems via clickers or cell phone live polling (e.g., Poll Everywhere) to assess student competency with certain concepts. They can assign creative, interactive projects using the camera functionality and photo- or video-sharing sites. Many teachers use Facebook and Twitter as supplemental instructional tools.[11] Indeed, one ninth-grade science teacher in Atlanta has even used the popular game Angry Birds to teach complicated physics principles.[12] The opportunities are as endless as the Web itself.

We love to see schools embrace technology to help students learn and to expand their educational horizons. Unfortunately, educators now also must deal with questionable, problematic, and even criminal behaviors perpetrated by teens via online technologies. However, you do not have to feel intimidated or discouraged from taking advantage of all technology has to offer at your school—as long as you do so in an informed and appropriate manner. This book seeks to help you along these lines.

## Delete Day

On May 6, 2011, The Mary Louis Academy in Jamaica Estates, New York, hosted a student-developed and student-led program called Delete Day. During Delete Day, 250 students came to the school's computer room during their lunch or unscheduled period. Once there, service-homeroom students helped participants do the following:

- Delete inappropriate pictures or comments from their Facebook pages.
- Delete "friends" whom they didn't know personally.
- Delete personal information that could be dangerous to share.
- Delete their membership in groups that might be hurtful or offensive.
- Delete Formspring pages.*

At each computer station was a "Delete Day Pledge" for the participant to sign and take home, as well as a comment card that solicited information, ideas, and reactions about the student's experience at the event. Fifty-four percent of participants deleted friends and disengaged from certain Groups on Facebook, 21 percent deleted comments, 20 percent deleted photos, and 17 percent deleted personal information from their profiles. Forty-four students deleted their Formspring pages completely, and nine students deleted their entire Facebook profiles. Upon completion of her participation in Delete Day, each student was given a pin with the Delete Day logo (designed and assembled by the student leaders) and a cookie (baked by student leaders).

According to student organizers, the purpose of the event was "to offer members of the Mary Louis community the opportunity to delete pictures, information, or other content from the Internet that may prove hurtful, offensive, or dangerous." Their motto for the event was "IT IS TIME TO TAKE RESPONSIBILITY. IT IS TIME TO TAKE ACTION. IT IS TIME TO DELETE!"

While no piece of the program was formally dedicated to cell phone usage, the leaders of and participants in Delete Day were invested in making all of their digital connections with others reflective of their best selves. The commitment of the organizers and participants alike created a newfound dedication to and appreciation of the obligation and responsibility they have to themselves, one another, and their school. All of the participants came of their own volition and during their free or lunch periods, as they were excited to join the community of students who had volunteered their time to make a difference. It was the student organizers who pushed hardest to make Delete Day happen—even those seniors who had already been accepted to college and had finals, AP exams, and other activities competing for their time wanted to host this event—and it created an extremely high energy level at the school.

Delete Day is a program that can be done at any school. It takes education, dedication, commitment, and an organized effort on the part of students, faculty, and staff to engage with the issues facing their community and work on them together. As is clear from the success of the event at The Mary Louis Academy, student-led programs have the capacity to impact school climate in amazing and valuable ways.

—Alison M. Trachtman Hill, founder and managing partner
Critical Issues for Youth (http://ci4y.com)

*Students decided to delete their Formspring pages completely (rather than solely remove inappropriate content) because they felt that everything on their Formspring pages was cruel, hostile, and unkind.

## Why Schools Must Respond to Cyberbullying and Sexting

We believe that schools across our nation should be sacred institutions for learning, where students feel secure and free to focus and interact without threat of harm or violence. School personnel are morally and legally obligated to provide a safe educational environment for all students—one that is free from discrimination. Title IX of the Educational Amendments of 1972 requires schools to prevent and address sexual harassment and sex discrimination, and its interpretation has been broadened in the decades since its passage.[13] It is safe to say that any form of discrimination occurring on campus that undermines a child's ability to feel safe and concentrate on learning must be addressed if it is made known to school officials. Not only is addressing such behavior mandated by law, but not dealing with it could lead to claims of negligence and financial liability (as well as reputational damage) if harm to a student occurred based on discrimination. It is important to remember that all forms of peer harassment—on a fundamental level—involve some type of discrimination. This could be discrimination based on how someone looks, dresses, acts, speaks, or simply "is." Youth can take the smallest difference and magnify it to cause drama, to build themselves up while tearing another down, or to indulge an impulse—in other words, just because they feel like it.

**Prevention Point**: Schools have a moral, ethical, and legal responsibility to prevent and respond to cyberbullying and sexting.

We remember that when we were in school that we couldn't wear T-shirts with inappropriate slogans or depictions. Occasionally, we heard of another student being sent to the principal's office and forced to wear the shirt inside out or made to wait until his parents brought another shirt to wear for the rest of the day. This might not seem like that big a deal, but there is logic behind these rules and actions. First, inappropriate content on T-shirts compromises the positive, safe, wholesome atmosphere that schools strive to provide. Second, such shirts can be offensive to other students and staff at school and therefore infringe upon their civil rights. The US Court of Appeals recently upheld a Tennessee school's decision to punish students for wearing Confederate flag T-shirts, agreeing with school administrators that the shirts would cause a substantial disruption among students and staff on campus.[14] Third, they unnecessarily attract negative attention and thereby distract students from learning. Schools, then, can respond to problematic content—or the behavior that creates such content—if its effects are detrimental to their purpose and goals. Such content and behavior range from inappropriate clothing all the way to severe forms of interpersonal harm. And this is just one way that a supportive environment can be fostered and institutionalized.

# TECHNOLOGY ISN'T THE PROBLEM

As much as this book is about the trouble teens can cause and get into when misusing technology, it must be made clear at the outset that *the vast majority of teens use technology safely and responsibly*. As you will learn in Chapter 3, approximately one in five teens admits to have participated in cyberbullying. Of course, this means that 80 percent of students have not bullied others online! Our research also shows that about 7 percent of students have sent a nude or seminude image of themselves to a classmate (see Chapter 4). Again, this means that 93 percent of students have not. Does this mean we should ignore these problems? Definitely not. Rather, it suggests that we should keep a sense of perspective. It also indicates that we need to approach these problems from a data-driven viewpoint—one informed by what research says about what teens are actually doing (see Chapter 8). We need to fully understand what electronic misbehaviors our students and children are involved in and be intentional and strategic in how we empower and educate them to do the right thing, both online and offline, no matter what.

To be clear, technology isn't the problem. There is nothing inherently problematic about cell phones; they are amazing devices that have revolutionized the way we communicate. Similarly, there is nothing fundamentally dangerous about Facebook. Social networking through that site has allowed interpersonal relationships to start, restart, and thrive, generating many emotional and psychological benefits. However, some will choose to use technological enhancements to cause harm to others or, intentionally or unintentionally, cause harm to themselves. This harm is often not physical—although there might be physical ramifications and side effects. Rather, it tends to manifest in less visible but possibly even more damaging ways. It is those behaviors that we should focus on—not the technology.

According to the US Centers for Disease Control and Prevention, motor vehicle crashes are the number one cause of death of teens. In 2009, approximately 3,000 teens died in car accidents.[15] Does this mean we should ban teens from driving? Of course not. But we do need to take steps to prevent accidents from happening, such as providing driver's education classes, encouraging parents to model appropriate driving habits, establishing safety guidelines, and so forth. The same approach needs to be taken with technology. You wouldn't just throw your teenager the keys to the family sedan and say, "Good luck and be safe!" But this is often what we do with technology: we assume that children will be safe and smart because we tell them to do so (or because they *had* to have heard and internalized all of the lessons from school and on the news!).

We need to be much more deliberate and comprehensive than that and regularly remind teens about issues they may run into. They are adolescents. How many times did you learn the lesson on the first go-around when you were a teenager? Probably not as often as you would like. Neither did we, so don't feel bad. This should serve to inspire us in the ways we deal with and instruct teens. Parents have to do this in their households, and we believe they bear the largest load when it comes to teaching their kids to use technology wisely. However, school personnel unquestionably share a good portion of the responsibility as well, since those kids are their captive audience for much of the day. Most schools now realize that they need to educate students about appropriate online behaviors and take steps to prevent students from misusing technology at school. Educators also know that what happens online—whether during school hours or on evenings and weekends—often directly impacts what happens *at school*. We propose that schools can take significant strides to prevent cyberbullying and sexting by developing and maintaining a positive, respectful, and nurturing classroom and school climate.

## THE POWER OF A POSITIVE SCHOOL CLIMATE

The National School Climate Center defines *school climate* as "the quality and character of school life. School climate is based on patterns of students', parents', and school personnel's experience of school life and reflects norms, goals, values, interpersonal relationships, teaching and learning practices, and organizational structures."[16] In general, a positive climate is one that engenders respect, cooperation, trust, and a shared responsibility for the educational goals that exist there. Educators, students, and *everyone* connected to the school consequently take ownership of the mission of the school and work together toward a shared vision. If a climate like this is established, everything else seems to fall into place. For instance, it will definitely lead to more academic success and greater educational exploration.

> *No one program, policy, or practice can address all of the reasons why young people harm themselves and others. No single strategy can prevent strangers or staff members from jeopardizing the well-being of students. The most prudent course of action for all schools is to address safety comprehensively.*
>
> —Daniel L. Duke, author of *Creating Safe Schools for All Children*[17]

More to the point of this book, though, is that there will be fewer problems at school and online, because students will not want to damage the positive relationships they have at school by doing anything that will disappoint or upset the educators or other students to whom they are strongly bonded.

"I am not going to post that online—Mrs. Smith is my favorite teacher and is really awesome and I don't want her to think badly of me!"

"I don't want my friends at school to think I was a moron for sending that message."

"I am totally going to keep my profile page clean, since everyone else at my school does it too."

"I don't want to miss out on any opportunities and fall behind my peers, and so I have *got* to build a positive online reputation!"

"I don't want to stand out for doing the wrong thing when everyone else is doing the right thing!"

We know that teens are more likely to be deterred from engaging in inappropriate behaviors by a fear of how their friends or family members (or others in their lives they look up to) might respond than by adult nagging. Indeed, we know from experience (and you will likely agree) that this deterrent effect is much stronger than laws, policies, and other rules. Therefore, by developing strong relationships between the school and students, among students themselves, and between the school and their families, this principle can be used to dissuade negative behaviors and encourage positive behaviors even when adults aren't around—such as when teens are online. And the vast majority are online, which has revolutionized the way they communicate and the way we have to handle behavioral problems.

## SUMMARY

We know that many youth have been the victim of cyberbullying or have done things to others that could be characterized as cyberbullying. We also know that some youth have sent and/or received sexually suggestive images of themselves or someone else to others, actions that could have substantial consequences. Finally, we know that all of these behaviors and experiences meaningfully affect the ability of students to learn and feel safe at school. As such, it is imperative that educators do what they can to prevent and effectively respond to the aforementioned behaviors so that a positive environment at school can be maintained. Moreover, as we will assert and affirm throughout this book, *educators who do establish a nurturing and caring classroom and school climate will make great strides in preventing a whole host of problematic behaviors, both at school and online.*

**Prevention Point:** A respectful climate at school will produce students who are safe, smart, honest, and responsible at school and online.

In addition to concisely detailing the scope, prevalence, and nature of cyberbullying and sexting, throughout this book we will encourage educators to marshal the powers of peer influence and the school environment to curtail these behaviors. We will also introduce and cover specific, pragmatic school climate initiatives that educators can implement in their schools. These include social norming, youth grassroots campaigns, peer mentoring, data-driven action plans, and multipronged policy and programming approaches by adults. Through these efforts, we hope to enlighten educators, parents, and teens about the tremendous importance of cultivating a positive school climate, not only to enhance student achievement, success, and productivity but also *to produce students who are safe, smart, honest, and responsible while using technology.*

## DISCUSSION QUESTIONS

1. Besides the ability to make a call from almost any location, what are some other benefits that teens derive from their mobile phones?

2. What are the risks and benefits of having students bring their own devices to your school? How do you minimize the risks and increase the benefits? Do the risks outweigh the benefits, or vice versa?

3. What misperceptions have adults historically had about teen behaviors that may negatively influence the way they address new technology problems?

4. In what positive ways are the Internet and electronic devices used in classrooms at your school? On the other hand, what are the most common problems or complications arising from this use?

5. If technology is not the problem and teen behavior with technology is, what behaviors warrant the most attention? Where should you even start?

## REFERENCES

1. R. M. Kowalski and S. P. Limber, "Electronic Bullying Among Middle School Students, *Journal of Adolescent Health* 41 (2007): S22–S30; S. C. McQuade III and N. Sampat, "Survey of Internet and At-Risk Behaviors," 2008, http://www.sparsa.org/res/research/SurveyOfInternet.pdf; J. Wolak, K. Mitchell, and D. Finkelhor, "Does Online Harassment Constitute Bullying? An Exploration of Online Harassment by Known Peers and Online-Only Contacts," *Journal of Adolescent Health* 41 (2007): S51–S58.

2. A. Lenhart, M. Madden, A. Smith, K. Purcell, K. Zickuhr, and L. Rainie, *Teens, Kindness and Cruelty on Social Network Sites: How American Teens Navigate the New World of "Digital Citizenship"* (Washington, DC: Pew Research Center's Internet & American Life Project, 2011), http://pewinternet.org/Reports/2011/Teens-and-social-media.aspx

3. A. Lenhart, K. Purcell, A. Smith, and K. Zickuhr, *Social Media & Mobile Internet Use Among Teens and Young Adults* (Washington, DC: Pew Internet & American Life Project, 2010), http://pewinternet.org/Reports/2010/Social-Media-and-Young-Adults.aspx

4. Lenhart, Madden, et al., *Teens, Kindness and Cruelty.*

5. Lenhart, Madden, et al., *Teens, Kindness and Cruelty.*

6. A. Lenhart, R. Ling, S. Campbell, and K. Purcell, *Teens and Mobile Phones* (Washington, DC: Pew Internet & American Life Project, 2010), http://pewinternet.org/Reports/2010/Teens-and-Mobile-Phones.aspx

7. "New Mobile Obsession: U.S. Teens Triple Data Usage," *NielsenWire*, December 15, 2011, http://blog.nielsen.com/nielsenwire/online_mobile/new-mobile-obsession-u-s-teens-triple-data-usage/

8. Lenhart, Ling, et al., *Teens and Mobile Phones.*

9. C. Norris and E. Soloway, "One-to-One Computing Has Failed Our Expectations," *District Administration* (2010); M. N. M. Khambari, W. S. Luan, and A. F. M. Ayub, "Teachers' Concerns of Laptop Ownership From the Malaysia Laptop Initiative," *Malaysian Journal of Educational Technology* 11, no. 1 (2011): 15–24; J. Lei and Y. Zhao, "One-to-One Computing: What Does It Bring to Schools?" *Journal of Educational Computing Research* 39, no. 2 (2008): 97–122.

10. The Richard W. Riley College of Education and Leadership at Walden University, "Educators, Technology and 21st Century Skills: Dispelling Five Myths; A Study on the Connection Between K–12 Technology Use and 21st Century Skills," 2010, p. 6, http://www.waldenu.edu/Documents/Degree-Programs/Full_Report_-_Dispelling_Five_Myths.pdf

11. K. Walsh, "Facebook in the Classroom. Seriously," *EmergingEdTech*, March 27, 2011, http://www.emergingedtech.com/2011/03/facebook-in-the-classroom-seriously/

12. J. Burk, "Why You Should Wait to Teach Projectile Motion Part 2: Introducing Projectile Motion Using Angry Birds," *Quantum Progress* [blog], February 17, 2011, http://quantumprogress.wordpress.com/2011/02/17/why-you-should-wait-to-teach-projectile-motion-part-2-introducing-projectile-motion-using-angry-birds/

13. S. Hinduja and J. W. Patchin, "Cyberbullying: A Review of the Legal Issues Facing Educators," *Preventing School Failure* 55, no. 2 (2010): 1–8; S. Hinduja and J. W. Patchin, *Bullying Beyond the Schoolyard: Preventing and Responding to Cyberbullying* (Thousand Oaks, CA: Corwin, 2009).

14. *Barr v. Lafon* (538 F.3d 554 (6th Cir. 2008) 2008).

15. Centers for Disease Control and Prevention, "Injury Prevention & Control: Motor Vehicle Safety. Teen Drivers: Fact Sheet," updated October 18, 2010, http://www.cdc.gov/motorvehiclesafety/teen_drivers/teendrivers_factsheet.html

16. National School Climate Center, "School Climate," accessed September 24, 2011, http://www.schoolclimate.org/climate/

17. D. L. Duke, *Source: Creating Safe Schools for All Children* (Boston: Allyn & Bacon, 2002), 122.

# 2

## School Climate

### *Where It Begins and Ends*

*We simply have not taken the problem of bullying seriously enough. . . . A school where children don't feel safe, is a school where children struggle to learn.*

—Arne Duncan, US Secretary of Education[1]

When we think of climate, we immediately think of the weather and either sunny days or rainy days. Sunny days may tend to make us more happy, upbeat, and even productive, generally speaking, while rainy days may make us more lethargic, introspective, and perhaps even a bit bummed out. This seems so basic but rings true for so many (sufferers of seasonal affective disorder know what we mean!). The outdoor climate can affect and shape our attitudes and behaviors, and those of us who have ever worked in an organizational setting also know that the "indoor" climate can as well. If the people you work with are optimistic, cheerful, supportive, selfless, trusting, and kind—and these traits have manifested in a somewhat constant environment that you look forward to each day—you are happier and probably do a better job. Well, all of this is completely relevant to how students feel, live, and hopefully thrive within your schools every day. A welcoming, cooperative, and trusting climate can insulate schools from a variety of problems and lead to greater student success.

## WHAT EXACTLY IS SCHOOL CLIMATE?

School climate generally relates to the social atmosphere of a "learning environment"[2] or the "'feel' of the school as perceived by students and teachers."[3] School climate has been defined as "the unwritten beliefs, values, and attitudes that become the *style of interaction between students, teachers, and administrators* [emphasis added]. . . . [It] sets the parameters of acceptable behavior among all school actors, and it assigns individual and institutional responsibility for school safety."[4] It has also been characterized as "the quality and consistency of interpersonal interactions—including feelings of trust and respect—within the school."[5] You are probably thinking that these definitions demonstrate that the idea of school climate is somewhat complex. You would be right; numerous researchers and educators have proposed multiple components of school climate. *Climate* is an intangible concept, but each definition attempts to capture a feeling or tone within a school.[6] Or, perhaps better stated, if an individual has a personality, an organization (such as a school) has a climate.[7]

> **Prevention Point:** The academic, affective, and social environment of a school tend to more strongly affect student performance and satisfaction than the physical environment and rule enforcement.

Some authors distinguish between school climate and culture. For example, according to a summary on the topic published by Michigan State University, *school culture* "reflects the shared ideas—assumptions, values, and beliefs—that give an organization its identity and standard for expected behaviors."[8] *School climate,* on the other hand, "reflects the physical and psychological aspects of the school that are more susceptible to change and that provide the preconditions necessary for teaching and learning to take place."[9] Stover (2005) states that "how students and staff members feel about their school is climate. Why they feel the way they do is determined by culture—by the values and behaviors of those in the school."[10] Our use of the term *climate* throughout this book reflects our perspective that the environment can in fact change, though we would include perceptions of the school's identity in our conceptualization.

## ASSESSING YOUR SCHOOL'S CLIMATE

Climate can be considered in terms of components that educators know from experience are related to positive behavioral choices and academic

### A Positive School Climate Makes Everything Possible

"The climate in a school can either make everything possible or not make everything possible." That quote is one of the most profound statements about schools that I have ever heard. It is true that instruction and curriculum are important, but neither can be effective unless the climate of the school/classroom is centered on respect, clear expectations, personal responsibility, and recognition.

Every school has a climate that is developed through the actions of the school leader. Therefore, it is vitally important that the school leader purposefully works to establish the climate in the way that he or she knows will best benefit the students and staff. The other option is for the school leader to do nothing, thus leaving it up to others to set the tone and develop the climate. That climate may not be positive, empowering, or productive. Instead, it may be demeaning, unclear, and non–student focused.

A school that has a positive climate rooted in clear expectations, and supported with recognition and respect, leads to students and staff making decisions that are in the best interest of not only the school but also themselves. Roy Disney once said, "When your vision is clear, decisions are easy." It is so true within a school. When your climate, vision, and expectations are clear, deciding whether or not to do the right thing is easy. It leads to the thought process of "that's the way we do it here." When students are faced with a choice of going onto a website that is inappropriate or not, whether at home or school, the climate they are most exposed to at school comes into play. Therefore, making the right decision is easier to make.

True, it doesn't work all the time. Within my building are many students who get into "trouble" with social networks, inappropriate websites, connecting with dangerous people online, and making poor choices in the photos they post on the Internet. Two years ago, we had a large spike in the number of issues and disciplinary action related to Internet behavior. Approximately 25 to 35 percent of discipline during the school year was Internet related. The following year, we implemented a morning homeroom meeting. During this 30 minutes once a week, two adults in each classroom would lead an activity or discussion that focused on the vision and expectations of the school. This practice, once a week, continued consistently throughout the school year. The results were amazing! The number of Internet-related disciplinary issues decreased significantly, and as did the number of overall discipline issues. Problems were either handled more often at the classroom level through discussion and guidance of the teachers, or the lessons learned and reinforced during those morning meeting times guided the thought processes of the students when opportunities to behave inappropriately came up.

At the end of each marking period, my administrative team would look at the discipline report and say, "Wow!" We did not start an anti-Internet campaign or increase the amount of Internet safety training. All we did was connect with students and purposefully strengthen the climate within our building around positive clear expectations and recognition. The end result was students making better life decisions. "The climate in a school can either make everything possible or not make everything possible."

—Steven A. Bollar, principal
Hartford School, Mount Laurel, New Jersey

success among students (and the accomplishment of educational goals by staff). Let us focus on assessing four of these components—or environments— that seem to matter and that researchers have identified as highly relevant: the social, affective, academic, and physical.[11]

A *social environment* that promotes cooperation and healthy interactions would result in answering yes to the following questions:

1. Is interaction between staff and students encouraged and made convenient?

2. Are staff friendly and collegial—do they get along with each other?

3. Do staff work well with parents to help teach and instruct youth?

4. Is decision making shared, with input solicited and considered valuable from students, teachers, and administration?

5. Are students and staff trained to prevent and respond to bullying, harassment, conflicts, and fights?

An *affective environment* that promotes belongingness and fosters self-esteem would lead to answering yes to the following questions:

1. Are all interactions between staff and students courteous, respectful, friendly, and supportive?

2. Do students trust staff?

3. Is morale high among staff and students?

4. Do students, staff, and parents feel welcomed, valued, and appreciated, and are they invested in the success of the school?

5. Does the school have a sense of community and embrace diversity?

An *academic environment* that promotes learning and self-fulfillment would involve the following:

1. Excellence in academics is encouraged; achievements are commended and rewarded.

2. Teaching methods are implemented with a respect for the different ways that youth learn.

3. Progress is monitored and assessments are made regularly, with the findings communicated to students and parents.

4. Assessments shape refinements in teaching and instruction.

5. Expectations are high for both teachers and for students, with everyone encouraged to succeed.

A *physical environment* that promotes learning and positive behaviors would have the following characteristics:

1. Students and staff feel comfortable with regard to noise, light, space, temperature, layout, cleanliness, and order of the school and its rooms.

2. Students and staff feel safe in all areas of the school.

3. Students and staff have all of the equipment, books, supplies, and resources they need to act and perform well.

4. Overcrowding is not an issue.

5. The school has been intentionally designed and decorated to foster a sense of welcome, spirit, community, beauty, and focus.

Research has shown that the academic, affective, and social environments tend to more strongly affect student performance and satisfaction than the physical environment and discipline and rule enforcement.[12]

Schools or independent researchers can evaluate the climate of a particular school in several ways. The most common method is by surveying students, staff, parents, or other community members about their experiences in the school.[13] In Chapter 8 we provide information about how to survey your students. Additionally, trained observers can monitor the activities and interactions in a school to determine the overall climate over time. Finally, one can learn about the climate of a particular school by reviewing official reports of disorder, absenteeism, academic performance, or behavioral problems. While this latter method is indirect, it can point to issues due to deficiencies in the social, affective, academic, or physical environment that exists at school.

**Prevention Point**: How safe, supported, engaged, helpfully challenged, and joyful we feel in school powerfully colors and shapes learning and healthy development.

## Our School Climate Measure

In our most recent study, we used a modified version of the American School Climate Survey (Student Version–2006) to assess the extent to which students felt welcomed and cared about at their school. Specifically, students were asked to report their level of agreement with the following statements:

- I feel safe at my school.
- I feel that teachers at my school care about me.

- I feel that teachers at my school really try to help me succeed.
- I feel that students at my school trust and respect the teachers.
- I feel that teachers at my school are fair to all students.
- I feel that teachers at my school take bullying very seriously.

Students responded to each of these questions using a 4-point scale ranging from *strongly disagree* (0) to *strongly agree* (3). Scores from the six questions were averaged for each student, and each school was given an average score based on responses from a random sample of students in that school. Responses from the approximately 4,400 students ranged from 0 to 3 with an average of 1.70.

As you can see, we focused on the *social* and *affective* factors because we believe those are most relevant when considering the problem behaviors we are interested in. That said, educators would do well to also consider how the *academic* and *physical* environments directly or indirectly affect attitudes, values, perspectives, and actions by both staff and students on their campus. If educators have not done so yet, they likely will be surprised to realize how potent a strong school climate can be and how poisonous a weak school climate can be.

## SCHOOL CLIMATE AND BEHAVIORS AT SCHOOL

The benefits of a positive school climate are broad and have been identified through much research across a variety of academic fields over the last 30 years.[14] It contributes to improved attendance and higher student achievement.[15] It has also been linked to social and emotional growth, as well as a decrease of disorder, delinquency, and juvenile violence.[16] Moreover, school climate is inextricably tied to the educational mission of schools and strongly affects perceived and actual safety on campus.[17] According to Lawrence and Green, "individuals use cues from the physical environment to make judgments and predictions about the type of behaviors and social norms deemed acceptable and expected in the place they are in."[18] This points directly to the importance of a positive atmosphere at school, especially as it relates to promoting productive behavior and to maintaining an environment in which educational growth can happen.

In our research, we found that students who perceived their climate to be better also behaved more appropriately—both at school and away from school. For example, students from schools with better climates were less likely to skip school or steal something from someone at school. They were also less likely to report bringing weapons or drugs to school and get in fights at school. Finally, they were less likely to participate in a variety of deviant or delinquent behaviors away from school, including drug and alcohol use and shoplifting. It is important to acknowledge that our study was cross-sectional in nature (data were collected at one point in time) and we are therefore unable to say that a positive climate *caused* students to behave more appropriately. Instead, we are only able to point out that a positive perception of school climate was linked with lower participation in 15 different problem behaviors. Future research should move to determine if changes in climate do in fact lead to subsequent changes in behavior.

## The Social Bond

Schools with a positive climate also encourage the development of strong social bonds between staff and students. These bonds are extremely powerful in their ability to determine beliefs and behaviors. When youth are emotionally attached or socially bonded to others, they internalize those persons' norms and values and do not want to disappoint them by behaving in a way that is contradictory to those principles. Some argue that we all—kids and adults alike—are naturally bent toward selfish, short-sighted decisions and actions.[19] If this is true, then why do most people obey laws and refrain from inappropriate or deviant behaviors when our human nature really encourages impulsivity and narcissism? Sociologists argue that because we have developed a bond with someone else (or many others), we set our own personal interests aside for the betterment of the group and behave in a way that is consistent with or supported by others.

Certain institutions in society, such as our family, peer group, broader community, religion, and school, tend to influence our choices and counter our natural tendencies to act in deviant, criminal, or otherwise unwise ways. You may be thinking that this theory only seems relevant to those individuals who are bonded with—and who have some sort of allegiance to—the "right" way of doing things and the institutions that support and embrace that "right" way. That is one of the primary objectives of a school and its community: to foster strong ties with students so that as they mature into adults, they become productive, abiding members of society. To be sure, our society would degenerate if a critical mass of the population did not adopt conventional standards of behavior.

**Prevention Point:** One of the primary objectives of a school is to foster strong ties with students so that as they mature into adults, they become productive, abiding members of society.

So, let's summarize. We know that the school affects the socialization and developmental trajectory of adolescents in significant ways because of the many hours each week that students spend there and the interactions they have with staff and fellow students. Extensive research has found that a bond to school serves to promote allegiance to conventional institutions and activities and to discourage participation in unconventional behaviors.[20] For example, those students who have little success academically or socially tend to experience failure at school, which translates to feelings of detachment and isolation—as if they do not belong or fit in with the rest. This then can lead to their participation in questionable or problematic actions.[21] Supporting research has found that teenagers who are attached and committed to school and school values are significantly less likely to engage in delinquent and illegal behaviors.[22]

Along the same lines, schools can help to informally and formally guide and shape the behavior and choices of those who attend.[23] Here also, supporting research has found a link between the presence of a "community" at school and decreased student misbehavior, drug use, and delinquency.[24] This means that "supportive relationships between and among teachers, administrators, and students, a common set of goals and norms, and a sense of collaboration and involvement"[25] greatly impact attitudes and actions at school.

---

### School Climate and Its Effect on School Social Issues

As online problems have escalated in American high schools in the past five years, one constant remains the same in helping to alleviate these problems: a strong student-staff connection. Students need to know there is someone at the high school they have a strong personal bond with each and every day of their high school career. Many successful administrators speak of the importance of each high school student being assigned a staff mentor for their high school years. Keene High School developed an Advisory Program five years ago in which each incoming student is assigned a staff mentor for the next four years. Daily meetings with the students, advisors, and an upperclassman have led to strong personal connections with students. Upper-class students provide the go-to link freshmen need. Students participate not only in the interview process of teachers, staff, and coaches but vote to determine who is hired. Their perspective is invaluable to creating an instant relationship.

Four years ago, some of our student leaders redesigned the ninth-grade orientation day and had a 95 percent attendance rate, even though the program is optional. The event included a "what not to wear" fashion show, an athletic and extracurricular activities convention, and a cap-and-gown photo shoot.

High schools that involve students in the day-to-day operations of their schools, respect their opinions, seek out their advice, and offer strong adult role models have fewer incidents of bullying, either face-to-face or online. School climate takes time and effort, but we must never forget its powerful impact on student empowerment and connectedness. Empowering students to paint murals on their walls; individualizing final exam projects; and interviewing, mentoring, discussing, and listening are the most effective tools to develop positive school social climate.

—Alan Chmiel, principal
Keene High School, Keene, New Hampshire

# SCHOOL CLIMATE AND BULLYING

A great deal of research has been done on the importance of school climate in affecting student behavior, but only a few studies have concentrated specifically on bullying and interpersonal harm. For instance, one study based on data collected from students in New Brunswick found that "disciplinary climate"—the "extent to which students internalize the norms and values of the school, and conform to them"[26]—reduced bullying in both sixth and eighth grades. Also, a climate that condones bullying within a high-conflict, disorganized school environment tends to increase bullying.[27] Youth who are introduced to and adopt normative beliefs that support peer aggression are more likely to bully others.[28] Yet other research has identified the apathy or insensitivity of teachers toward bullies and bullying behavior and their lack of emotional support for victims as relevant to climate.[29]

In our work, it was clear that student experiences with bullying were correlated with climate. That is, those students who perceived their school's climate to be more positive were significantly less likely to bully others at school. Moreover, significantly fewer students reported experiencing bullying at schools that had a better climate. When considering this body of research, then, it is safe to conclude that failing to intentionally create a positive school climate contributes to increased instances of bullying and interpersonal conflict.[30] In Chapter 5 we will extend this

---

### The Benefits of a Positive School Climate

School climate is an idea that educators have been focused on for over a hundred years. And, although the country is still lacking in a national definition of school climate, there is growing empirical support for the notion that when students, teachers, parents/guardians, and community members learn and work together, they improve the social, emotional, civic, and intellectual dimensions of school life/climate. We can use that data to support the whole village, whole child concept, in wonderfully important ways.

Over the last 25 years, a growing body of empirical as well as ethnographic research has shown that when students are learning and growing up in a positive school climate or schools that are safer, more supportive, more engaging, more helpfully challenging, and fun, academic achievement dramatically increases, high school dropout rates dramatically decrease, and health-promotion and risk-prevention programs become more effective. We also see a significant increase in teacher retention rates. Very exciting research is coming out that supports how important it is to recognize the social, emotional, and civic dimensions of learning with school climate surveys. This research also underscores the need to take concrete steps to engage youth, parents, community members, and school personnel to learn and work together.

—Jonathan Cohen, cofounder and president
National School Climate Center

argument to the online behaviors of adolescents, and we will demonstrate the importance of school climate and strong social bonds between students and staff in this area.

## SUMMARY

As discussed throughout this chapter, years of research and experience clearly demonstrate the beneficial outcomes associated with a good climate at school. To reiterate, we know that students who report positive school experiences have fewer disciplinary problems, get better grades, use fewer illicit substances, and participate in fewer delinquent behaviors. What we argue in this book is that developing a welcoming climate at school will also lead to fewer behavioral problems *away from school*. Before we get into the details of our strategy, the next two chapters will explore the online experiences of adolescents, with particular focus on some of the trouble some teens get into. Cyberbullying, sexting, and other problematic online behaviors challenge adults on a daily basis, so it is important that we bring you up to speed about the nature, extent, and characteristics of these issues.

## DISCUSSION QUESTIONS

1. What characterizes "school climate"? In what ways can it be identified? In what ways can a negative school climate be identified?

2. What components (environments) should be considered when assessing school climate? How are each of these environments related to one another, and how are they different from one another?

3. In what ways can schools and/or independent researchers evaluate school climate? Are there any benefits to using one type of evaluation compared to another type?

4. What are the specific benefits of a positive school climate? More specifically, how does a positive school climate result in the socialization of youth and development of strong social bonds?

5. How is school climate linked to your school's educational mission and the behaviors of students at your school? Why is it important to understand the links between student behavior and school climate?

6. What aspects of school climate promote bullying and peer harassment? On the other hand, what aspects of school climate discourage bullying and peer harassment? Do you see these relationships at your school?

# REFERENCES

1. A. Duncan, "The Myths About Bullying" (US Secretary of Education Arne Duncan's remarks at the Federal Partners in Bullying Prevention Summit, Washington, DC, August 11, 2010), http://www.ed.gov/news/speeches/myths-about-bullying-secretary-arne-duncans-remarks-bullying-prevention-summit/

2. R. H. Moos, *Evaluating Educational Environments* (San Francisco: Jossey-Bass, 1979), 89.

3. R. A. Lawrence, *School Crime and Juvenile Justice*, 2nd ed. (New York: Oxford University Press, 2007), 138.

4. W. N. Welsh, J. R. Greene, and P. H. Jenkins, "School Disorder: The Influence of Individual, Institutional, and Community Factors," *Criminology* 37, no. 1 (1999): 89.

5. N. M. Haynes, C. Emmons, and M. Ben-Avie, "School Climate as a Factor in Student Adjustment and Achievement," *Journal of Educational and Psychological Consultation* 9 (1997): 322.

6. R. Owens, *Organizational Behavior in Education*, 5th ed. (Needham Heights, MA: Allyn & Bacon, 1995); A. Halpin and D. Croft, *The Organizational Climate of Schools* (Chicago: Midwest Administration Center, The University of Chicago, 1963).

7. A. T. Roach and T. R. Kratochwill, "Evaluating School Climate and School Culture," *Teaching Exceptional Children* 37, no. 1 (2004): 10–17.

8. E. Tableman, "School Climate and Learning," Michigan State University *Best Practice Briefs*, no. 31 (December 2004): 1, http://outreach.msu.edu/bpbriefs/issues/brief31.pdf

9. Tableman, "School Climate and Learning"; H. S. Adelman and L. Taylor, "Classroom Climate," in *Encyclopedia of School Psychology*, ed. S. W. Lee, P. A. Lowe, and E. Robinson (Thousand Oaks, CA: Sage, 2005).

10. D. Stover, "Climate and Culture: Why Your Board Should Pay Attention to the Attitudes of Students and Staff," *American School Board Journal* 192, no. 12 (2005): 2.

11. H. J. Freiberg, ed., *School Climate: Measuring, Improving, and Sustaining Healthy Learning Environments* (London: Falmer Press, 1999), 31.

12. J. Griffith, "School Climate as 'Social Order' and 'Social Action': A Multi-level Analysis of Public Elementary School Student Perceptions," *Social Psychology of Education* 2 (1999): 339–369.

13. G. P. Kuperminc, B. J. Leadbeater, C. Emmons, and S. J. Blatt, "Perceived School Climate and Difficulties in the Social Adjustment of Middle School Students," *Applied Developmental Science* 1 (1997): 76–88.

14. Moos, *Evaluating Educational Environments*.

15. Stover, "Climate and Culture"; Kuperminc et al., "Perceived School Climate and Difficulties in the Social Adjustment"; Haynes, Emmons, and Ben-Avie, "School Climate as a Factor in Student Adjustment and Achievement."

16. Freiberg, *School Climate*; W. N. Welsh, "The Effects of School Climate on School Disorder," *Annals of the American Academy of Political and Social Science* 567 (2000): 88–107; A. A. Payne, D. C. Gottfredson, and G. D. Gottfredson, "Schools as Communities: The Relationships Among Communal School Organizations, Student Bonding, and School Disorder," *Criminology* 41 (2003): 749–777.

17. Welsh, "The Effects of School Climate on School Disorder"; J. B. Sprott, "The Development of Early Delinquency: Can Classroom and School Climates Make a Difference?" *Canadian Journal of Criminology and Criminal Justice* 46, no. 5 (2004): 553–572; P. H. Jenkins, "School Delinquency and the School Social Bond," *Journal of Research in Crime and Delinquency* 34, no. 3 (1997): 337–367; D. Lockwood, *Violence Among Middle School and High School Students: Analysis and Implications for Prevention* (Washington, DC: US Department of Justice, Office of Justice Programs, 1997), ERIC Document Reproduction Service No. ED419040.

18. C. Lawrence and K. Green, "Perceiving Classroom Aggression: The Influence of Setting, Intervention Style and Group Perceptions," *British Journal of Educational Psychology* 74, no. 4 (2005): 590.

19. T. Hobbes, *Leviathan, or The Matter, Form & Power of a Common-Wealth Ecclesiastical and Civil* (London: Printed for Andrew Crooke, at the Green Dragon in St. Paul's Churchyard, 1651); T. Hirschi, *Causes of Delinquency* (Berkeley: University of California Press, 1969).

20. S. Kasen, K. Berenson, P. Cohen, and J. G. Johnson, "The Effects of School Climate on Changes in Aggressive and Other Behaviors Related to Bullying," in *Bullying in American Schools*, ed. D. L. Espelage and S. Swearer (Mahwah, NJ: Lawrence Erlbaum, 2004), pp. 187–210; J. Stockard and M. Mayberry, *Effective Educational Environments* (Newbury Park, CA: Corwin, 1992).

21. W. N. Welsh, "Effects of Student and School Factors on Five Measures of School Disorder," *Justice Quarterly* 18 (2001): 911–947.

22. Hirschi, *Causes of Delinquency*.

23. Welsh, Greene, and Jenkins, "School Disorder: The Influence of Individual, Institutional, and Community Factors"; Jenkins, "School Delinquency and the School Social Bond"; S. A. Cernkovich and P. C. Giordano, "School Bonding, Race, and Delinquency," *Criminology* 30 (1992): 261–291.

24. J. D. Morenoff, R. J. Sampson, and S. Raudenbush, "Neighborhood Inequality, Collective Efficacy, and the Spatial Dynamics of Homicide," *Criminology* 39, no. 3 (2001): 517–560; R. J. Sampson, J. D. Morenoff, and F. Earls, "Beyond Social Capital: Spatial Dynamics of Collective Efficacy for Children," *American Sociology Review* 64, no. 5 (1999): 633–660; R. J. Sampson, S. Raudenbush, and F. Earls, "Neighborhoods and Violent Crime: A Multilevel Study of Collective Efficacy," *Science* 227 (1997): 918–924.

25. Payne, Gottfredson, and Gottfredson, "Schools as Communities," 751.

26. X. Ma, "Bullying and Being Bullied: To What Extent Are Bullies Also Victims?" *American Educational Research Journal* 38, no. 2 (2001): 357.

27. D. Olweus, S. Limber, and S. F. Mihalic, *Bullying Prevention Program: Blueprints for Violence Prevention, Book Nine* (Boulder: Center for the Study and Prevention of Violence, Institute of Behavioral Science, University of Colorado, 1999); Kasen et al., "The Effects of School Climate on Changes in Aggressive and Other Behaviors."

28. D. Espelage and S. M. Swearer, "Research on School Bullying and Victimization: What Have We Learned and Where Do We Go From Here? *School Psychology Review* 32, no. 3 (2003): 265–383; L. R. G. Huesmann, N. G., "Social Norms and Children's Aggressive Behavior, *Journal of Personality and Social Psychology* 72 (1997): 408–419.

29. G. D. Gottfredson and D. G. Gottfredson, *Victimization in Schools* (New York: Plenum Press, 1985); I. Whitney and P. K. Smith, "A Survey of the Nature and Extent of Bullying in Junior/ Middle and Secondary Schools," *Educational Research* 31, no. 1 (1993): 3–25.

30. T. R. Nansel, M. Overpeck, R. S. Pilla, W. J. Ruan, B. Simons-Morton, and P. Scheidt, "Bullying Behaviors Among U.S. Youth: Prevalence and Association With Psychosocial Adjustment," *Journal of the American Medical Association* 285, no. 16 (2001): 2094–2100; V. E. Besag, *Bullies and Victims in Schools* (Milton Keynes, UK: Open University Press, 1989).

# 3

## Adolescent Mistreatment in the 21st Century

### An Introduction to Cyberbullying

*Today, bullying doesn't even end at the school bell—it can follow our children from the hallways to their cell phones to their computer screens. . . . We've got to make sure our young people know that if they're in trouble, there are caring adults who can help.*

—US President Barack Obama[1]

## BULLYING AT SCHOOL

Bullying has long been an issue of concern for educators and parents, and studies have demonstrated that a significant proportion of adolescents are negatively impacted by it. Nansel and her colleagues define *bullying* as aggressive behavior or intentional "harm doing" by one person or a group, generally carried out repeatedly and over time, that involves a power differential.[2] It can encompass a variety of forms, including physical aggression (hitting, kicking, taking items by force), verbal aggression (taunting, teasing, threats), and indirect actions such as excluding others from activities, spreading rumors, and manipulating friendships.[3] Most generally, bullying is equated to the concept of harassment, which is a form of unprovoked aggression often directed repeatedly toward another individual or group of individuals.[4] Bullying tends to become more insidious as it continues over time and therefore may be better equated to "violence" than to "harassment."

Identifying the extent to which students or staff face threats of violence is an essential first step before working to promote a safe school environment and climate. Based on data from 2008–2009 from an estimated 55.6 million preK through 12th-grade students, researchers at the Bureau of Justice Statistics (BJS) found 1.2 million nonfatal school-based victimizations, including 629,800 violent crimes (i.e., rape, sexual assault, robbery, aggravated assault, and simple assault).[5] While there were more total nonfatal crimes at school, the rate of serious violent crime was lower at school (i.e., inside the school building, on school property, or on the way to or from school) than away from school.[6] In addition, almost one-third of the students aged 12–18 indicated they had been bullied at school in the past year.[7] Most recently, the 2010 BJS *Indicators of School Crime and Safety Report* reported that approximately 32 percent of students between 12 and 18 years of age were bullied at school during the 2007–2008 school year.[8] Of those, 23 percent experienced bullying once or twice a month, 10 percent once or twice a week, and 7 percent almost daily.

## CONSEQUENCES OF BULLYING

Underscoring the importance of addressing the problem is the fact that those who are involved in bullying can suffer a number of moderate to serious consequences. Bullying takes a significant psychological and emotional toll on youth; research has found that the most frequent reactions of bullying victims include feelings of vengefulness, anger, and self-pity (with male victims more frequently experiencing vengefulness and female victims experiencing self-pity), while bullies most often experience emotions of sorrow or indifference.[9] According to an Office of Juvenile Justice and Delinquency Prevention (OJJDP) fact sheet on youth bullying, other detrimental consequences experienced by victims include feelings of loneliness, humiliation, insecurity, and fearfulness; poor relationships and trouble making friends; and a compromised ability to adjust emotionally and socially.[10]

Being the target of bullying or other violent behaviors may also be a risk factor for involvement in deviant or delinquent behavior. For example, research has found that youth who are victimized are at a greater risk to engage in delinquent behaviors, while other studies have pointed to a strong link between criminal victimization and criminal offending, particularly when considering violent behaviors.[11] While bullying may not always be considered criminal victimization, some variations can lead to further aggression and violence.

> **Prevention Point:** Research has found that youth who are bullied are at a greater risk to engage in delinquent behaviors.

Several high-profile school shootings in recent years highlight the need to identify and address peer harassment. For example, an investigation conducted by the US Secret Service of 37 school-shooting incidents involving 41 attackers between 1974 and 2000 found that 71 percent (29) of the attackers "felt bullied, persecuted, or injured by others prior to the attack."[12] It was also determined that being bullied played at least some role in their later violent outburst.[13] These findings, coupled with the increased use of technology among youth and the unique issues related to Internet-based violence, highlight the need for deeper inquiry into bullying and its latest form: cyberbullying.

## WHAT IS CYBERBULLYING?

When we started our work in this area more than ten years ago, we would begin our workshops by asking attendees how many had heard of the term *cyberbullying*. Very few had. These days, just about everyone has heard the term, but it still amazes us how many different ways it can be defined. You might get a different characterization if you ask a parent, a teen, or a teacher. In fact, we regularly correspond with some of the brightest "experts" on the topic of cyberbullying, and even some of them have different definitions of what it is! When we ask teens to tell us what cyberbullying is *to them*, they often define it very simply: cyberbullying is "bullying using technology." This sums it up nicely, if one knows what "bullying" is.

> *I broke up with this guy because I wanted to keep our relationship a secret. So after a week he all of a sudden started texting me and saying how me and my brother were brats and how I was a B\*\*\*\*. He said some pretty nasty things. I asked him why he said it and he said it was because I broke his heart and he was getting revenge from that. Me and my friends often get bullied its one thing if its at school but to bring it home was another. We have to stick up for each other. I thought school was supposed to be safe.*
>
> —15-year-old girl from undisclosed location

As we discussed above, bullying is intentional aggression that is carried out repeatedly by someone who has power over another. Recall that the aggression can be physical (e.g., hitting or pushing), psychological (e.g., verbal putdowns or "dissing"), or relational (e.g., exclusion or rumor spreading). To be sure, the power differential can be a complicated and nuanced matter. Physical stature doesn't necessarily translate into power on the playground. Moreover, one can have social power over another person (by being more popular) or even "technological power" by knowing how to use computers, cell phones, or other devices more proficiently.

One key aspect of all types of bullying, though, is repetition. One instance of harassment or pushing should not be labeled as bullying, no matter how bad it is. It does, of course, warrant a response, but the repetitive nature of bullying is what makes it potentially so much worse than a single experience. If a teen is being bullied regularly by a classmate, this is going to be on her mind *constantly*. In class, between classes, before school, and after school—the target of bullying is going to be thinking of ways to avoid interacting with the bully. Clearly this will detract from her ability to feel safe and learn while at school.

**Prevention Point**: Cyberbullying is willful and repeated harm inflicted through the use of computers, cell phones, and other electronic devices.

We define *cyberbullying* as willful and repeated harm inflicted through the use of computers, cell phones, and other electronic devices. While this is an imperfect definition, we believe it is the clearest and most comprehensive one that exists. For example, throwing a cell phone at someone multiple times would technically fall under our definition of "repeated harm

### A Teenaged Target's Cry for Help

The beginning of my sophomore year I had two friends I mainly hung out with. By midyear I had distanced myself from them since they would leave me out constantly until one day I decided to just stop talking to them. Since then one of the girls found it funny to shoulder me every time she saw me in school no matter where I was or who I was with. At first I didn't say or do anything—I found it very dumb and I wasn't allowed to get any trouble because I was playing a sport. I thought eventually she would stop. People would see her do it and ask me why I didn't do anything or say anything. Until one day I confronted her and told her to stop—we were 5 years old to be doing those things. She just laughed and continued push me or throw one of her friends at me. And again I continued to ignore her but it seemed pointless.

One day while I was getting ready to go away for a game my locker's lock was covered in some substance which I later found out was one of the girls' saliva. That day after school, since I was away with my team at a game, the girls opened my locker (I used to share my locker with one of the girls when we were friends and she still remembered

*(Continued)*

(Continued)

my combination). They went around asking some people to fill a cup with pee. Some people did it with no knowledge what it was for. The girls filled cups as well. They dumped the cups of urine all over my locker and things. For the next couple days my locker and part of the hallway smelled horrible but I didn't really pay much attention to it since the school always had a funky smell and I was sick. I used my things and locker with no knowledge of what had happened. Until one day at lunch everyone in my lunch table was talking about a locker number and what had been done to it. Right then I heard the number and said it was my locker. Everyone after refused to speak.

One of my teammates told me that she was sorry but she couldn't tell me who did it but they had told her they were going to do it but she doubted they would. Throughout the day people came confessing to me and apologizing. I talked to one of my teachers about it but told no one would tell me who did it. When people finally started to confess, I went to my dean's office and told him what had happen. He brought people to confess, and then brought the girls who clearly denied it. After he went to take a look at my locker and said he had no proof but that it did smell.

The next day I had Facebook messages from people saying the girls had done it and had asked them for a cup of urine. The school told me they would suspend them for the action. Turns out the school only suspended them for a day for supposedly not cooperating which was not what I was told. And their parents were not even called to be notified. The girls began writing very mean things about me on Facebook and Formspring. My parents talked to the principal and he refused to do anything about it and my parents demanded to talk to the board but they refused to let us contact them. We went to the police station to file a report on the girls, but the police station lied on filing the report.

After reading all of the constant Facebook and Formspring messages I was so upset I got two panic attacks. My parents printed all the messages that had been written by the girls. I was rushed to the emergency room where they calmed me down and asked what had happened and was referred to a psychologist. With the hospital papers we went to the police station where they discovered no one had done the report and one was actually made this time. The sheriff called the girls' parents and girls for a meeting the next day along with me and my parents. Parents had no clue of what their daughters had done but they denied their daughters did anything. The officer gave them a warning and told me they'd watch for any Facebook etc. messages involving me. The messages continued. The police station along with the school did not take action and the girls were let back into the school like nothing happened. Having this happen to me made me unsure of people. I have a hard time making friends now. I'd rather be by myself. I close people out now and I really don't like it but I can't help it. It all scares me now.

—16-year-old girl from Illinois

inflicted through cell phones." Of course we aren't talking about these kinds of behaviors. In fact, the best definition might really be the one that most teens provide to us: "cyberbullying is bullying using technology."

Even though cyberbullying can take on many different forms, the most common types of cyberbullying today include

- mean or hurtful messages sent online or via cell phones;
- rumors or threats posted or sent;
- humiliating pictures or videos being posted online; and
- imposter profiles on social networking websites.

## THE CYBERBULLIED

There has been no shortage of cyberbullying incidents reported in the media over the last few years. These are instructive reminders about the potentially tragic consequences of cyberbullying left unchecked:

- *September 19, 2011.* Fourteen-year-old Jamey Rodemeyer struggled with his sexuality and was repeatedly bullied at school and online. He posted an "It Gets Better" video on YouTube seemingly trying to convince himself as much as anyone else that his situation would improve over time. Several anonymous comments on his Formspring page encouraged him to kill himself, including this one: "I wouldn't care if you died. No one would. So just do it :) It would make everyone WAY more happier!!"[14]
- *September 19, 2010.* Eighteen-year-old Tyler Clementi was secretly recorded having a sexual encounter with another man in his Rutgers University dorm room. The video was then apparently streamed live online for others to see. Two nights later he was recorded again with the man, and the video was once again streamed online. The next day Clementi committed suicide. Ten minutes before he died, he posted this to Facebook: "Jumping off the gw bridge sorry."[15]
- *March 21, 2010.* Seventeen-year-old Alexis Pilkington of Long Island, New York, committed suicide allegedly following numerous online assaults on social media sites (especially Facebook and Formspring). The torrent of hurtful comments continued even after her death. "She was obviously a stupid depressed—who deserved to kill herself. she got what she wanted."[16]
- *January 14, 2010.* Fifteen-year-old Phoebe Prince of South Hadley, Massachusetts, committed suicide after experiencing months of bullying and cyberbullying, which included name-calling (e.g., "Irish slut") on Facebook and Twitter.[17]
- *January 19, 2009.* Fifteen-year-old Megan Gillan of Cheshire, United Kingdom, committed suicide after repeated bullying and cyberbullying, including messages on her Bebo page making fun of her appearance. Her last text message to a friend was "I love you, never forget that."[18]

**Prevention Point**: At least one in five middle and high school students has experienced cyberbullying.

Thankfully extreme cases like these are rare, but that doesn't mean we should ignore or discount the problem.

In an analysis of 35 articles published in peer-reviewed journals that included cyberbullying victimization rates (as of January 2011), we found that the number of youth who experience cyberbullying ranges from 5.5 to 72 percent (average: 24.4 percent).[19] Much of the variation in these figures is due to how each study was carried out (e.g., differences in how cyberbullying was defined and measured, the age of the respondents, whether surveys were administered at school or online, and if students were reporting lifetime or more recent experiences). In one of the earliest cyberbullying studies, Michele Ybarra and Kimberly Mitchell found that 19 percent of youth between the ages of 10 and 17 had experienced cyberbullying as either a victim or an offender.[20] In 2005, data collected from 3,767 middle school students from 6 schools demonstrated that 11 percent had been cyberbullied in the last 2 months, 4 percent were cyberbullies, and almost 7 percent were both a cyberbullying victim and offender.[21] More recently, data from 2007 indicated that almost 10 percent of middle school students had been cyberbullied in the last 30 days, with around 17 percent experiencing cyberbullying over their lifetime.[22] In this same study, 8 percent of students had cyberbullied others over the last 30 days, while 18 percent had done so over their lifetime. Finally, 12 percent of middle schoolers in this sample reported having been both the victim and offender at some point in their lifetime.

Research also indicates that just about anyone can be the target of cyberbullying. Boys and girls of all backgrounds have told us about their painful experiences. While no student is immune from being bullied, we do tend to see some patterns when looking at particular demographic characteristics. For example, much of the research demonstrates that girls are more likely than boys to be cyberbullied.[23] This difference is more pronounced when looking at lifetime experiences versus more recent experiences. For example, in our most recent study, we found that 7.0 percent of boys and 7.9 percent of girls had been cyberbullied in the previous 30 days. When looking at lifetime experiences, 16.6 percent of boys and 25.1 percent of girls said they had been cyberbullied.

Age also appears to be related to experiences with cyberbullying, with the majority of studies indicating these problem behaviors seem most prominent in the middle school years. We should also point out, however, that experiences with cyberbullying continue through high school and into college and beyond. In fact, we receive a significant number of emails and phone calls from *adults* who are being harassed online. That said, early adolescence can be a particularly challenging developmental stage for a variety of reasons, meaning that being cyberbullied at that age can be especially hurtful.

Very few studies have examined the role that race plays in cyberbullying incidents, but those that have included it as a variable largely show that it isn't a significant factor. In our studies, we have repeatedly found that teens of all races experience cyberbullying at roughly the same rate. While the differences are relatively small, white and Asian students report more recent experiences with cyberbullying than African American and Hispanic students.

In addition to these demographic characteristics, we have examined other factors that are known to be related to traditional bullying. For example, we found that over 72 percent of lesbian, gay, bisexual, and transgendered (LGBT) students report being the target of a bully at some point in their lifetimes compared to 63 percent of heterosexual students. The difference is even more striking when one focuses on cyberbullying: almost twice as many LGBT students report experiencing cyberbullying compared to heterosexual students (36.1 percent compared to 20.1 percent). We also have learned that students who were struggling in school—both academically and behaviorally—were more at risk to be a victim of cyberbullying. Students who reported to us that they typically earn Ds and Fs were twice as likely to have been the victim of cyberbullying compared to students who earned Cs and above.

Even though we know more now than we did just five years ago about who is more likely to be the target of cyberbullying, this phenomenon needs much more exploration and analysis. More research is necessary to examine whether experience with cyberbullying is associated with other circumstances, such as socioeconomic status, family structure, and mental health issues, to name a few. It is also important to look at personality characteristics (such as introversion/extroversion, internal/external locus of control, and self-control) and even behavioral disorders and their relation to victim populations. It would also be useful to identify the strongest buffering or insulating factors that keep an adolescent resilient in the face of peer conflict and harassment and thereby differentiate those who might be most susceptible to internalizing the harm rather than shrugging it off.

## THE CYBERBULLY

Just as any student can be bullied, anyone can easily become a bully. Often, it seems, the person engaging in the bullying behaviors doesn't see his or her actions as "bullying." The student sees these actions as a joke or "not that big of a deal." Teens can often get "caught up" in bullying when pressured by peers or when a particular incident gets out of control. For example, maybe a group of teenage girls is hanging out, and one of them suggests they send a classmate a sarcastic text message. Depending on how that message is received and the recipient's response, the incident could escalate to more cruel messages or other electronic or in-person bullying. We see many examples of comments made on social networking sites that are perhaps taken out of context or misinterpreted, leading to subsequent hurtful comments—and the next thing you know, there is a blowup at school.

Approximately 17 percent of students have admitted to us in anonymous surveys that they have cyberbullied others at some point in their lifetimes. This figure is consistent with the average across 27 other published studies that asked students to report their cyberbullying behaviors.[24] So on average, slightly less than one in five students has cyberbullied others. Some research has demonstrated that boys are slightly more likely to report involvement in cyberbullying, though other studies have been inconclusive.[25] Youth from different racial backgrounds report similar involvement in cyberbullying.

Very little is known about what causes a teen to engage in cyberbullying. We do know that the most commonly reported reason students tell us they cyberbully others is revenge. The student who admits to cyberbullying often feels justified in this behavior because she or he was bullied first or the target did something to warrant the abuse (at least in the eyes of the bully). In fact, almost half of the students who identified as victims of cyberbullying also reported that they had cyberbullied others. Other times, respondents told us that they were just joking around and only after someone told them did they realize that what they were doing could be defined as cyberbullying.[26]

> I bullied because I was bullied before. I assumed that because I felt it, everyone else had to know. The cycle continued. I said things that weren't true to get the attention away from me. I was hoping that people would forget what they were saying about me and focus on someone else. Little did I know that I myself had turned into one of them.
>
> —14-year-old from Virginia

So the good news is that most students do not engage in cyberbullying. This is an important message that will be stressed even more in Chapter 7. And many of the 20 percent or so who cyberbully do so rarely and don't engage in particularly egregious forms. Of course, just because the number of teens who are cyberbullying others is small doesn't mean that the impact isn't great.

## WHERE DOES CYBERBULLYING OCCUR?

Cyberbullying happens across a variety of venues and mediums in cyberspace, and it shouldn't come as a surprise that it occurs most often wherever teenagers regularly congregate. Ten years ago, many teens hung out in chat rooms, and as a result that was where most harassment took place. In recent years, most youth have been drawn to social networking websites (e.g., Facebook) and video-sharing websites (e.g., YouTube).

This trend has led to increased reports of cyberbullying occurring in those environments. Instant messaging on the Internet or text messaging via cell phones also appear to be common ways in which youth harass others.

Journalists and others often ask us to identify the "worst websites for cyberbullying." This is a difficult question. We usually ask for clarification, already knowing that the person posing the question simply wants to know where most cyberbullying is happening today. Well, when we respond by saying that a lot of cyberbullying is happening on Facebook, the reporter often concludes that "it is Facebook's fault that there is cyberbullying!" Of course, that isn't any more accurate than saying that it is the school's fault that bullying happens. Just as some schools have more bullying problems than others and some schools are doing more to effectively prevent and respond to bullying, some social networking sites have more problems than others or are doing more to prevent and respond to cyberbullying. Facebook is probably above average in that regard: as are many schools, it is doing more than some but could be doing more. Cyberbullying is common on Facebook because that is where kids hang out these days. If teens spent eight hours per day in the library, you can bet that there would be problems there. And if adults were hesitant or afraid to go into that library (as some adults seem to be hesitant about or afraid of Facebook), there *definitely* would be problems. The moral of the story is that more adults need to be hanging out on Facebook (and other social sites) so they can model appropriate behaviors and intervene in incidents before they get out of hand.

In addition, since many youth now carry smartphones (e.g., iPhones and Droids), they often have full computing, recording, and Internet capabilities on a device that is *always* with them. As a result, cyberbullying can take place almost anywhere at any time. For example, teens have taken pictures in a bedroom, a bathroom, or another location where privacy is expected and posted or distributed the photos online. More recently, some teens have recorded unauthorized videos of others and uploaded them for the world to see, rate, tag, and talk about. We are also seeing this happen with portable gaming devices, in 3-D virtual worlds, and on social gaming sites. To reiterate, wherever youth are hanging out online, cyberbullying is likely there as well.

## CORRELATES OF CYBERBULLYING

It is important to note that the effects of cyberbullying, like those of traditional bullying, are not insignificant. Experiences with cyberbullying have made victims angry, frustrated, and sad, and these negative emotions often lead to self-harm or other forms of aggression (more on this later).[27] In previous research, we found relationships between cyberbullying and low self-esteem, suicidal ideation, and school problems—both for the bully and the bullied.[28] These relationships are discussed in more detail below.

## Cyberbullying and Self-Esteem

Social psychologist Dr. Manny Rosenberg defined *self-esteem* as "a favorable or unfavorable attitude toward the self."[29] Research consistently finds that youth who are bullied tend to have lower self-esteem than those who are not bullied.[30] Despite the consistency of this finding among social science studies, it is still unclear whether experience with bullying *causes* a target to have lower self-esteem or if teens with lower self-esteem are seen as better targets by the bully. It could also be that low self-esteem and bullying are both related to some third variable, such as poor school performance or lack of social competence. That is, students who do poorly at school or who struggle to communicate with others might have low self-esteem *and* be targeted for bullying. No matter what the precise relationship is, we know that bullying and self-esteem are related.

Our recent research has extended this body of knowledge by linking low self-esteem with experiences with cyberbullying. In our study involving approximately 2,000 randomly selected middle schoolers from one of the largest school districts in the United States,[31] cyberbullying victims *and offenders* both had significantly lower self-esteem than those who had not experienced cyberbullying. This relationship persisted even while controlling for gender, race, and age, though our results did suggest that males, non-Whites, and older middle schoolers tend to have lower levels of self-esteem than their peers. Of note is that the relationship between cyberbullying *victimization* and self-esteem was stronger than that of cyberbullying *offending* and self-esteem.

Just as in the previous studies discussed above, our work wasn't able to specifically determine that experience with cyberbullying *caused* low self-esteem. Nevertheless, these results are yet another reminder that educators and parents should make a concerted effort to prevent and respond to all forms of bullying—whether it is manifested in fistfights on school property or in disparaging and threatening instant messages in cyberspace, since both directly or indirectly affect the psychosocial well-being of the youth involved.

*It started after me and my boyfriend broke up and all of his friends started to call me a whore, skank, slut, etc. At first I didn't let it bother me but then the whole school started calling me it and I became known as the class whore. They even made a song for me. It came so bad that I had no friends and I was the one walking alone in the halls knowing that everyone was staring and talking about me. There was a Facebook page made about me but then was later deleted. I thought about just ending my life because I thought that would be easier . . . .*

—15-year-old girl from Michigan

## Cyberbullying and Suicide

Much of the media attention surrounding cyberbullying has focused on teens who have committed suicide after being bullied (recall the tragic examples described above). These incidents are heartbreaking and should deepen our resolve to do everything in our power to prevent bullying from escalating to this point. That said, does experience with cyberbullying *cause* a teen to commit suicide? While no direct evidence supports this conclusion, volumes of literature have been written on the relationship between traditional bullying and suicide, and our previous research has linked experience with bullying and cyberbullying with higher levels of suicidal thoughts and attempts among victims.[32] Specifically, traditional bullying victims were 1.7 times more likely and traditional bullying offenders were 2.1 times more likely to have attempted suicide than those who were not traditional victims or offenders. Similarly, cyberbullying victims were 1.9 times more likely and those who reported involvement in cyberbullying were 1.5 times more likely to have attempted suicide than those who were not cyberbullying victims or offenders.

> **Prevention Point:** Students who were cyberbullied were almost twice as likely to have attempted suicide than those who had not experienced cyberbullying.

It should be acknowledged that many of the teenagers who committed suicide after experiencing bullying or cyberbullying had other emotional and social issues in their lives. For example, one victim attended special education classes in elementary school and struggled socially and academically.[33] Another suffered from low self esteem and depression and was on medication when she took her life.[34] As mentioned earlier, it is unlikely that experience with cyberbullying *by itself* leads to youth suicide. Rather, it tends to exacerbate instability and hopelessness in the minds of adolescents already struggling with stressful life circumstances.

## Cyberbullying and School-Related Delinquency and Violence

One of our earliest studies involved determining if cyberbullying was related to delinquency, school violence, and other offline behavioral problems.[35] We believed this would be true, because traditional bullying has been linked to antisocial behaviors such as vandalism, shoplifting, truancy, dropping out of school, fighting, and drug use as well as negative emotions that are sometimes resolved in deviant ways.[36]

This led us to collect data to assess if being mistreated repeatedly online led to what we called "self-reported offline problem behaviors." These included whether students had consumed liquor, cheated on a school test, skipped school without an excuse, assaulted a peer, damaged property, shoplifted, smoked marijuana, assaulted an adult, run away from home, carried a weapon, or been sent home from school. As you can see, the behaviors range from relatively minor forms of deviance to serious delinquency. Results from our analysis suggest that youth who experience cyberbullying are more likely to report they have participated in the offline problem behaviors listed above. Recent data released by the US Department of Education corroborated our findings, showing that students involved in cyberbullying were more likely than their peers to have been involved in a fight at school.[37] To be sure, cyberbullying does not occur in a vacuum and is often related to other problem behaviors, including school violence and delinquency.[38]

## UNIQUE FEATURES OF CYBERBULLYING

While bullying and cyberbullying are comparable with respect to their nature (both can involve harassment, threats, rumors, etc.), some characteristics that are unique to cyberbullying may make it a categorically distinct form of adolescent aggression.[39] For instance, the ubiquity of technology has enabled would-be bullies to access their targets around the clock. When we were growing up, if we had a disagreement with a classmate late in the school day, often we wouldn't see that person until the next day. By then we might have forgotten what we were so mad about. Today, impulsive teens can act immediately and speak their mind without that time to cool down.

Those who engage in cyberbullying are also able to hide behind the anonymity of a computer screen or cell phone and can perpetrate their acts even when they are physically separated from the target. As noted psychologist Kenneth Gergen and his colleagues pointed out decades ago,

> Anonymity itself does not seem to be a social ill. Rather, the state of anonymity seems to encourage whatever potentials are most prominent at the moment—whether for good or for ill. When we are anonymous we are free to be aggressive or to give affection, whichever expresses most fully our feelings at the time. There is liberation in anonymity.[40]

Traditional bullying, on the other hand, often occurs when the victim and offender are in the same physical space (though this is not always the case). The physical distance between the victim and the bully enabled by technology seemingly allows the latter to say and do what she wants with little fear of reprisal or consequence. *Seemingly* is a key word, though, since in reality very little done online is completely anonymous. Just about everything can be traced and tracked online using Internet service providers, cell phone service providers, and Internet Protocol (IP) addresses.

> ### Decoding Your Digital Footprint
>
> When individuals are online, they are assigned an Internet Protocol (IP) address by their Internet service provider (e.g., Earthlink, AOL, Qwest, Comcast, their school) or cell phone service provider (e.g., Sprint, AT&T, Verizon). This IP address is unique and is bound to a person's current online session—whether it is via a computer, cell phone, or other portable electronic device. It is continually associated with the data transactions (sending [uploading] and receiving [downloading], interacting, communicating) that are made between one's device and the rest of the World Wide Web and between one's social networking site, email, instant message, and chat software and the existing population of Internet users. All data transactions are stamped with one's IP address and the exact date and time (to the millisecond) that it occurred, and they are kept in log files on computers owned by Internet service providers, cell phone service providers, and content providers (Facebook, Google, Hotmail, Yahoo!, etc.).
>
> When attempting to discover the aggressor behind the keyboard, it is vital to know the IP address bound to the malicious message or piece of content. Once that is discovered, the relevant provider can assist school police (or local, state, or federal law enforcement) in identifying the online session in question, which points to the Internet service provider or cell phone service provider through whom the online connection was made, then to the person connected to that specific account (by way of the billing information), and finally to the family member who was logged in at the time the cyberbullying took place.

Related to anonymity is the concept of disinhibition. Adolescents may be disinhibited, again due to the physical distance afforded by technology, to say things they normally would not say to a person when face to face. For instance, if we bump into someone while walking down the hall, almost all of us would say "Excuse me," or "I'm sorry." But when someone cuts us off in traffic, even the most patient among us sometimes curses or makes inappropriate gestures. This is the disinhibition effect—our social restraints are weakened (or temporarily eliminated) because we aren't acting as ourselves toward another person; we are simply acting on impulse with little thought of the consequences. The distance afforded by technology allows bullies to be disinhibited in their behaviors. Indeed, many youth who have admitted to us that they have bullied others really didn't see the harm in the behavior.

Cyberbullying also tends to be more viral than traditional bullying. Even though rumors seemingly circulate very quickly throughout a school via traditional methods, they travel at lightning speeds with the aid of technology. A cyberbully can send an email containing disparaging or hurtful remarks about a target to wide audience with a single click of the computer mouse (or touch of the touchscreen on a phone or tablet). In short, technology has allowed bullies to avoid the social conventions and pressures of

---

**Unique Characteristics of Cyberbullying**

- 24/7 access to technology and the target
- Perception of invincibility while online
- Reduced restraint and increased freedom due to physical distance
- Extent of victimization quickly spreads far and wide
- Difficult to recognize the harm that is being inflicted

---

face-to-face communication and post or send malicious, embarrassing, or threatening content more easily and to wider audiences than ever before.

## THE RELATIONSHIP BETWEEN TRADITIONAL BULLYING AND CYBERBULLYING

Even though cyberbullying has some characteristics that differentiate it from traditional schoolyard bullying, we find that a meaningful amount of bullying occurs in both environments. This shouldn't be all that surprising given the overlapping online and offline worlds of teens. While it is difficult to determine whether being a bully or being bullied at school causes similar experiences in cyberspace (or vice versa), a clear relationship between the two forms exists. For example, Michele Ybarra and Kimberly Mitchell found that about half of cyberbullying victims and those who engage in cyberbullying report also experiencing traditional, offline bullying.[41] In one of our previous studies, we found that traditional bullies were more than twice as likely to be both the targets and the perpetrators of electronic forms of bullying compared to those who do not engage in traditional bullying.[42] Moreover, we learned that victims of offline bullying were 2.7 times as likely to be the victim of cyberbullying.

Based on our data from 2010, almost two-thirds of the youth who reported being cyberbullied in the previous month said they were also bullied at school within that same time period. Similarly, over three-quarters of those who admitted to cyberbullying others also admitted to bullying others at school in the previous 30 days. It appears that with this phenomenon, we are often dealing with a population of targets who are doubly susceptible to victimization—both online and off—and a population of aggressors who do not discriminate when it comes to whom they mistreat—and where.

---

**Prevention Point**: Students who are bullied at school are bullied online; students who bully at school, bully online.

## SUMMARY

Cyberbullying is a significant problem affecting far too many students on a regular basis. While it is not yet at epidemic levels, as some media reports suggest, it no doubt will increase in frequency and seriousness if ignored. The nature of cyberbullying can make it more challenging to deal with than the more visible forms of harassment, but the signs that indicate a student is struggling with it are often hard to miss. It took too many generations for adults to recognize the serious consequences associated with bullying at school. By dismissing or ignoring this new form of bullying, educators risk significant and irreparable harm to a school's climate. At the same time, we offer a model that promises to prevent all types of bullying, wherever students are interacting. We believe that cultivating a positive and caring culture at your school will go a long way to prevent bullying and cyberbullying from happening in the first place. The fact that you are reading this book is evidence enough that you have a good understanding of what you are up against. In the chapters that follow, we will equip you with a variety of specific strategies and comprehensive approaches that we hope will result in fewer and/or less serious incidents of cyberbullying at your school. We hope that you will see how powerful a positive school climate is not only in preventing various forms of bullying but also in reducing the frequency of other online problematic student behaviors, such as sexting.

## DISCUSSION QUESTIONS

1. *Bullying* can be defined in a variety of ways. What are the primary behaviors associated with the term? How does *harassment* fit into the concept of bullying?

2. What are the consequences of bullying? How do these consequences affect victims as well as bullies themselves? How do you see these consequences play out among students at your school?

3. What is the relationship between bullying and cyberbullying? What are some similarities between the two concepts? What are the differences?

4. What are the different forms of cyberbullying? In your eyes, is any form more serious than the other? What repercussions can you see arising from the different forms? Share and discuss some recent incidents that have occurred at your school.

5. Who can be a target of cyberbullying? Are the demographic characteristics (gender, age, etc.) of victims the same as those of the general public, or do they represent a specific subgroup of students?

Conversely, who can become the cyberbully? Are there distinguishing characteristics of a "typical" cyberbully? What do the aggressors at your school look like? What do the targets look like?

6. Do the cyberbullying incidents in which individuals committed suicide have factors in common? How do these cases fit into the overall victimization rates? How can you prevent cyberbullying from resulting in suicide?

7. Which do you think is happening more often among students at your school: bullying or cyberbullying? Have you seen the behaviors occur together?

# REFERENCES

1. J. Lee, "President Obama & the First Lady at the White House Conference on Bullying Prevention," *The White House Blog*, March 10, 2011, http://www.whitehouse.gov/blog/2011/03/10/president-obama-first-lady-white-house-conference-bullying-prevention/

2. T. R. Nansel, M. Overpeck, R. S. Pilla, W. J. Ruan, B. Simons-Morton, and P. Scheidt, "Aggression Behaviors Among US Youth: Prevalence and Association With Psychosocial Adjustment," *Journal of the American Medical Association* 285, no. 16 (2001): 2094–2100.

3. D. Olweus, *Aggression in the Schools: Bullies and Whipping Boys* (Washington, DC: Hemisphere Press, 1978); S. P. Limber and M. M. Nation, "Bullying Among Children and Youth," *Juvenile Justice Bulletin* (April 1998), http://www.ojjdp.gov/jjbulletin/9804/bullying2.html

4. M. Manning, J. Heron, and T. Marshal, "Style of Hostility and Social Interactions at Nursery School and at Home: An Extended Study of Children," in *Aggression and Antisocial Behavior in Childhood and Adolescence*, ed. A. Lionel, M. B. Hersov, and D. Shaffer (Oxford, UK: Pergamon, 1978), pp. 29–58.

5. T. D. Snyder and S. A. Dillow, *Digest of Education Statistics 2010* (NCES 2011-015), (Washington, DC: National Center for Education Statistics, US Department of Education, 2011), http://nces.ed.gov/pubs2011/2011015.pdf

6. S. Robers, J. Zhang, J. Truman, and T. D. Snyder, *Indicators of School Crime and Safety: 2010* (NCES 2011-002, NCJ 230812) (Washington, DC: US Department of Education and US Department of Justice, 2010), http://nces.ed.gov/pubs2011/2011002.pdf

7. Robers et al., *Indicators of School Crime and Safety.*

8. Robers et al., *Indicators of School Crime and Safety*.

9. F. Esbensen and D. Huizinga, "Juvenile Victimization and Delinquency," *Youth & Society* 23, no. 1 (1991): 202–228; M. G. Borg, "The Emotional Reaction of School Bullies and Their Victims," *Educational Psychology* 18, no. 4 (1998): 433–444; R. J. Sampson and J. L. Lauritsen, "Deviant Lifestyles, Proximity to Crime, and the Offender–Victim Link in Personal Violence," *Journal of Research in Crime & Delinquency* 27, no. 1 (1990): 110–139; J. L. Lauritsen, R. J. Sampson, and J. H. Laub, "The Link Between Offending and Victimization Among Adolescents," *Criminology* 29, no. 2 (1991): 265–292; J. N. Shaffer and B. Ruback, *Violent Victimization as a Risk Factor for Violent Offending Among Juveniles* (NCJ 195737) (Washington, DC: Office of Juvenile Justice and Delinquency Prevention, Office of Justice Programs, US Department of Justice, 2002).

10. Shaffer and Ruback, *Violent Victimization as a Risk Factor*.

11. Shaffer and Ruback, *Violent Victimization as a Risk Factor*; Borg, "The Emotional Reaction of School Bullies and Their Victims"; Sampson and Lauritsen, "Deviant Lifestyles, Proximity to Crime, and the Offender–Victim Link in Personal Violence"; Lauritsen, Sampson, and Laub, "The Link Between Offending and Victimization Among Adolescents"; D. P. Tattum, "Violence and Aggression in Schools," in *Bullying in Schools*, ed. D. P. Tattum and D. A. Lane (Stoke-on-Trent, UK: Trentham, 1989), 7–19.

12. B. Vossekuil, R. A. Fein, M. Reddy, R. Borum, and W. Modzeleski, *The Final Report and Findings of the Safe School Initiative: Implications for the Prevention of School Attacks in the United States* (Washington, DC: US Secret Service and US Department of Education, 2002), p. 21, http://www.secretservice.gov/ntac/ssi_final_report.pdf

13. Vossekuil et al., *The Final Report and Findings of the Safe School Initiative*.

14. S. Tan, "Teenager Struggled With Bullying Before Taking His Life," *Buffalo News*, September 27, 2011, http://www.buffalonews.com/city/schools/article563538.ece

15. E. Pilkington, "Tyler Clementi, Student Outed as Gay on Internet, Jumps to His Death," *The Guardian*, September 30, 2010, http://www.guardian.co.uk/world/2010/sep/30/tyler-clementi-gay-student-suicide/

16. E. Martinez, "Alexis Pilkington Brutally Cyber Bullied, Even After Her Suicide," CBS News, March 26, 2010, http://www.cbsnews.com/8301-504083_162-20001181-504083.html

17. E. Bazelon, "What Really Happened to Phoebe Prince?" *Slate .com,* July 20, 2010, http://www.slate.com/articles/life/bulle/ features/2010/what_really_happened_to_phoebe_prince/could_ the_south_hadley_schools_have_done_more.html

18. A. Taylor, "Teen Suicide Over Bebo Posts," *The Sun,* July 29, 2009, http://www.thesun.co.uk/sol/homepage/news/2561880/ Teenager-Megan-Gillan-commits-suicide-over-Bebo-posts.html

19. J. W. Patchin and S. Hinduja, *Cyberbullying Prevention and Response: Expert Perspectives* (New York: Routledge, 2012).

20. M. L. Ybarra and J. K. Mitchell, "Online Aggressor/Targets, Aggressors, and Targets: A Comparison of Associated Youth Characteristics," *Journal of Child Psychology and Psychiatry* 45 (2004): 1308–1316.

21. R. M. Kowalski and S. P. Limber, "Electronic Bullying Among Middle School Students," *Journal of Adolescent Health* 41 (2007): S22–S30.

22. S. Hinduja and J. W. Patchin, *Bullying Beyond the Schoolyard: Preventing and Responding to Cyberbullying* (Thousand Oaks, CA: Corwin, 2009).

23. Patchin and Hinduja, *Cyberbullying Prevention and Response.*

24. Patchin and Hinduja, *Cyberbullying Prevention and Response.*

25. Patchin and Hinduja, *Cyberbullying Prevention and Response.*

26. Patchin and Hinduja, *Cyberbullying Prevention and Response.*

27. S. Hinduja and J. W. Patchin, "Offline Consequences of Online Victimization: School Violence and Delinquency," *Journal of School Violence* 6, no. 3 (2007): 89–112.

28. Hinduja and Patchin, *Bullying Beyond the Schoolyard;* S. Hinduja and J. W. Patchin, "Bullying, Cyberbullying, and Suicide," *Archives of Suicide Research* 14, no. 3 (2010); J. W. Patchin and S. Hinduja, "Cyberbullying and Self-Esteem," *Journal of School Health* 80, no. 12 (2010): 616–623.

29. M. Rosenberg, *Society and the Adolescent Self-Image* (Princeton, NJ: Princeton University Press, 1965), 15.

30. L. G. Wild, A. J. Flisher, A. Bhana, and L. Carl, "Associations Among Adolescent Risk Behaviours and Self-esteem in Six Domains," *Journal of Child Psychology and Psychiatry* 45 (2004): 1454–1467; D. Glover, G. Gough, M. Johnson, and N. Cartwright, "Bullying in 25 Secondary Schools: Incidence, Impact and Intervention," *Educational Research* 42, no. 2 (2000): 141–156; L. A. Beaty and

E. B. Alexeyev, "The Problem of School Bullies: What the Research Tells Us," *Adolescence* 43, no. 169 (2008): 1–11.

31. Patchin and Hinduja, "Cyberbullying and Self-Esteem."

32. B. High, *Bullycide in America—Moms Speak Out About the Bullying/ Suicide Connection* (Rocky Mountain House, Alberta, Canada: JBS, 2007); Hinduja and Patchin, "Bullying, Cyberbullying, and Suicide."

33. J. Flowers, "Cyber-Bullying Hits Community," *Addison County Independent*, October 2006, http://www.addisonindependent .com/node/280/

34. K. Zetter, "Dead Teen's Mother Testifies About Daughter's Vulnerability in MySpace Suicide Case—Update," *Wired.com*, November 20, 2008, http://www.wired.com/threatlevel/2008/ 11/lori-drew-pla-1/

35. Hinduja and Patchin, "Offline Consequences of Online Victimization."

36. N. Ericson, "Addressing the Problem of Juvenile Bullying," *OJJDP Fact Sheet*, no. 27 (June 2001); D. Olweus, "Norway," in *Nature of School Bullying: A Cross-National Perspective*, ed. P. K. Smith, Y. Morita, J. Junger-Tas, D. Olweus, R. Catalano, and P. Slee (London: Routledge, 1999); Borg, "The Emotional Reaction of School Bullies and Their Victims."

37. J. DeVoe and C. Murphy, *Student Reports of Bullying and Cyber-Bullying: Results From the 2009 School Crime Supplement to the National Crime Victimization Survey* (NCES 2011-336) (Washington, DC: National Center for Education Statistics, 2011), http://nces .ed.gov/pubsearch/pubsinfo.asp?pubid=2011336

38. Hinduja and Patchin, "Offline Consequences of Online Victimization."

39. Hinduja and Patchin, *Bullying Beyond the Schoolyard.*

40. K. J. Gergen, M. M. Gergen, and W. H. Barton, "Deviance in the Dark," *Psychology Today* 7 (1973): 130.

41. Ybarra and Mitchell, "Online Aggressor/Targets, Aggressors, and Targets"; Hinduja and Patchin, *Bullying Beyond the Schoolyard.*

42. S. Hinduja and J. W. Patchin, "Cyberbullying: An Exploratory Analysis of Factors Related to Offending and Victimization," *Deviant Behavior* 29, no. 2 (2008): 1–29.

# 4

# *Adolescent Relationships in the 21st Century*

## *An Introduction to Sexting*

*From my freshman year to my sophomore year I dated the same boy. I naively thought that we were in love, going to get married, and live happily ever after, as many 16 year olds think of their boyfriends and girlfriends. But my sophomore year we broke up and we didn't speak for two months. One night I was hanging out with my two best friends when he texted me saying "If you send me a naked picture of yourself I'll get back together with you." I didn't think about what I was doing, and impulsively, wanting to do everything I could do to get him back, I quickly took a topless picture with my head cropped out and my two best friends faces in the picture. I didn't know that by clicking send I would be changing my life and who I was forever.*

—Allyson Pereira, (then) 16-year-old girl from New Jersey

Teens in today's society have extensive access to cell phones, with 77 percent of those between the ages of 12 and 17 owning one.[1] This number has been growing steadily over the years—from 63 percent in 2006 and just 45 percent in 2004—and such a trend should continue as entry costs decrease and as cell phone service providers increase their coverage areas. Cell phones allow youth to keep in regular contact with parents and friends alike, and they serve as a communication safety line in difficult situations (like when a new driver has a flat tire).

Sending and receiving text messages via one's cell phone has become extremely popular, especially among adolescents. A survey by Nielsen found that teens send or receive an *average* of 3,400 text messages each month (or approximately 7 texts per waking hour!).[2] In addition to sending text-based messages, most cell phones also transmit pictures and video. While there are many positives associated with this instant ability to connect, communicate, and share, it also creates several potential problems. One such issue of concern that has emerged is referred to as "sexting."

> **Prevention Point**: Sexting is the sending or receiving of sexually explicit or sexually suggestive nude or seminude images or video, usually via a cell phone.

We define *sexting* as "the sending or receiving of sexually explicit or sexually suggestive nude or seminude images or video" (generally occurring via cell phone). Others have characterized it as "the creating, sharing, and forwarding of sexually suggestive nude or nearly nude images by minor teens."[3] Still others prefer to focus on "youth-produced sexual images."[4] Most commonly, the term has been used to describe incidents where teenagers take nude or seminude (e.g., topless) pictures of themselves and distribute those pictures to others using their cell phones (although it is also possible to distribute such images via social networking sites, email, instant messaging programs, and video chat). The images are often initially sent to romantic partners or interests but can find their way into the hands of others, causing problems. While the public is most concerned about these behaviors as they occur among adolescents, there is evidence that many adults participate in sexting as well.[5] The purpose of this chapter is to provide readers with a fundamental understanding of the problem and its consequences, both on an individual and societal level. We then provide guidance to educators and parents to reduce the acceptability and prevalence of this activity.

## SEXTING IN THE NEWS

> *It's really not something that should be happening in middle school, but unfortunately it does.*
>
> —13-year-old girl from Florida

A steady stream of news stories continues to inform and alarm us about the problem of sexting. For instance, three girls (ages 14 and 15) were charged with creating, disseminating, or possessing child pornography after they allegedly sent nude or seminude images of themselves via cell phone to three male class-mates (ages 16 and 17) in 2009. In this Westmoreland County, Pennsylvania, case, the boys were also charged with possession of child pornography since they had the incriminating images on their phones.[6] In March of the same year, a 14-year-old boy was arrested and accused of sending a picture of his genitalia via cell phone to a female classmate in his high school;[7] a similar case occurred in Fort Wayne, Indiana.[8] Around the same time, a 14-year-old girl from Passaic County, New Jersey, was charged under child pornography laws for posting almost 30 nude photos of herself on MySpace.[9] In another case, two

**Figure 4.1**

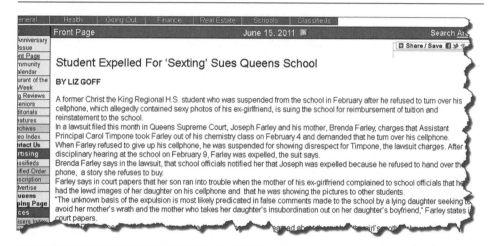

**Figure 4.2**

**Figure 4.3**

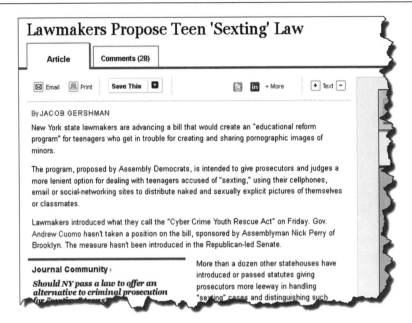

**Figure 4.4**

teenagers from Ohio were charged with "contributing to the delinquency of a minor," a first-degree misdemeanor, when school administrators found nude photos of two 15-year-old classmates on another student's phone.[10] Figures 4.1–4.4 show similar stories "ripped from the headlines."

# HIGH-PROFILE INCIDENTS

Apart from these incidents, which garnered significant media attention, the suicides of Jesse Logan and Hope Witsell catapulted adolescent sexting behaviors to the forefront of the national social conscience. Jesse Logan was an 18-year-old girl from Ohio whose ex-boyfriend circulated nude pictures of her to a large number of their high school peers, leading to extensive and unremitting verbal cruelty. In an attempt to get the behaviors to stop and to educate others about the problem, Jesse appeared on a Cincinnati television program to talk about her ordeal. Unfortunately, that didn't improve her situation. Two months later, she committed suicide after suffering socially and academically as a result of the humiliation and abuse she received from classmates. As MSNBC.com reported, "the girls were harassing her, calling her a slut and a whore. She was miserable and depressed, afraid to even go to school."[11]

Hope Witsell was a 13-year-old from Florida when she sent a topless picture of herself to a boy she liked. The image quickly found its way onto the phones of other students. Her journals indicated the vicious name-calling (e.g., "slut," "whore") she endured for weeks before it became too much for her to handle. "Tons of people talk about me behind my back and I hate it because they call me a whore! And I can't be a whore. I'm too inexperienced. So secretly, TONS of people hate me."[12] She ended her life two weeks into her eighth-grade year.

## Why Do Teens Engage in Sexting?

We recently saw a girl (who looked to be around nine years of age) wearing a shirt that proclaimed "Born to be SEXY." Not to be prudes, but it is bothersome that cultural messaging strategies continue to induce girls to think of themselves primarily (or even partially) as a commodity that can possibly (or actually) sexually benefit others. This shirt would be problematic even if a grown woman was wearing it. Along the same lines, reality shows like *Toddlers and Tiaras* and *Dance Moms* at best condone and at worst promote a certain image that young girls should aspire toward and even obsess over. This also can contribute to girls and women adopting an oversexualized approach to attracting attention from others.

We have seen anecdotally, through screenshots collected by our research team as they scour Facebook and MySpace, that girls who present themselves in line with these messages seem to have more online "friends" and receive more Wall posts and comments on their profiles. This attention and feedback consequently reinforces and promotes the behavior by providing the affirmation and validation that we are all looking for and hoping to receive—albeit in different ways. The major concern we (and many others) have is that feelings of self-worth and identity will be tied exclusively to physical attractiveness and sexual exploration/experimentation. This, as psychological research has

### Adolescent Anger Lands Teen on the Sex Offender Registry

Eighteen-year-old Phillip Alpert was convicted of child pornography charges and appears on the official offender/predator website of the Florida Department of Law Enforcement (FDLE) because of his role in a sexting incident. After an angry phone call, Alpert signed onto his 16-year-old ex-girlfriend's email account using her password (that she had provided to him), located the nude images she had sent him in the past, created a personal email list, attached the photos, and then sent the images to about 70 individuals. With the seconds that it took to click "Select All" and "Send," Alpert went from a "foolishly behaving teenager to a child pornographer and a sex offender."[13]

Alpert and his family cooperated fully with the police, and their home was searched and all electronic storage devices were seized. The authorities that spoke to Alpert noted that the 18-year-old was not the typical suspect who would face child pornography charges, but this didn't matter in the long run. After the charges were filed against Alpert, the prosecution warned him that if he did not accept the plea offer, he would likely spend most of his life in prison.[14] Not knowing what to do and thinking the criminal justice system would know what was best, he accepted the deal. The deal included semiannual polygraph tests, five years of probation, and five years of forced attendance at weekly sexual offender classes designed to ensure that he does not reoffend. According to his lawyer, Lawrence Walters:

> Here, he's being trained not to reoffend and deal with his pedophilia or sexual deviance, which does not exist. He's stuck with people who did terrible things with minors, and he's forced to tell his story over and over again and can't move beyond it. For a 19- to 20-year-old kid, that's not a healthy thing. The more he does this and the longer he goes to these classes, the more he concludes, "I guess I am one of them. I must have done something so horrible to be considered like the dregs of society." It has a terrible impact on his self-worth.[15]

Finally, Alpert is now a registered sex offender, a label he will have to carry until he is 43 years old.[16] Due to the charges against him, Alpert was forced out of the community college he was attending and was unable to keep employment for any length of time. Alpert takes responsibility for the harm that he caused to his girlfriend and does not believe that he should "escape all punishment for his behavior." However, he does not believe that the punishment fits the crime or that he should be labeled as a sex offender for simply making one late-night mistake shortly after reaching the age of majority (i.e., chronologically becoming an "adult" according to the law). Whether the prosecutorial and legal response was appropriate or not, the details of this entire case are a sad commentary on the difficulties involved in sexting between and among developmentally immature youth.

shown, may lead to future victimization—or, at least, unhealthy and even exploitative attraction and interest from boys and men.[17] A deeper discussion of this issue is warranted to couch the current analysis of sexting in its proper context.

It seems helpful to view and interpret sexting among adolescents through a developmental lens. Youth seek to figure out who they are and what they stand for during this tenuous period of life, and the process by which this occurs depends greatly upon cues from their social environment. That is, peer perceptions and cultural norms are a large determinant of their self-worth. As such, adolescents often seek to present themselves to their peers in a way that attracts positive attention and increases social status. This then serves to meet their inherent needs for affection, affirmation, and validation.

A teenage girl might hesitate for a moment when asked to send a semi-nude or nude picture of herself to a boyfriend or boy she's interested in, but if it may improve that boy's perception of her and consequently her perception of herself—and if it is deemed socially acceptable behavior—she may do it. This problem is exacerbated by incessant cultural messages that describe and promote teen sexuality in arguably unhealthy ways—where "hooking up" may be preferred to "dating" and where having personal privacy boundaries is viewed as "old-school" and "lame." Many factors—such as self-respect (or the lack thereof), locus of control, self-esteem, and immaturity—contribute to this problem.[18]

**Prevention Point:** Teens tell us that they engage in sexting because it is safer than sex: they won't get a disease or get pregnant. They need to understand the real, lasting consequences of taking and sending suggestive or explicit pictures.

A recent study observed that we live in a culture that condones a media environment replete with sexual content.[19] The results demonstrated that

> by the end of middle school, many young people have seen sexually explicit content on the Internet, in X-rated movies, or in magazines. Early exposure is related to subsequent attitudes about gender roles, personal sexual norms, sexual harassment, and sexual behaviors.[20]

In such a society, then, sexting can be misconstrued as a way for adolescents to explore their sexuality without actually participating in the act of sex. Indeed, several teens have told us that they engage in sexting because "it is safer than having sex." They don't have to worry about getting pregnant or contracting a disease. "I can trust my boyfriend," they say. "It's not a big deal, and everyone in a relationship is doing it."

Adolescents are overcome with images every day, in numerous media and press outlets online and offline, in which celebrities are ostentatiously posing in bikinis or low-cut clothing and are otherwise showing off their body in sexual ways. This colors the conceptions of young women by defining what is "sexy" and what will seemingly help in obtaining popularity and attention. If youth learn that sexualized behavior and appearance are approved of and rewarded by society and by the people whose opinions matter most to them, they are likely to internalize these standards and consequently engage in "self-sexualization."[21]

> *When one considers our society, it's no surprise that our children have lost all sense of modesty. Not only do social networking sites like Facebook, MySpace, and Bebo encourage teens to share information about themselves; but when they are not taking their clothes off, their role models are spilling their guts about their "private" lives all over the pages of every national newspaper, magazine, and on television.*

—Television Producer and Director Olivia Lichenstein[22]

There is no shortage of examples of celebrities participating in sexting behaviors. For example, a hacker reportedly accessed Miley Cyrus's email account and found pictures that had been sent to her boyfriend. Even though the pictures were not nude, they were still considered provocative. Topless images of actress Vanessa Hudgens that she allegedly sent to her boyfriend were also released on the Internet. Pop superstar Rihanna has also publicly endorsed the activity, despite the media fallout surrounding topless pictures of her that surfaced online. In a *Rolling Stone* interview, she stated, "When you're not with the person you want to be intimate with, a picture is the next best thing. Well, Skype is safer. But a picture lasts a long time. When you're alone . . . pictures can be very handy."[23]

To be sure, adults have not presented themselves as good examples when it comes to the distribution of sexually explicit material. Male celebrities such as golfer Tiger Woods, actor Jesse James, Tony Parker of the NBA's San Antonio Spurs, and retired quarterback Brett Favre have also been involved in sexting scandals. Several politicians (including most famously New York Representative Anthony Weiner) were forced to resign due to their sharing of explicit photos. Whether they want to be or not, these public figures are role models to preteens and teens. As such, adolescents may see the attention that famous people receive following these exploits as positive (bad publicity is better than no publicity!) and even start to normalize the behavior in their mind as more incidents appear in the media. Moreover, some adolescents in the 21st century may participate in sexting in order to emulate the celebrity, much as they want to dress in the same way and talk in the same manner. The American Psychological Association found in its "Report of the APA Task Force on the Sexualization of Girls" that

> as girls participate actively in a consumer culture (often buying products and clothes designed to make them look physically appealing and sexy) and make choices about how to behave and whom to become (often styling their identities after the sexy celebrities who populate their cultural landscape), they are, in effect,

sexualizing themselves. Keen observers of how social processes operate, girls anticipate that they will accrue social advantages, such as popularity, for buying into the sexualization of girls (i.e., themselves), and they fear social rejection for not doing so.[24]

According to psychologist Dr. Judith Paphazy, it is predictable that teens and twenty-somethings reared on a diet of reality television will conclude that giving up some aspects of personal privacy is normal and even offers many rewards. Yet the teens who bare their souls, or skin, don't necessarily see themselves as willfully giving up their privacy. They just construe the concept differently and believe that their Facebook participation and texting conversations are private adolescent places.[25] This said, though, adolescents are "group animals," and their requirements for privacy are not the same as in adult-to-adolescent communications. Rather, they openly share "risky" material within their social group—especially electronically.

In a society in which a woman dressed up as a "pig-tailed schoolgirl" has evolved into a sexual fantasy for some, one cannot be surprised that sexting among adolescents serves a similar fantasy role. However, in the adolescent's mind, which prioritizes the "here and now," consequences are rarely considered, and once that Send button is clicked, there is no going back. No longer do teens pass notes to each other, asking the recipients to circle "yes" or "no" to innocent questions such as "Do you like me?" Instead, sexting has become the newest form of flirting, where images are sent in order to display one's attractiveness. Both males and females see sexting as a way to keep the attention and excite the emotions and passions of the people they are interested in attracting. To be sure, sexting is also considered appealing to the younger generation because it is taboo. It represents a risqué act that doesn't actually go as far as sexual intercourse or even "fooling around" in person, but it feels pretty close on a psychological level. Plus, it is done behind their parents' and teachers' backs and would be forbidden if an adult found out about it—which adds another level of excitement.

## Sexting Images Go Viral

Most teens who engage in sexting assume that only one person (at most) will see the images that they took. As pointed out above, they typically send the image to a romantic partner or interest and believe it will not be seen by anyone else. Of course, if that were the case, we probably wouldn't find out about it or be talking about it today. Some recipients of the images distribute them to others, deliberately or inadvertently, potentially resulting in significant social and emotional consequences for the person pictured. The subject of the image may experience a great deal of mental anguish, embarrassment, shame, and regret after (1) taking the nude or seminude image of himself or herself and (2) sending it to his or her romantic interest. The betrayal that accompanies discovery that one's picture is "out in the wild" may also compromise that teen's ability to trust others and to be relationally vulnerable in the future. These feelings may undermine a teen's desire to go to school, work, or even social events and may lead to self-imposed isolation and loneliness in order to avoid stares, comments, and further harassment by those who have seen or heard about the circulating pictures.

Fear may be another dominant emotion: fear of being ostracized, fear of continued social stigma, or fear of additional sexual exploitation if the images are distributed across the Internet as child pornography. Outside of these consequences, the child might be punished by his or her parent(s), by school administrators, and by the state (through criminal prosecution).[26] With so many weighty ramifications, you would think that youth would be deterred if only they could consciously think through the consequences of their actions. Unfortunately, due to biological and social immaturities, they may ignore the potential consequences of sexting and act without much forethought, driven largely by emotions.[27] These emotions include the desire to be liked and loved by someone or everyone, the hope that this relationship is the one that will last forever, the feeling that their picture won't be viewed by unwelcome third parties, the belief that they are invincible and unsusceptible to things turning out badly, and the notion that this is what the rest of their peer group is doing. With regard to the last point, we now turn our attention to identifying how much sexting is really going on across adolescent populations. This should clue us in to how widespread the problem is and ideally even inform a subsequent plan of action based on identifying who is more likely to participate and how it takes a toll on the lives of victims.

**Prevention Point**: Due to biological and social immaturities, teens may ignore the potential consequences of sexting and act without much forethought, driven largely by emotions.

## HOW MANY TEENS REALLY PARTICIPATE IN SEXTING?

Five major studies have been completed that have collected data on the frequency of sexting among teens (including our own preliminary work). Figure 4.5 summarizes the data from these various studies.

### National Campaign to Prevent Teen and Unplanned Pregnancy

First, the National Campaign to Prevent Teen and Unplanned Pregnancy and CosmoGirl.com released data from late September and

**Figure 4.5**

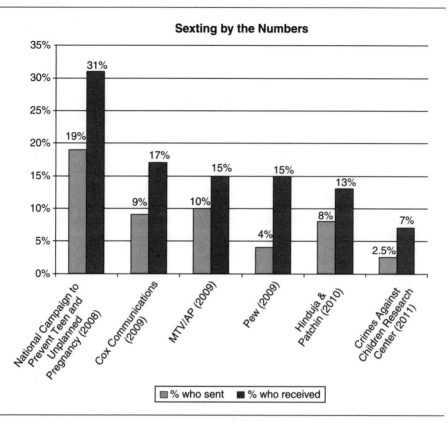

**Sexting by the Numbers**

Legend: ▨ % who sent   ■ % who received

early October of 2008 from a total of 653 teenagers aged 13 to 19.[28] In this study, titled "Sex and Tech: Results From a Survey of Teens and Young Adults," almost one out of five (19 percent; 22 percent of girls and 18 percent of boys) of the respondents revealed that they had sent a sexually suggestive picture or video of themselves to someone via email, cell phone, or another form of online interaction. Approximately 40 percent of teens said they sent sexually suggestive messages (not images) via text, email, or instant message.

Of note, of those who sent sexually suggestive content, 21 percent of girls and 39 percent of boys admitted that they did so to someone they wanted to date or "hook up" with.[29] The survey revealed that many of the teenagers were aware of the risk that their pictures could be forwarded to someone else. Three out of four of the teens noted that sending sexually suggestive content "can have negative consequences." One-quarter of the girls and one-third of the boys said that they have had nude or seminude images shared with them that were originally intended for someone else. In this survey, teens were also asked to share their reasons for participating in sexting. The following justifications were provided: to be "fun and flirtatious," as a "sexy present to their boyfriend/girlfriend," in response to content that they had received, as a "joke," to "feel sexy," and in some instances due to feeling pressured.

It is very important to move past the percentages and look carefully at the thought processes of youth as they decide to send a compromising picture of themselves that can prove to be their downfall. The above feedback seemingly reveals the lack of maturity that many teenagers possess (through little fault of their own), as well as an inability to think beyond the moment in which they are sending the pictures.[30] It also demonstrates a deep, visceral desire to draw and receive the sexual attention of another, ostensibly to meet certain felt needs that likely tie into their identities and values.

## Cox Communications

Cox Communications released findings from a sexting study conducted in April 2009 indicating that 9 percent of 655 teenagers ages 13–19 surveyed had sent sexually suggestive pictures via text or email, 3 percent had forwarded one, and 17 percent had received one.[31] Of those who have either sent or received sexts, 43 percent have done both, and nearly all those who have sent sexts have received them. Among these respondents, only 6 percent have sent a sext and never received one, 51 percent have received a sext and never sent one, and 43 percent of those who have either sent or received sexts have done both.

With regard to the relationship between senders and recipients, 60 percent of those who sent texts or emails with a nude or nearly nude/sexually suggestive photo of themselves did so to their boyfriend or girlfriend. Three out of four (75 percent) received one or more of these messages from their boyfriend or girlfriend. Interestingly, 21 percent sent such a message to someone they had a crush on, while 49 percent received it from someone they had a crush on. A final notable statistic from this study is that 19 percent sent a sext to their ex-boyfriend or ex-girlfriend, while 20 percent received one from their ex-boyfriend or ex-girlfriend.

Stated reasons for sending sexts included the following:[32]

- To have fun (43 percent)
- To impress someone (21 percent)
- To feel good about myself (18 percent)
- To try to date someone (8 percent)
- As a joke (4 percent)
- As a dare (1 percent)

Most surprisingly, 43 percent of those who have sent such a message did so simply because someone asked them to do so. Whether this points to the historically powerful pressure of peer influence, signals a population of current-day youth who are looking for quick validation from others, or highlights a generation who believes that this behavior is commonplace and they are just doing what "everyone" else is doing, this finding is somewhat shocking. Perhaps, though, it shouldn't be if we once again put ourselves in the shoes of American adolescents today.

## MTV/AP

MTV and the Associated Press explored the issue of sexting in September 2009 and found that 10 percent of those between the ages of 14 and 24 had sent a naked picture of themselves to others and 15 percent had received naked pictures or video from someone directly.[33] Respondents stated they had sent a naked picture to a boyfriend or girlfriend (53 percent), someone they had a crush on (15 percent), someone they dated or hooked up with (22 percent), someone they had just met (10 percent), someone they wanted to date or hook up with (25 percent), or someone they only knew online and had never met in person (29 percent). Interestingly, many respondents characterized the sending of naked pictures to someone else as "stupid" (64 percent), "dangerous" (54 percent), "uncomfortable" (48 percent), and "gross" (41 percent), while some considered it "hot" (10 percent), "fun" (10 percent), "sexy" (14 percent), "flirty" (12 percent), and "trusting" (10 percent).[34] Finally, underscoring the point that one really never knows what the recipient of a naked picture does with it, 68 percent said they don't think their photos were shared with anyone else, 19 percent said they weren't sure, and 14 percent said that the pictures intended for only one person were indeed shared with others without permission.

## Pew Internet & American Life Project

The Pew Internet & American Life Project collected data from 800 teens June–September 2009 and found that 4 percent of youth (ages 12–17) who owned cell phones had sent sexually suggestive nude or nearly nude images of themselves to someone else, while 15 percent had received such images of someone that they knew. In addition, the survey found that older teens were more likely to participate, with 8 percent of 17-year-olds having sent and 30 percent having received these images. Teens who pay their own cell phone bill are more likely to engage in sexting; 17 percent of teens who paid their own cell phone bill admitted to sexting compared to 3 percent of teens who did not pay their own bill.[35]

## Crimes Against Children Research Center

The Crimes Against Children Research Center collected data in late 2010 from a nationally representative sample of over 1,500 Internet users between the ages of 10 and 17.[36] Results indicated that about 7 percent of youth had received "nude or nearly nude" images of others, while 2.5 percent admitted to have posed nude or nearly nude in a picture or video. Girls and older students were more likely to have appeared in and received sexually explicit images.

Overall, the authors of this study concluded that far fewer students are participating in sexting than previously thought. Moreover, the proportion of teens who participate in a way that is potentially subject to child pornography laws (sexually explicit images that include naked breasts, genitals, or someone's bottom) is extraordinarily low (only about 1 percent). It was also discovered, however, that parents, teachers, and law enforcement officers never found out about 72 percent of the images that the youth had received or appeared in. Given that this study utilized the most rigorous research methodologies of all sexting studies to date, the results should not be dismissed.

### Our Own Survey

Finally, in our most recent (2010) survey, we found that 12.9 percent of youth aged 11–18 had received a naked or seminaked image of someone from their school.[37] Moreover, 7.7 percent admitted that they had sent a naked or seminaked image of themselves to someone else from their school. We found that males were more likely to have *received* a naked or seminaked image of someone from their school via cell phone (see Figure 4.6); specifically, about 16 percent of males had received a naked or semi-naked image compared to about 10 percent of females (this was statistically significant). Males were also slightly more likely to have *sent* a naked or seminaked image via cell phone (8.1 percent of males versus 7.2 percent of females).

Sexting behaviors appear to increase in frequency as teens get older—which makes sense because their real-world sexual experimentation also tends to increase.[38] It is clear from our work that participation in sexting steadily increases as students progress through middle and high school (see Figure 4.7). It is also evident that sexting does not end when teens graduate from high school. Another study conducted by Pew found that 6 percent of adults over the age of 18 admitted to having sent a nude or seminude image of themselves to others, while 15 percent reported that they had received such an image.[39]

**Prevention Point**: Boys are significantly more likely to receive sexts and slightly more likely to send them.

It is clear from the studies described above that a meaningful number of youth have participated in sexting. The actual number of students is somewhat uncertain when looking across existing studies for a number of reasons. First the rates reported above vary depending on how

Figure 4.6

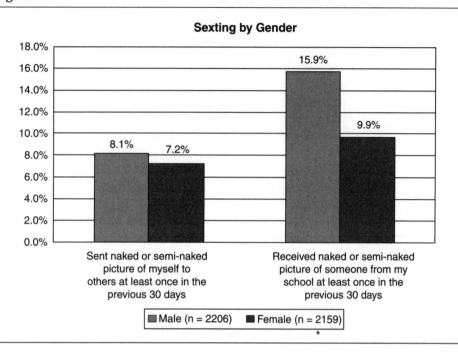

Figure 4.7

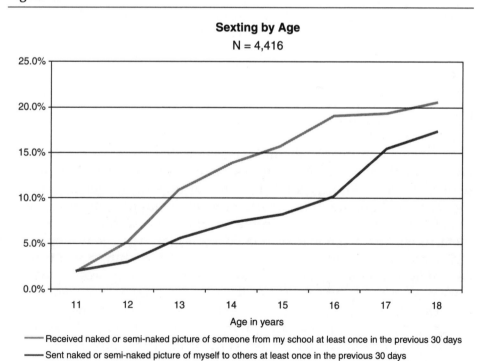

sexting was defined, whether that definition included only cell phone use or also included other forms of online communication, the specific age group studied, and the study's methodology and sampling. For example, the studies conducted by the National Campaign to Prevent Teen and Unplanned Pregnancy and MTV both included adults in their samples (18- to 24-year-olds), while Pew and our work include only students who were 18 years old or younger. To be sure, more research is necessary, and those of us who study this problem need to better coordinate our efforts so the results can be more meaningfully interpreted.

## SEXTING: A CONTINUUM OF BEHAVIORS

It appears that sexting occurs along a continuum, ranging from what could arguably considered typically teenage behavior to significant and intentional victimization of others.[40] First, the behavior of sending and receiving sexually suggestive or explicit pictures—as it occurs between two consenting teenagers where there is a shared romantic interest—very well may be developmentally normative behavior.[41] Adolescents tend to explore and experiment with their sexual identity and boundaries while growing into full adulthood and may simply be utilizing the technology with which they have grown so comfortable to accomplish that end. Next on the continuum would be sexting that involves some measure of harassment, pressure, or ill will. An example of this would be when a boy compels a girl to send a topless photo of herself with the argument that "if you really loved me, you would do it." Another instance would be when a girl breaks up with a boy because he cheated on her and then sends a private picture he sent to her to the rest of her friends. Even though the boy shouldn't have messed around with another girl, the former partner is still distributing a sexual picture intended only for her with the malicious intent to get back at him.

Further along this line would be sexting that involves active solicitation, either by a boy or a girl, for attention (in particular, that of a sexual nature).[42] Adolescents who attempt to present themselves in a certain sexualized way may create nude or seminude pictures or videos of themselves—under no influence of others—and may distribute them to convey a number of related messages. They may hope that recipients consequently view them as hot, sexy, fun, adventurous, risk taking, "up for a good time," and worth pursuing sexually. While clearly misguided, this may be done in a relatively innocent manner. That said, some instances of sexting as solicitation may involve a teenager willingly prostituting him- or herself through the sending and posting of self-created sexual content to attract buyers of sexual services.

*Young people just look at it as another way to have fun with a cell phone. They don't consider the end consequences.*

—Joe Showker, instructional technology resource teacher
Rockingham County, Virginia

Finally, this continuum ends in the most serious type of sexting behavior—that involving the intentional exploitation of others for sexual or material benefit. One example would be the case of Anthony Stancl, a New Berlin, Wisconsin, 18-year-old high school senior who impersonated two girls ("Kayla" and "Emily") on Facebook, befriended and formed online romantic relationships with a number of boys from his high school (again, while posing and interacting as a girl). He then convinced 31 of those boys to send him nude pictures or videos of themselves. As if that weren't bad enough, Anthony—still posing as a girl and still communicating through Facebook—tried to convince more than half to meet with a male friend and let him perform sexual acts on them. If they refused, "she" told them that the pictures and videos would be released across the Internet for all to see. Seven boys actually submitted to this horrific request and allowed Stancl to perform sex acts on them or performed sex acts on him. He also took numerous pictures of these encounters with his cell phone, and the police eventually found over 300 nude images of male teens on his computer. He was charged with five counts of child enticement, two counts of second-degree sexual assault of a child, two counts of third-degree sexual assault, possession of child pornography, and repeated sexual assault of the same child—and received a 15-year prison sentence in early 2010.

Another example of exploitation—this time for material gain—occurred in a Maryland suburb of Washington, DC, where 50 boys were involved in inducing, pressuring, or coercing twenty 14- and 15-year-old girls to send them sexually explicit pictures and video. The pictures that were received were then uploaded to a password-protected website, with the password sold to students at their local high school and middle school. Individual pictures were also exchanged for money between students via cell phones and email. The girls who participated regretted their choices immensely and knew what they were doing was wrong even while doing it, but they still went through with it at the request of the boys involved.

## Crimes Against Children Research Center Typology

Janis Wolak and David Finkelhor from the Crimes Against Children Research Center at the University of New Hampshire developed a typology of sexting cases reviewed from law enforcement reports (see Figure 4.8).[43]

**Figure 4.8**    Typology of Sexting Cases

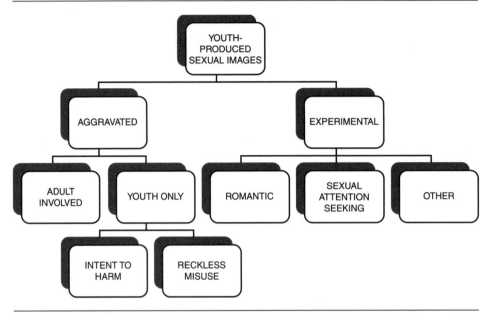

Source: Janis Wolak & David Finkelhor, 2011, *Sexting: A Typology.*[45]

A distinction was made between "experimental" and "aggravated" cases, with the former involving youth sending images to other youth and with no malicious or perverse intentions and with no privacy violations. The latter tended to involve either (1) the involvement of adults (e.g., sending pictures to them or solicitation by them of pictures) or (2) malicious or criminal conduct tied to images, such as abuse, extortion, or deception.[44] Wolak and Finkelhor's analysis revealed that there are many different types of sexting cases, and that it would be a mistake to treat all with the same child pornography laws.

## Sexting and the Law

One of the biggest concerns regarding sexting behaviors among school-aged youth is the fact that many still formally fall under existing child pornography statutes. Strictly speaking, a 15-year-old boy who takes a naked picture of himself and sends it to a romantic partner technically could be charged with the creation and distribution of child pornography. Some have argued that these convictions overstep appropriate bounds and are outside of the original intent of legislators, who formulated the laws to prosecute adults who prey on youth.[46] Others believe that such strict interpretation of the law (where it is a felony to take, send, or keep any sexually explicit image of a minor) is necessary to prevent tragedies like the suicides of Jesse Logan and Hope Witsell.[47]

**Prevention Point:** Youth  who create and distribute sexting images may be violating state and federal law.

Child pornography, of course, falls outside the scope of First Amendment protections, namely because of the harm victimized minors suffer at the hands of the adults who create or distribute it. In fact, federal child pornography law defines sexually explicit conduct depicting a minor as either (a) one of several specifically enumerated sexual acts (e.g., actual or simulated sexual intercourse, oral-genital, etc.) or (b) a lascivious exhibition of the genitals or pubic area.[48] Federal law also defines child pornography as "visual depiction of sexually explicit conduct." According to those guidelines, a "minor" is someone who is under the age of 18, and "conduct" refers to intercourse, oral sex, bestiality, masturbation, and "lascivious exhibition of the genitals or pubic area of any person."[49] A naked picture of a minor doesn't *necessarily* qualify as child pornography if it does not display any of the above characteristics. For example, a toddler in a bathtub would presumably not meet the standard of "lasciviousness." Alternatively, a picture of a minor who is completely clothed could theoretically qualify as pornography if, for instance, the image lasciviously focuses on the genital area. Therefore, the question becomes whether youth should be labeled as child pornographers or even sexual predators if they are taking pictures of themselves (creation, possession) and then making the choice to distribute (dissemination) the images to the phone of a boy or girl they like (possession).

When lawmakers consider kids and virtual worlds, the urge to legislate appears overwhelming, as the intersection of children and new media has always inspired calls for a crackdown as an efficient way of doing "something" about a problem.[50] However, criminally prosecuting children for sexting can be likened to a modern-day witch hunt in which punishment is exacted but those who "offend" never really learn from the experience. With this in mind, we are encouraged to see many states moving away from aggressive stances that treat teen sexters as child pornographers and toward more instructive stances to help teens understand the gravity and implications of their actions. If sexting merely amounts to a new form of sexual expression, self-exploration, and high-tech foreplay and flirting, then punishing minors who engage in it with child pornography laws seems overly harsh and largely unproductive.

Furthermore, many legal and political authorities are beginning to factor in the age of participants and the relational context in which the sexting incident occurred when considering sanctions.[51] The vast majority of instances seem to occur as part of adolescent courtship rituals during an era where cell phones, texting, and sending digital pictures are mainstays of youth culture.[52] As mentioned earlier, teens who engage in sexting often

## Selected State Sexting Bills

Arkansas (2011)—A proposed law addresses the problem of sexting, defined as using wireless communication to stalk a child and communicating improperly with a minor. A person can be charged with a Class A or B felony depending on whether a meeting occurred between a person over age 20 years and another less than age 15 years. Communicating improperly with a minor who is under the age of 18 years with use of wireless communication is a Class A misdemeanor.[57]

California (2011)—Under this bill, if a minor is found guilty of committing an offense deemed sexting as described in the bill, the minor can be fined up to $1,000 and be required to undergo counseling. The court can charge any other fine, sentence, or probation according to the offense. The current law states that any person can be charged with a felony for possessing or distributing images of a minor under the age of 18 years engaging in or simulating sexual conduct.[58]

Florida (2011)—A new law (effective October 2011) reduces the penalty for first-time teen sexting from a felony to a noncriminal offense punishable by a $60 fine and up to 8 hours of community service.[59]

Hawaii (2011)—Law concerns a minor promoting or possessing electronically communicated indecent material. A minor can be found guilty if he or she has intentionally or knowingly transferred to another person a nude depiction of him- or herself. A minor can be charged with a misdemeanor offense and will have the offense expunged after reaching 18 years of age. If an adult is found guilty, the adult can be charged with a Class C felony.[60]

Indiana (2011)—In this bill, exceptions are provided for defenses in disseminating matter (pictures, etc.) to minors. The following exceptions that are provided for defense must all apply: (1) a cellular phone, another wireless device, or social networking account was used for the picture; (2) the defendant is not more than four years older or younger than the person in the picture; (3) the relationship between the two persons was or is a dating relationship; and (4) the crime was committed by a person under the age of 22 years.[61]

Ohio (2011)—A minor is guilty of a misdemeanor in the third degree and a misdemeanor of the first degree for subsequent offenses and can be adjudicated as an unruly child for committing the offense of sexting. No minor shall knowingly send, post, exchange, or share a photograph or video of him- or herself or another minor in a state of nudity. A minor is not in violation if the material is used for an educational, a scientific, an artistic, etc. reason and the minor's parents give consent.[62]

Oregon (2011)—An individual can be convicted of inappropriately using a sexual image and punished with a maximum of 1 year imprisonment and/or a $6,250 fine. This does not apply to individuals in some cases whose ages are less than three years different from that of the victim.[63]

South Carolina (2011)—It is unlawful for a minor who is at least 12 years of age and not more than 18 years to knowingly use communication to send, etc. a nude image of another minor. This civil offense is punishable by not more than a $100 fine, and the offender must take an educational program relating to sexting. If he or she fails to do this, his or her driver's license will be taken away for a period of time.[64]

"think that it's all in good, clean fun or, for some, part of a mating ritual."[53] As such, the growing sentiment is that youth should not be prosecuted using laws that were intended to protect them from predatory adults.[54] We agree with this perspective, as teenagers who naively engage in this behavior should not be placed on sexual offender registries as that will largely ruin their life potential. Prosecutors seem to be retreating from their hard-nosed stances, but they still are pressing formal charges that include "disorderly conduct," "illegal use of a minor in nudity-oriented material," and felony "sexual abuse of children . . . , criminal [use] of a communications facility, or open lewdness."[55] Criminal charges in general, though, may not be the best tack to take.

It has been suggested that once the media buzz that surrounds the problem of sexting fades, legislators should take the opportunity to determine whether it is sufficiently widespread, "given the context of a sex-saturated society and the normal proclivities of teenagers, so as to justify new statutes regulating it."[56] Therefore, if teens are using these types of messages as sexual expression, it is up to peers, educators, and parents to educate adolescents about the true meaning of empowerment, values, equality, and mutual respect within the confines of a relationship. Such efforts are critical in order to change prevailing mentalities among youth regarding what is acceptable and unacceptable.

Our prevention and response efforts are going to be less than ideal if we cannot effectively counter what society is hammering into the minds of adolescents. If the dominant message our kids are hearing is that teen sexuality leads to romantic love, personal fulfillment, popularity, and celebrity status with very little (if any) public or personal fallout, they will continue to push the proverbial envelope, and the line between right and wrong will be increasingly obscured. Cultivating in youth a deeper measure of self-respect, for example, is one way to insulate them against participation in sexting and help them to stand firm when faced with very strong peer and cultural pressures. This can occur within immersive school climate initiatives that support, guide, and strengthen youth to do what is best for *them* in order to accomplish their academic and personal goals—rather than being swayed in other directions.

## SUMMARY

*Sexting* is a buzzword that often strikes fear in adults. Research shows that a minority of youth are involved in the behavior but that when it does occur, big problems can result. It is essential, then, that adults educate themselves about why teens engage in sexting and convey to them the consequences of taking, possessing, or distributing sexually explicit images of themselves or their classmates. We definitely need to handle this issue with care. The number-one priority is to minimize the distribution of sexting images and express to teens the seriousness of such behaviors. The tragic examples of teens who have committed suicide after sexting incidents is a stark reminder that we need to handle these cases better in the future than we have in the past. Of course, it is best if sexting doesn't happen at all. The remainder of this book will lay out a specific plan to help minimize sexting, cyberbullying, and a wide variety of other adolescent problem behaviors online and off. And it all starts with what you are doing in your classroom.

## DISCUSSION QUESTIONS

1. Why do individuals send sext messages? What might an individual who receives a sext say or do in response?

2. How do celebrities perpetuate the behavior of sexting? Why do teens model their behavior after the actions of these individuals? Should celebrities, who are adults, be punished for these behaviors or, at the very least, publicly chastised?

3. What consequences should be available for a person who sends a sext when the message is then forwarded on to others? What kinds of psychological and emotional problems might develop for the original and secondary sender(s)? How does fear play a role in feelings of those individuals who sent the sext?

4. What are some of the crimes a teen can be charged with for sending and/or receiving a sext in your state? Do you think these are appropriate and necessary? What impact do criminal penalties have on the teenager? How should states respond to sexting?

5. What are your school policy and procedures concerning sexting? How should you respond if a student shows you a sexting image of another student? How should you respond if a teen comes to you in tears after she discovers an image of her is being circulated around the school?

## REFERENCES

1. A. Lenhart, M. Madden, A. Smith, K. Purcell, K. Zickuhr, and L. Rainie, *Teens, Kindness and Cruelty on Social Network Sites: How American Teens Navigate the New World of "Digital Citizenship"* (Washington, DC: Pew Research Center's Internet & American Life Project, 2011), http://pewinternet.org/Reports/2011/Teens-and-social-media.aspx

2. "New Mobile Obsession: U.S. Teens Triple Data Usage," *NielsenWire*, December 15, 2011, http://blog.nielsen.com/nielsenwire/online_mobile/new-mobile-obsession-u-s-teens-triple-data-usage/

3. A. Lenhart, *Teens and Sexting* (Washington, DC: Pew Internet & American Life Project, 2009), p. 3, http://www.pewinternet.org/~/media//Files/Reports/2009/PIP_Teens_and_Sexting.pdf

4. J. Wolak and D. Finkelhor, *Sexting: A Typology* (Durham, NH: Crimes Against Children Research Center, University of New Hampshire, 2011), http://www.unh.edu/ccrc/pdf/CV231_Sexting%20Typology%20Bulletin_4-6-11_revised.pdf

5. A. Lenhart, *Teens and Sexting*; J. Leshnoff, "Sexting Not Just for Kids: Plenty of Older Adults Send Racy Messages on Their Cellphones—but It's Usually a Private Matter," AARP, June 2011, http://www.aarp.org/relationships/love-sex/info-11-2009/sexting_not_just_for_kids.html

6. C. A. Courogen, L. Brenckle, and D. Victor, "Police Call 3 Teen Girls' 'Sexted' Photos 'Dumb Stuff.'" *The Patriot-News* (PA), January 30, 2009, http://www.pennlive.com/patriotnews/stories/index.ssf?/base/news/1233292214107320.xml

7. A. Meacham, "Sexting-Related Bullying Cited in Hillsborough Teen's Suicide," *Tampa Bay Times*, November 29, 2009, http://www.tampabay.com/news/humaninterest/article1054895.ece

8. M. Irvine, "Porn Charges for 'Sexting' Stir Debate," Associated Press, MSNBC.com, February 4, 2009, http://www.msnbc.msn.com/id/29017808/ns/technology_and_science-tech_and_gadgets/t/porn-charges-sexting-stir-debate/

9. B. DeFalco, "Teen Girl Facing Porn Charge for Photo Posts—Megan's Law Creator Appalled at Prosecutor," *The Commercial Appeal* (Memphis, TN), March 27, 2009.

10. "Two Mason Teenagers Charged in 'Sexting' Case," WLWT.com, March 4, 2009, http://www.wlwt.com/news/18855563/detail.html

11. M. Celizic, "Her Teen Committed Suicide Over 'Sexting,'" *TODAY*, MSNBC.com, March 6, 2009, http://today.msnbc.msn.com/id/29546030/

12. M. Inbar, "'Sexting' Bullying Cited in Teen's Suicide," *TODAY*, MSNBC.com, December 2, 2009, http://today.msnbc.msn.com/id/34236377/ns/today-today_people/t/sexting-bullying-cited-teens-suicide/

13. R. D. Richards and C. Calvert, "When Sex and Cell Phones Collide: Inside the Prosecution of a Teen Sexting Case," *Hastings Communications and Entertainment Law Journal* 32, no. 1 (2009): 8.

14. Richards and Calvert, "When Sex and Cell Phones Collide."

15. G. Kaufman, "Sexting Leads to Teen Having to Register as a Sex Offender," MTV.com, February 11, 2010, http://www.mtv.com/news/articles/1631734/sexting-leads-teen-having-register-sex-offender.jhtml

16. Richards and Calvert, "When Sex and Cell Phones Collide."

17. American Psychological Association, "Report of the APA Task Force on the Sexualization of Girls," 2007, http://www.apa.org/pi/women/programs/girls/report-full.pdf

18. S. Lamb, *The Secret Lives of Girls: What Good Girls Really Do—Sex Play, Aggression, and Their Guilt* (New York: The Free Press, 2001).

19. J. D. Brown and K. L. L'Engle, "X-Rated: Sexual Attitudes and Behaviors Associated With U.S. Early Adolescents' Exposure to Sexually Explicit Media," *Communication Research* 36, no. 1 (2009): 129–151.

20. Brown and L'Engle, "X-Rated," 144.

21. American Psychological Association, "Report of the APA Task Force on the Sexualization of Girls."

22. O. Lichtenstein, "How the Faceless and Amoral World of Cyberspace Has Created a Deeply Disturbing . . . Generation SEX," *The Daily Mail*, January 28, 2009. http://www.dailymail.co.uk/femail/article-1129978/How-faceless-amoral-world-cyberspace-created-deeply-disturbing--generation-SEX.html

23. J. Eells, "Rihanna, Queen of Pain," *Rolling Stone*, June 6, 2011, http://www.rollingstone.com/music/news/rihanna-queen-of-pain-rolling-stones-2011-cover-story-20110606/

24. American Psychological Association, "Report of the APA Task Force on the Sexualization of Girls," 17.

25. L. Porter, "Malice in Wonderland," *The Age* (Australia), August 10, 2008, http://www.theage.com.au/articles/2008/08/09/1218139163632.html

26. *Miller v. Skumanick* (605 F.Supp.2d 634, 643 (M.D.P.A. 2009)).

27. J. Arnett, "Reckless Behavior in Adolescence: A Developmental Perspective," *Developmental Review* 12 (1992): 339–373; D. B. Ruder, "The Teen Brain: A Work in Progress," *Harvard Magazine,*

September–October 2008, http://harvardmag.com/pdf/2008/09-pdfs/0908-8.pdf

28. The National Campaign to Prevent Teen and Unplanned Pregnancy, "Sex and Tech: Results From a Survey of Teens and Young Adults," 2008, http://www.thenationalcampaign.org/sextech/PDF/SexTech_Summary.pdf

29. The National Campaign to Prevent Teen and Unplanned Pregnancy, "Sex and Tech: Results From a Survey."

30. Arnett, "Reckless Behavior in Adolescence."

31. Cox Communications, "Teen Online & Wireless Safety Survey," 2009, http://www.cox.com/takecharge/safe_teens_2009/research.html

32. Cox Communications, "Teen Online & Wireless Safety Survey."

33. A Thin Line, "2009 AP-MTV Digital Abuse Study," 2009, http://www.athinline.org/MTV-AP_Digital_Abuse_Study_Executive_Summary.pdf

34. A Thin Line, "2009 AP-MTV Digital Abuse Study."

35. Lenhart, *Teens and Sexting*.

36. K. J. Mitchell, D. Finkelhor, L. M. Jones, and J. Wolak, "Prevalence and Characteristics of Youth Sexting: A National Study," *Pediatrics* 129, no. 1 (2012): 13–20, http://pediatrics.aappublications.org/content/129/1/13.full.pdf+html

37. S. Hinduja and J. W. Patchin, "Sexting: A Brief Guide for Educators and Parents," 2010, http://www.cyberbullying.us/Sexting_Fact_Sheet.pdf

38. M. Waites, *The Age of Consent: Young People, Sexuality, and Citizenship* (Basingstoke, UK: Palgrave Macmillan, 2005); A. Thornton, "The Courtship Process and Adolescent Sexuality," *Journal of Family Issues* 11, no. 3 (1990): 239–273.

39. Lenhart, *Teens and Sexting*.

40. N. E. Willard, "School Response to Cyberbullying and Sexting: The Legal Challenges," Center for Safe and Responsible Internet Use, 2010, http://csriu.org/documents/documents/cyberbullyingsextinglegal_000.pdf

41. Thornton, "The Courtship Process and Adolescent Sexuality"; J. Arnett, "Emerging Adulthood: A Theory of Development From the Late Teens Through the Twenties," *American Psychologist* 55, no. 5 (2000): 469–480.

42. Willard, "School Response to Cyberbullying and Sexting."

43. Wolak and Finkelhor, *Sexting: A Typology.*

44. Wolak and Finkelhor, *Sexting: A Typology.*

45. Wolak and Finkelhor, *Sexting: A Typology.*

46. *In re Angelia D. B.* (564 N.W.2d 682 (Wis. 1997)).

47. M. K. Ludwig, "School Resource Officers, the Special Needs Doctrine, and *In Loco Parentis*: The Three Main Attacks on Students' Fourth Amendment Rights Within the Schoolhouse Gate," *ChildLaw and Education Institute Forum* (2010): 1–13, http://www .luc.edu/law/academics/special/center/child/childed_forum/ pdfs/2010_student_papers/Mary_Ludwig.pdf; *In re William V* (4 Cal. Rptr. 3d 695 (Cal. App. 1 Dist. 2003)).

48. "Certain Activities Relating to Material Involving the Sexual Exploitation of Minors" (*18 U.S.C. 2252*, 1996), accessed September 7, 2011, http://www.law.cornell.edu/uscode/text/18/2252/

49. "Child Pornography" (*18 U.S.C. 2256*, 2010), accessed July 30, 2011, http://www.law.cornell.edu/uscode/text/18/2256/

50. J. Fairfield. "The End of the (Virtual) World," *West Virginia Law Review* 112, no. 1 (2009), 53.

51. Lenhart, *Teens and Sexting*; *People v. Dilworth* (661 N.E.2d 310 (Ill. 1996)).

52. Wolak and Finkelhor, *Sexting: A Typology.*

53. C. Machniak, "*Flint Journal* Editorial: Law, Civility Lag Behind 'Sexting,'" *Flint (Michigan) Journal*, April 30, 2009, http://www .mlive.com/opinion/flint/index.ssf/2009/04/flint_journal_ editorial_law_ci.html

54. J. Wolak, D. Finkelhor, and K. J. Mitchell, "How Often Are Teens Arrested for Sexting? Data From a National Sample of Police Cases," Pediatrics 129, no. 1 (2012): 4–12, http://pediatrics .aappublications.org/content/129/1/4.full.pdf+html

55. Lenhart, *Teens and Sexting*, 3.

56. C. Calvert, "Sex, Cell Phones, Privacy, and the First Amendment: When Children Become Child Pornographers and the Lolita Effect Undermines the Law," *The Catholic University of America CommLaw Conspectus: Journal of Communications, Law, and Policy* 18, no. 1 (2009): 22, http://firstamendment.jou.ufl.edu/pubs/ sexcellphonesprivacyarticle.pdf

57. http://www.arkleg.state.ar.us/assembly/2011/2011R/Bills/SB741.pdf

58. http://www.leginfo.ca.gov/pub/11-12/bill/asm/ab_0301-0350/ab_321_bill_20110209_introduced.html

59. http://articles.latimes.com/2011/oct/01/nation/la-na-1001-sexting-20111001/

60. http://www.capitol.hawaii.gov/session2011/Bills/HB573_.HTM

61. http://www.in.gov/legislative/bills/2011/HB/HB1042.1.html

62. http://www.legislature.state.oh.us/bills.cfm?ID=129_HB_80

63. http://www.leg.state.or.us/11reg/measures/sb0600.dir/sb0677.intro.html

64. http://www.scstatehouse.gov/sess119_2011-2012/bills/3130.htm

# 5

## *School Climate and Online Misbehaviors*

*You can't separate climate from instruction. You can't separate climate from leadership. You can't separate climate from the purposeful things you do to build a relationship with students. If a school is doing great on one thing, it tends to all fall in line.*

—John Shindler, director of the Western Alliance
for the Study of School Climate[1]

Chapter 2 outlined the power of a positive climate in cultivating an environment at school where wrong attitudes and choices simply aren't accepted (by staff or other students). Chapters 3 and 4 focused on two major ways in which adolescents misuse technology—through cyberbullying and sexting. This chapter moves to connect these seemingly disparate discussions by arguing that a positive climate at school will help to reduce and prevent student problems, not only at school but also online.

During the last several years, school staff have become well aware that what happens online often significantly impacts the environment at school and the ability of students to learn. In fact, many states have recently passed legislation requiring that schools take notice of online issues that disrupt learning. For example, a New Jersey law that took effect on September 1, 2011, states that any bullying or harassment that occurs at school or a school-sponsored event or "off school grounds . . .

that substantially disrupts or interferes with the orderly operation of the school or the rights of other students"[2] is subject to school discipline. New Hampshire, Massachusetts, Connecticut, and several other states include similar language in recently passed legislation. There is little question that what happens among youth via electronic devices affects what happens at school. It is also true that what goes on at school influences the nature and content of students interactions while away from school. That means that a lack of connectedness, belongingness, peer respect, school pride, and other climate components may very well increase the likelihood of technology misuse off-campus by teens.

---

### School Climate and Cyberbullying

There is a definite link between school climate and student online behavior. Without question, problems that occur between students in an online environment become issues at school. These issues often include a large number of students, as they can quickly share their opinions online with many of their classmates. Usually, the concern is brought to my attention by a student who reports being bullied or a parent who wants to know "What are YOU going to do about it?"

We have worked hard to educate our students and parents regarding online safety. Recently, we added a curricular unit at the seventh-grade level (soon to start in fifth grade). Each grade level participates in activities regarding cyberbullying. Additionally, we have had experts come in and talk to our students, staff, and parents about how to be more aware of online issues and how to respond appropriately. We are currently working on steps to communicate and practice online behavior expectations as part of the overall system of Positive Behavior Interventions and Supports (PBIS) at our school.

We try to assist students in resolving cyberbullying issues even if the behaviors did not occur at school. We have had our counselor or trained peer mediators meet with students who are involved in online conflicts to work toward a resolution. As the principal, I have met with several parents to inform (and often educate) them about their child's online behavior. By confronting the issue, I believe our school climate has improved. Students (and parents) know that we care about them beyond the school walls. They know we believe a safe, bully-free environment is critical to providing the best education possible.

—Dr. Barry Kamrath, principal
Bloomer Middle School, Bloomer, Wisconsin

---

## SCHOOL CLIMATE AND BEHAVIORS ONLINE

To our knowledge, only one previous study has specifically looked at how school climate influences cyberbullying. In that study, climate was measured by assessing the degree to which students felt personally connected to the school.[3] A few thousand Colorado youth in Grades 5, 8, and

11 completed questionnaires during the fall of 2005 (with two-thirds of the original sample participating in a follow-up study in the spring of 2006). Here, the researchers found that the more positively students rated their school climate (e.g., staff were trusting, supportive, and fair and the overall environment at school was pleasant), the less frequently they indicated they participated in verbal, physical, and online bullying. The researchers concluded that "preventive interventions that target school bullying by changing norms about bullying and school context may also impact Internet bullying"[4]—which of course supports the main theme of this book. Based on that study and our own research and experiences working with schools for the past decade, we sought to empirically explore the relationship between school climate and online behavioral problems in our own work.

## OUR RESEARCH

In Chapter 3, we defined *cyberbullying* as "willful and repeated harm inflicted through the use of computers, cell phones, and other electronic devices." These elements include "willful" (the behavior has to be intentional, not accidental); "repeated" (bullying reflects a pattern of behavior, not just one isolated incident); "harm" (the target must perceive that harm was inflicted); and "computers, cell phones, and other electronic devices" (this, of course, is what differentiates cyberbullying from traditional bullying). Electronic devices can be used to create and transmit text, sketches, diagrams, images, audio, and video. It is important to point out that this is a *conceptual* definition: a group of words strung together used to provide a mental picture of cyberbullying that we have in our heads. Others if asked to define the term might have different mental pictures. However, we've sought to come up with a definition that others would largely agree is accurate, concise, and comprehensive.

It also bears mentioning that conceptual definitions like ours can be vague and therefore difficult to use in research. How do you distinguish harm that is willful from that which is not willful? What is meant by "repeated" harm? Twice? Five times? Twenty times? Over how long a period? Should we consider and include psychological, emotional, mental, physical, or financial "harm"? Does the definition include words spoken in voice data over a headset that a youth uses while playing a first-person shooter video game over the Internet against other teenagers across the world? Does it include video recorded over a phone, digital camera, or digital video camera, or all of the above? Does it cover stick-figure drawings made on paper and then run through a scanner? How do you convey all of these varieties and variations to the adolescents whose cyberbullying experiences you want to learn about?

In our research, we needed to create an *operational* definition of cyberbullying to clarify our mental picture to youth—so they would know what indicates its existence or presence or qualities. Keeping all of these issues in mind, when we survey school-aged youth about their experiences with cyberbullying, we clearly inform them that the following is what we are talking about:

> Cyberbullying is when someone repeatedly makes fun of another person online or repeatedly picks on another person through email or text message or when someone posts something online about another person that they don't like.

In addition to this specific definition, we also ask teens to report their experiences with nine specific behaviors:

- I have been cyberbullied.
- Someone posted mean or hurtful comments about me online.
- Someone posted a mean or hurtful picture of me online.
- Someone posted a mean or hurtful video of me online.
- Someone created a mean or hurtful web page about me.
- Someone spread rumors about me online.
- Someone threatened to hurt me through a cell phone text message.
- Someone threatened to hurt me online.
- Someone pretended to be me online and acted in a way that was mean or hurtful.

After explaining what we mean by *cyberbullying* and asking about several specific behaviors, we invite students to tell us in as much detail as they feel comfortable about their most recent experience with cyberbullying (you have already seen many excerpts from these stories in this book). By approaching these behaviors from multiple vantage points, we are able to better understand exactly what teens are experiencing and how it is affecting, and is affected by, their school climate. For this book, we use our most comprehensive measure of cyberbullying and consider students who have experienced at least one of the above nine behaviors, two or more times, to be a target of or participant in cyberbullying.

As discussed in Chapter 4, *sexting* is also defined and measured in various ways. Our conceptual definition, "the sending or receiving of sexually explicit or sexually suggestive nude or seminude images or video via one's cell phone" could be misunderstood by adolescents, so in our research we specifically ask them about several specific behaviors, including the following:

- How often in the last 30 days have you experienced the following while using your cell phone: Someone text messaged you with a naked or seminaked picture or video of someone from your school?

- How often in the last 30 days have you done the following on your cell phone: Text messaged someone with a naked or seminaked picture or video of yourself?

You can see that these questions are perhaps narrower than others that have been used to ask students about sexting behaviors. That said, we feel they are very direct and as unambiguous as you can get when trying to ask about a behavior like sexting.

The data for the following analysis were drawn from our most recent study, a random sample of about 4,400 students from 33 middle and high schools in one very large school district in the southern United States. While we acknowledge the preliminary nature of this research (more students and more schools from around the United States would be much better!), we feel that this initial empirical analysis coupled with the theoretical foundation laid throughout this book serves as a compelling basis for believing school climate is related to experiences with cyberbullying and sexting.

**Prevention Point:** Students who reported a better climate at their school also reported fewer online behavioral problems.

Consistent with expectations, we found that in schools where students reported a better climate, students also reported fewer cyberbullying and sexting incidents. As illustrated in Figure 5.1, schools that were rated by students to have relatively "low" school climate had more reports of cyberbullying and sexting than those rated as "medium" or "high." As described in Chapter 2, the climate score was based on student responses to six statements:

- I feel safe at my school.
- I feel that teachers at my school care about me.
- I feel that teachers at my school really try to help me succeed.
- I feel that students at my school trust and respect the teachers.
- I feel that teachers at my school are fair to all students.
- I feel that teachers at my school take bullying very seriously.

Students responded to each of these questions using a 4-point scale ranging from strongly *disagree* (0) to *strongly agree* (3). Scores from the six questions were averaged for each student, and each school was given an average score based on responses from a random sample of students in that school. School climate scores ranged from 1.41 to 2.16, and the three groups were created by looking at natural breaks, which placed roughly one-third of the schools in each group. Average climate scores for each group were low (1.55), medium (1.71), and high (1.90).

**Figure 5.1**

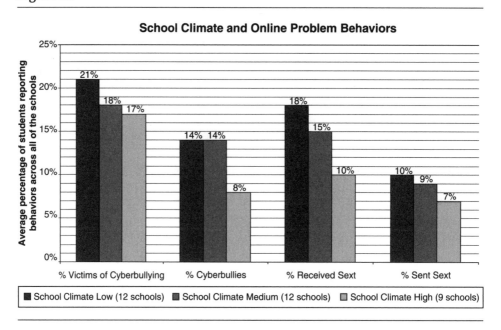

Again, an important caveat is in order. These differences are modest at best, and since our sample included only 33 schools from 1 district, it would be problematic to apply these results to all schools across the United States. It is also quite likely that there are schools out there with much better or significantly worse climates, based on our measure. To be sure, more research is necessary. That said, clear theoretical reasoning and emerging empirical data support the notion that positive school climates are associated with fewer problem behaviors at school and online.

### Educators' Efforts Matter

We also found that teachers who talk about these issues with their students are making a difference. Even though almost half (46 percent) of students said their teacher never talked to them about being safe on the computer and 69 percent of students said their teacher never talked to them about using a cell phone responsibly, when these conversations happen, they seem to have a positive impact. Students who told us that a teacher had talked to them about being safe on the computer were significantly less likely to report cyberbullying others (see Figure 5.2). Moreover, those who told us that a teacher had recently talked to them about using their cell phone responsibly were significantly less likely to say that they had sent a sext to another student (see Figure 5.3). Of course the content of those conversations is also important. Once again, we call for more research to clarify what works in terms of teachers talking with students about safely and responsibly using computers and cell phones.

**Figure 5.2**

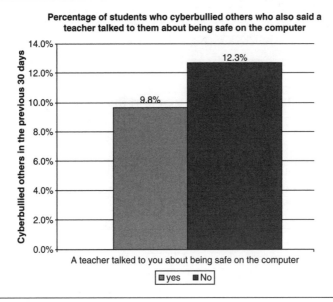

Percentage of students who cyberbullied others who also said a teacher talked to them about being safe on the computer

**Figure 5.3**

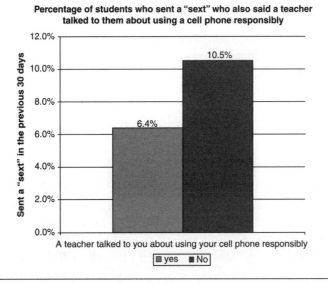

Percentage of students who sent a "sext" who also said a teacher talked to them about using a cell phone responsibly

## Whom Do Targets Tell About Their Experiences With Cyberbullying?

It is also noteworthy that fewer than 10 percent of targets of cyberbullying told a teacher or other adult at school about their experience (about 19 percent of the targets of traditional bullying told an adult at school).

**Prevention Point:** Only about half of the students in our study said a teacher had talked to them about being safe online. But these students were significantly less likely to cyberbully others than those who hadn't been talked to.

Much of the reluctance of students to report these kinds of behaviors stems from their skepticism that the teacher will actually do anything useful to stop the behavior. In fact, most students we speak to suggest that telling a teacher (or other adult) will often make matters worse. In our study, 75 percent of students felt that the teachers at their school took bullying seriously, but fewer (66 percent) felt that the teachers at their school took *cyberbullying* seriously. So clearly adults in school have some work to do to convince students that these problems can be resolved effectively. How can a school or classroom hope to have a positive climate if students are afraid or hesitant to talk to adults about these issues? This is just one aspect of school climate that must be corrected if school administrators hope to develop and maintain an environment where youth can freely learn and thrive.

> *One of my friends started hassling me on msn messenger. She was sending me nasty messages and text messages and this carried on at school. I told my parents, my friends, and a teacher. She was spoken to a few times but it still carries on a bit now. . . . This really affected me at home and at school; I couldn't concentrate on school work and I was always upset and down now I just ignore it and get on with it. I have plenty more friends and I don't need her anymore. Maybe one day she will give up and grow up.*
>
> —15-year-old girl from the United Kingdom

### Expectation of Discipline

In our most recent survey, we asked students to tell us how likely it would be for someone at their school to be caught and punished for cyberbullying. In general, about half (51 percent) of the students said that it was likely that a student from their school would be punished for cyberbullying. Interestingly, this number dropped to less than 40 percent among the students who had actually been victims of cyberbullying. When we examined this question from the perspective of different school climates, we found that students from the schools with more positive climates reported a higher likelihood of a response (see Figure 5.4). Specifically, 65 percent of the students at the schools that scored "high" on our scale (as defined above) said that cyberbullies would be punished at their school compared to only 35 percent of the students at the "low-scoring" schools. Here again, the quality of the climate at school shapes student perceptions of accountability for behaviors online.

**Figure 5.4**

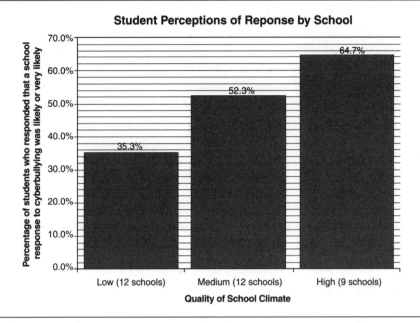

Student Perceptions of Reponse by School

SUMMARY

There are fewer behavioral problems and higher academic performance in schools with a positive climate, and as this chapter has demonstrated, the influence of climate extends beyond the school walls. Students who feel they are part of a welcoming environment will largely refrain from engaging in behaviors that could risk damaging the positive relationships they have at school. Now that we better understand the online experiences of our students, and know that the climate at school is related to those experiences, the next step is to work to transform your classroom and school into a place where students feel safe, respected, involved, and connected. The remainder of this book provides you with a road map for doing just that. Even though it is not an easy path to travel, we are confident that you will not be disappointed when your efforts materialize into happier students and staff and an overall better place to learn and teach.

DISCUSSION QUESTIONS

1. What components comprise the definition of cyberbullying used in our research? Why is this definition *conceptual* in nature? How can one make a more useful *operational* definition of cyberbullying? Do you think cyberbullying should be defined differently than the bullying that occurs at school?

2. In reviewing the study of school climate and online problem behaviors, what conclusions can be drawn from the findings and data?

Why do you think the data suggest that a positive school climate influences online behaviors by students?

3. How do teachers and other adult role models influence student behaviors outside the classroom? How extensive should the role of a teacher be in educating students about online behavior and cell phone use? What is your school doing to teach students about the responsible use of technology? What are you doing?

4. Why do students fear telling a teacher or administrator about problems they are facing online? How might a student benefit from speaking up and talking to an adult at school? What can you do to make it easier for students to talk to you?

5. Why are targets of cyberbullying reluctant to tell non-school-based adults about their experiences? How might a positive school climate indirectly improve this trend?

## REFERENCES

1. D. Stover, "Climate and Culture: Why Your Board Should Pay Attention to the Attitudes of Students and Staff," *American School Board Journal* 192, no. 12 (2005): 32, http://www.nsba.org/Board-Leadership/Governance/KeyWork/Climate-Resources/climate-and-culture.pdf

2. New Jersey State Board of Education, "Administrative Code: Comment/Response Form," April 6, 2011, p. 39, http://www.nj.gov/education/sboe/meetings/2011/April/public/Item C.%20%20Programs to Support Student Development.doc

3. K. R. Williams and N. G. Guerra, "Prevalence and Predictors of Internet Bullying," *Journal of Adolescent Health* 41, no. 6 Suppl. 1 (2007): S14–S21.

4. Williams and Guerra, "Prevalence and Predictors," S14.

# 6

## *Strategies for Improving Your School Climate*

*I have come to a frightening conclusion. I am the decisive element in the classroom. It is my personal approach that creates the climate. It is my daily mood that makes the weather. As a teacher I possess tremendous power to make a child's life miserable or joyous. I can be a tool of torture or an instrument of inspiration. I can humiliate or humor, hurt or heal. In all situations, it is my response that decides whether a crisis will be escalated or de-escalated, and a child humanized or de-humanized.*

—Haim G. Ginott,[1] child psychologist and author
of *Teacher and Child*

By now you know how important school climate is and understand how some teens are misusing technology in ways that can undermine and disrupt the positive learning environment you've sought to create. Schools *must* build and maintain a positive atmosphere that promotes appropriate behaviors and facilitates healthy interactions, as this will contribute strongly to reducing the frequency of many problematic behaviors at school and online, including bullying and harassment. But where do we begin? How do we improve the quality of life on campus to make this happen? Well, let's break it down in a general (though not fixed!) order in which we think you might proceed. This is not an exact formula for every school district, as different districts are probably in varying stages of cultivating a positive school climate already (even if you don't formally call it that). But if you have never embarked on this type of journey, which seeks to clear the air, freshen things up, and revolutionize the way interacting, socializing, and learning are done on your campus, here's what we suggest.

## TOP-DOWN APPROACH

When constructing a concerted effort to improve school climate, it is crucial to begin with a top-down approach. At the district level, you first must recognize that this objective is preeminent and serves as the springboard for success in all other goals of public education (academic achievement, socio-emotional health, adolescent development, character education, etc.). Then you must enumerate clearly what you are currently doing from the district offices to support efforts to promote a safe school environment and connectedness among and between students and adults at school—and see how those initiatives can be expanded or modified to address teen technology misuse.

Moving down to the school level, it is critical to train all staff (educators, counselors, nurses, coaches, administrators) on issues that promote the personal, social, and academic growth of students. This necessarily involves the creation and maintenance of an environment incredibly supportive of common dignity, peer respect, and the appropriate use of communication technologies—and one completely unsympathetic to online bullying or other unwitting or intentional demonstrations of immaturity and irresponsibility via technology. Here, students must know unconditionally that adults are there who understand their desire to exploit technology for all of its positive uses; who encourage those uses; and who believe in teens' ability to take advantage of computers, cell phones, and other portable electronic devices to do great things both in school and in life.

Tied to this is the element of cohesion—promoting a kind of collegiality among peers, as well as between teachers and their students in a mentoring capacity.[2] Purposed pairing of students with adult mentors on campus demonstrates that each child can excel and that none are irredeemable, regardless of past academic disappointments or behavioral missteps. Strategic efforts to promote bonding among students should be in place, as this is related to personal, emotional, behavioral, and scholastic success. Teens must therefore have a true connection with *at least* one adult on campus who periodically checks in on them, builds them up with encouraging words, asks meaningful questions about their lives, and issues gentle reminders that he or she is there if the student ever has any need for help—or even if the student just wants to chat about how things are going (which typically involves expressing socio-emotional needs that the adult can help meet). Everyone who successfully navigated middle and high school had *someone* who got them through. We suspect that for you it was an educator, which in part might help explain your chosen life's work.

---

**Prevention Point:** Every student needs to have a true connection with at least one adult at school. Could that be you?

---

Adults at school should also make an effort to take part in various activities with students (apart from just teaching them in class). Talk to them at lunch, become an advisor to an afterschool club, go to football games and say hi to them there. Be proactive in creating opportunities for building relationships and engaging in dialogue about issues they are confronting—otherwise, these conversations won't readily happen.

School spirit also must be intentionally fostered and fertilized to motivate and induce youth to bond with their school and consequently be more likely to align with and adhere to the norms and conventions in place among those who go to that school (such as, of course, appropriate participation in cyberspace). Part of a positive school climate also involves building morale through the ways in which adults interact with each other. Adults must intentionally (if not naturally) demonstrate collegiality and a contagious esprit de corps before the youth they care for. It's no secret that adults in the workplace sometimes do not get along, but faculty or staff who talk badly about a colleague in the presence of students send the (wrong) message that it is okay to publically make fun of or degrade a peer.

## KNOW THEIR NAMES

The climate of a school matters because, if cultivated positively, it engenders an environment in which students feel welcomed, supported, and cared for. This means that they believe that school personnel are kind, invested in their success, and personally looking out for them. Most of us can remember at least one (or more, if we are lucky!) administrator or teacher from our elementary, middle, or high school years who seemed to take a meaningful interest in our lives—who saw something special in us and who gave extra time and effort to encourage us, assist us, or otherwise just cheer for us as we made our way through a class or grade level. This starts with adults at school simply learning the names of students. For example, one assistant principal in Ohio takes home student photos and starts memorizing the names that go with faces at the beginning of every school year.[3] He then takes the time to greet kids by name, ask them how they are doing, and encourage them to get involved in school-based activities.

*I don't even know how he knew me or knew my name. . . . He makes me want to be more involved and makes me want to do better at my school. If all the teachers were like him, we'd probably have the best school. . . . It's almost like I don't think he's a principal to 2,000 kids. I think he's a principal to me.*

—sophomore from Ohio

*Absolutely hands-down every session, students wished that teachers would know their names and something about them. . . . Kids have said that to us for years. "Know my name. I know you get 120 kids a year, but know my name, and say my name right. And know something about me."*

—Wendy Constantine, Peaceable School coordinator, Anchorage, Alaska

Knowing your students' names and expressing interest in their activities and experiences is a powerful way to develop a lasting bond with them. Anonymity can leave students with a feeling that they don't matter—and one consequence among many other negatives is that they feel they can do what they want without anyone at school noticing, let alone caring. If students are not acknowledged by name, they may feel anonymous. On the other hand, if they feel as though the adults at school know who they are, and care about them, they may think twice about posting that hurtful comment about another student online. They become a person instead of just a face in the crowd whose behavior is invisible and immaterial. When they are noticed, though, they have a presence and hopefully also a standard of behavior to which they are now accountable. Furthermore, if you demonstrate a genuine concern for them, they will begin to value and seek out your indirect and direct approval and esteem—which ideally preempts behavioral problems down the road!

## COMMUNITY BUILDING

Building upon the simple act of learning of student names, teachers should organize community-building activities to remind students that they are individually important and that what they have to say has value. This can be as easy as asking meaningful questions about their lives and recognizing and rewarding right behavior and random acts of "rightness"—when a student does something that demonstrates character. Then community building can be tied to their online participation and interaction. Perhaps you ask them to brainstorm about positive, life-affirming things they can do online, and one student decides to create a Facebook Fan Page to raise awareness about human trafficking in the United States or breast cancer because her mother was recently diagnosed. Start to commend her for doing so in front of other students—hopefully inducing other students to engage in similar initiatives, leading in turn to more recognition and reward. All of these actions collectively underscore the intrinsic worth of each student, which motivates them to behave well, achieve more, and mature into teenagers and young adults who don't just exist but actually make a difference with their lives. And all of this tends to enhance the social and behavioral atmosphere among students. Students become aware that they are an integral member of the school community, and they start to take ownership and responsibility over everything that is happening in the classroom, building, and broader district. In turn, they will come to expect and demand that others not disrupt the "great thing" that is going on in their school.

## SMALL TEACHER–STUDENT RATIOS

Small teacher–student ratios, as well as teacher availability before or after school (or during certain times in the school day), can go a long way toward reminding youth that they are not just another butt in the seat but rather someone whose academic and social success greatly matter to all of the adults on campus. School and classroom size has been linked to a number of student performance, behavioral, and attitudinal measures. For example, it affects students' interest in going to school and continuing on to college, their participation in extracurricular activities, their specific scholastic achievement, how well they like school, their self-concept and feelings of belongingness, and a number of discipline and substance use problems.[4]

As we have stressed throughout this chapter, it is imperative that students feel that their teachers care about them and are personally invested in their success. This becomes more difficult when students feel like they have to compete among each other for attention. Furthermore, a teacher simply can't stay engaged with every student as a class gets bigger and bigger. Some students will become distracted, if only due to room size and not the skills of the teacher, and begin to drift away or play with their smartphones instead of paying attention. If this affects one child, it can affect a handful—which can consequently affect the entire school climate. It is much easier to ensure that 20 students are paying attention than 35 students.

> *There is a natural predilection in American education toward enormity, and it does not serve schools well.*
>
> —William J. Fowler Jr.

Large class sizes have become an unfortunate, but in many cases necessary, response to funding deficiencies as districts work to survive during difficult budgetary times. Even though smaller class sizes are preferable to bloated classrooms, creative and determined teachers can counteract the negative effects of large class sizes by intentionally interacting with every student on a regular, even daily, basis if possible. Frequently touching base with every student reminds each young person that he or she has not been forgotten and that you genuinely care about his or her success. It will certainly take more effort with 35 students than with 20, but it will be worth it when they remember the positive experiences in your class at the 20-year class reunion.

## STAY IN THE LOOP

To paraphrase Kay Burke[5] with regard to classroom conversations, not being "in the know" or current on the newest technologies puts teachers at a disadvantage. Failing to understand the technology and places where cyberbullying, sexting, and other forms of online harassment occur prevents teachers from knowing what to do and how to do it. We really want adults who work with youth to feel encouraged rather than overwhelmed when it comes to staying familiar with new technologies and sites being used by students. You already have a ton on your plate, and you don't know where you can carve out time to learn more about specific Facebook privacy settings, how Twitter is being used, or what personal gaming devices can and cannot access the Web. But these things are important, and they are worth learning about.

We first recommend that an exclusive formal educator training is held at least once every school year at which the latest information about how teens are using technology is presented to administrators from all schools in your district. Building a meeting around teen technology misuse will clearly establish this issue as a priority area for your district. Moreover, it can be used to identify point persons whom educators can consult for guidance and can allow for pipelines of information exchange to be set up.

Second, setting aside 1 hour per week—just 60 minutes—to intentionally educate yourself about what your students are using (or misusing) will help even more. Then you can broach the topic with confidence in class and have students help you more fully understand it by filling in the gaps. Ideally, they will respect you a bit more because they see you are putting in the effort to familiarize yourself with something that is highly relevant to them. Over time, your efforts will also identify you to your students as someone they can talk to openly about any concerns they have (involving technology or not).

**Prevention Point:** Take the time to learn what interests your students—both online and off.

Also, one educator's improper or uneducated response casts the rest of the adults at school in a bad light.[6] This can then discourage youth from approaching you (or other adults) with any problems they are having because "you just don't understand." As Burke[7] points out, making light of a student being victimized online reinforces to the bully that what he is doing is either funny or, at the very least, trivial and insignificant. It also demonstrates to the target that *something is wrong with her* since she can't laugh or shrug it off. It further perpetuates the idea that public humiliation of another person is acceptable. One of us vividly remembers an incident in middle school when a teacher laughed along with most of the class when his pants' zipper was noticed to be down. This particular teacher missed a valuable opportunity to demonstrate to the class that such ridicule wasn't appropriate.

Also according to Burke,[8] teachers who ignore or fail to recognize warning signs from students such as a sudden drop in educational performance, absenteeism, withdrawal and isolation, and other related indicators cannot help victims. You must be keyed into the psycho-emotional health of students, especially those in your classes. You know when something is awry; trust your gut and investigate.

Sometimes when an instance of teen technology abuse is discovered, teachers may be reluctant to get involved and/or report the incident. They may discount the seriousness of the incident, fear retaliation, be unsure of the legal implications, or just be too busy dealing with everything else going on. None of these are valid excuses; all instances must be looked into.[9] An ambivalent attitude sets a negative tone for students, who may see adult ambivalence as a basis for forming a similar perspective. Responses must also be consistent, equitable, nonemotional (not knee-jerk reactions), and very calmly implemented so as not to lose instructional momentum.

You should always remember that the environment you build should not be punitive and draconian. Instead, it should be supportive, trust promoting, educational, and empowering. Students (and adults!) sometimes make mistakes and should not be vilified. Rather, you should provide enough assistance to make it less likely that the person will make the same mistakes in the future. And your intervention should lead to behavioral self-regulation for that student, as well as others who know about and learn from the incident.

## Clearly Define What Is "Not Cool"

Schools must create and promote an environment in which certain behaviors and language simply are not tolerated—by students or staff. Within a positive school climate, students know what is appropriate and what is not and behave accordingly. We believe it is extremely important to work to develop a climate in which cyberbullying or other misuses of technology are simply viewed as "not cool" among the student

**Staying in the Loop: What I've Learned by Listening and Understanding**

**Language: "Post in the cut and shoot the ones."**

A major obstacle for school administrators who want to combat cyberbullying is lacking an understanding of the language the participants on Facebook use to communicate with their peers. Constant monitoring of online communication is futile unless the monitor can comprehend what is being said. For example, take this statement: "If you keep muggin' me, I'm gonna go ham." Translated, this simply means if you continue to look at me in a menacing manner, I will cause you a great deal of discomfort (*ham* = *mayhem*). Or if one reads that students will "post in the cut and shoot the ones," the message implies that students will meet behind the school or an apartment and fight one-on-one with fists (no weapons). Keeping up with adolescent vocabulary is a daunting task. It seems like as soon as we figure out what something means, the kids change their vocabulary.

**Female majority: "He said–she said," is actually usually "She said–she said."**

The overwhelming majority of cyberbullying incidents I deal with involve females. Following are the two main issues:

1. Gossip or "talking smack/trash" regarding another online. I especially deal with many of these types of issues on Mondays after parties and other social gatherings that occur on the weekend.

2. Arguing over a relationship with a boy. I am also finding disputes over a girlfriend becoming more prevalent.

It is important for educators to understand that anyone can be involved in cyberbullying and sometimes it is the people you would least expect.

**There is no distinction between cyber and traditional bullying: "Meet me on the playground at recess."**

My experience indicates that bullying and cyberbullying are no longer exclusive of one another. The lines are blurred. All bullying I deal with *includes* cyber incidents meshed with what we know as traditional or playground bullying. If it is happening online, it is likely also happening at school (and vice versa).

**High-priority areas: "Can I please have a pass to the bathroom?"**

Most large schools have introduced some type of camera/video system to aid with discipline. The proliferation of cameras in schools, while helpful at times, also poses its own set of problems. Privacy laws do not allow for this type of security precaution in certain areas. School bathrooms fall into this category. The students realize this. As a result, kids ask for a pass to the bathroom, where they can text a message or threat, and fighting resulting from cyber and/or traditional bullying occurs in this area. This is very difficult to defend against, especially in a high school when females fight. Most who break up these fights are males. Fighting in the girls' bathroom is a problem. At least when fights took place in the open, male administrators could break them up. We are extremely hesitant to EVER enter into a female restroom!

*(Continued)*

(Continued)

**School status: "Facebook/Fight Club."**

An interesting phenomenon has recently come to our attention. Students are creating Facebook pages that depict their own school "fight club." Students record fights with their cell phones and post to these sites within seconds. I would suggest educators search their high school name followed by "fights" to see what comes up. You may be very surprised. You will also notice where many of the altercations take place (e.g., school bathrooms).

—Mark Trachtenbroit, assistant principal
Wheeler High School, Marietta, Georgia

population. How can this be done? Well, there is no quick solution, but if inappropriate behaviors are immediately and consistently addressed, over time they should disappear. We remember in elementary school that we heard the "*n*-word" as a form of name-calling. This occurred rarely—but it happened enough that we remember it. It was unacceptable back then, but it wasn't yet collectively considered completely "uncool." Twenty years later, we would assert that use of that horrible word remains unacceptable but also has seemingly been deemed completely "uncool" as an insult in many, if not most, environments. Perhaps growing societal condemnation of racism and prejudice, coupled with positive attention toward embracing all forms of diversity, has affected our vernacular and culture to such an extent that children learn very early in life what words they can and cannot use. In one generation, we have seen positive change in the appropriateness of words due largely to education and awareness. This example gives us hope that the same systemic change can take place as it relates to cyberbullying and sexting, particularly through the paradigmatic approach of improving climate.

## MONITOR BEHAVIORS AND RESPOND FAIRLY AND CONSISTENTLY TO PROBLEMS

District personnel have a responsibility to accomplish certain educational and social goals and to foster a positive school climate in which students can achieve these goals. In addition, schools must provide an empathic and nonthreatening environment where youth are comfortable to speak candidly to staff if they are dealing with interpersonal problems. Information technology has permeated educational institutions at all levels, and whether schools provide access to specific devices or not, you have an obligation to give basic instruction on how to utilize technology properly and conscientiously. To be sure, your climate will suffer if you don't. We just do not believe that you should give students laptops, email addresses, or access to computers in school labs; deliver curriculum over the Web or assign classwork or homework that requires search engines; or facilitate discussions and research projects online if you are not also willing to take the time to define, demonstrate, and differentiate between acceptable and unacceptable use of computers and the Internet.

Just about every school has some type of policy in place against bullying and cyberbullying (48 states require schools to have bullying policies as of March 2012). Does your school have a sexting policy? Simply having a policy, however, without proper enforcement, can be counterproductive to your efforts to establish a positive climate. Often, students will perceive certain administrators to be "pushovers" and will take advantage of the situation. That said, it is sometimes difficult to interpret whether certain forms of online speech constitute bullying or are protected under a student's First Amendment rights. Therefore, school personnel must educate themselves about cyberbullying and sexting laws to know when and how to intervene without feeling like they are "policing" every one of their students' online interactions.

On a practical level, educators must also properly supervise their students' usage of on-campus computers and personal cell phones to avoid inadvertently allowing them to engage in cyberbullying or fall victim to it while on school grounds. Leaving students unsupervised in a computer lab, for example, is risky for a number of reasons—not the least of which is the concern that they will use the technology to harm or harass others.

It is also important to remember that adolescents are very "now focused"—that is, they are concerned with what is right in front of them at this very moment. They rarely consider the long-term implications of their actions. Even though they may know that cyberbullying is wrong or that sending an explicit image to another is potentially risky, they may engage in the behavior anyway because they often do not have to deal with any *immediate* consequences. If not closely monitored, the behaviors may not be noticed by adults and may be reinforced by peers. To the extent possible, there needs to be swift and certain response so that teens learn that it is not okay to engage in those types of behaviors.

As a final point, when a teacher does intervene in an attempt to resolve a cyberbullying or sexting incident, he or she must be careful not to allow a favorable (or unfavorable) opinion of one student to prevent pursuit of a resolution that is fair to all those involved. A biased mediation by a teacher or administrator may deter targets from seeking help in the future.[10] School staff cannot be viewed as ineffective adults who simply give the proverbial "slap on the wrist" to those who threaten, humiliate, or harm other students using computers or cell phones. They must draw a firm line and stick to it. This does not mean that you need to have zero-tolerance, mandatory policies that don't allow for flexibility and discretion, but rather that policies and corresponding responses must be reasonable yet sufficiently weighty to be effective (see Chapter 9 for more on this). Enforce school policy fairly and consistently across situations, keeping in mind, again, that the goal is to get the inappropriate online behaviors to stop.

> **Prevention Point:** Be careful not to be perceived as playing favorites when responding to inappropriate behaviors. Respond fairly and reasonably no matter who is involved.

## ENCOURAGE ACTIVE STUDENT PARTICIPATION IN DECISION MAKING

Students should also feel that they have a voice at school. This means that their input on school activities, curriculum, teaching styles, field trips, behavioral issues on campus, and other matters is valued and taken into consideration. Administrators should regularly meet with student leaders or even consider convening a "student advisory board" comprised of students who want to get involved in the governance of their school. Administrators should take student perspectives into account and adapt accordingly to reassure students that their opinions do matter.

Educators need to periodically review their policies and programming concerning student behaviors. And we encourage you to enlist the assistance of students from your school to help. They know—perhaps better than anyone else—what devices, programs, or sites are being used and misused. They can clue you in to the latest popular social networking fad, the newest interactive software being exploited, and the hottest technology tools (along with all of their capabilities). Students can inform adults about some of the problems they are seeing with technology, including cyberbullying, sexting, academic cheating, or general distractedness in the classroom. Ask both older and younger student leaders to sit at the table with administrators and provide feedback on the tech-related (mis)-behaviors they see and hear about (or even participate in). Does your policy cover all possible types, forms, and varieties? Since the majority of students use technology safely and responsibly, it is in their best interest to assist adults in identifying inappropriate uses and getting them dealt with so that one malicious student does not ruin it for the others. Further, policies should focus on specific behaviors rather than particular technologies. As discussed in Chapter 1, the problem isn't necessarily the cell phone—it is how some students choose to use their cell phones. Students can identify the problems most likely to disrupt their ability to learn so that creative and comprehensive policies can be adopted.

All students need to know and understand the acceptable-use policies for school-owned devices. Students who are involved in reviewing the policies cannot say that they "didn't know" that what they were doing was wrong, and using students to help define the behaviors (and even possible response options) will ensure that the policies are up to date and applicable to contemporary concerns. Plus, if students are a part of policy development, they have a stake in the policies' successful implementation. When new or revised policies are developed, use students to help get the word out. The student advisory board could go into individual classes for a few minutes to talk about the purpose of new policies, or they could collaborate on an article for the school paper or website. We've found that the more you educate students about potential issues and concerns, the more willing they are to take ownership of reasonable policies to prevent the misuse of technology.

It is also a good idea to give youth an opportunity to offer constructive criticism on the wording of your formal rules, as well as the informal and formal penalties tied to various transgressions. Allow them to articulate their thoughts and suggestions about what will really work to change prevailing mentalities across campus and meaningfully promote a school climate that is all about appropriate and responsible behaviors (at school and online). Adults know a lot, but many teens know a lot, too, that can inform and guide what is being done in schools, since they are fully immersed in all things technological and social. This is their life—marshal their perceptive minds to assist in determining how best the school can equip students with the skills and knowledge to be responsible digital citizens, how best to pitch mature online behavior as the "cool" thing to do, and how best to get everyone on board.

## STUDENT–TEACHER EVALUATIONS

Students should also have the opportunity to evaluate teachers (or other staff). Oftentimes we think we are doing an ideal job, but we never solicit any feedback or constructive criticism. The years go by with us doing the same thing over and over again without ever getting better (and probably getting worse over time!). This trend can be remedied if you can regularly obtain from students their suggestions, opinions, and thoughts. Typically, educators can distribute an anonymous survey in class or use an online survey (many programs are free and easy to use) that can be emailed to students or posted on the school's website.

One teacher we know sends out the following to his students each year:

> I would like some feedback concerning your experience in my class during the first half of the school year, primarily so that I can get better at teaching. Therefore, I've developed a SurveyMonkey questionnaire to allow you to rate me as your instructor and also provide any suggestions or comments you feel would be useful to me—either for the rest of the school year or for subsequent classes I teach. This is completely anonymous and voluntary, and it is NOT

possible for your responses to be linked to your individual identity. Basically, I'm just looking for you to take the time to constructively comment/critique the first half of your school year with me. Don't tell me what you think I want to hear. Provide comments that I can learn from. Remember, the survey is completely anonymous.

One of his past students stated:

He not only works with students, but also takes advice from them on how to be more effective. . . . This is done through an anonymous survey he himself creates and distributes, making it more personalized to his teaching styles, class, and concerns. The feedback on these surveys is discussed in class and changes are implemented. I have seen it actually make a difference!

How does this relate to a positive school climate? Overall, it conveys to students that you value their input and are being proactive in understanding concerns that they have. They might not feel comfortable raising their hands and voicing concerns about your performance or about other issues with the class. But they may be willing to click through a hyperlink to load a web-based survey simply because they are naturally inclined toward web-based ways of sharing information. By stepping out of your comfort zone, you are reaching them where they are. This will matter to them because it shows you are willing to enter their world. This is one way you can make youth feel welcome in your classroom environment—by valuing their perspectives and doing everything in your power to address their concerns (even concerns they have about you!).

## ENCOURAGE REPORTING OF ANY INAPPROPRIATE BEHAVIOR

As we've discussed, many youth don't tell adults about their negative online experiences: they don't want to be blamed and, as a consequence, lose their Internet privileges or otherwise be forced to miss out on all of the benefits of the Internet. A 13-year-old girl from Virginia expressed this to us, stating, "I wanted to tell my parents but I was afraid that they would never let me chat again, and I know that's how a lot of other kids feel." Knee-jerk, restrictive reactions to difficult experiences a child has bravely shared with a parent will likely close off a candid line of communication that must instead be preserved.

As part of a positive school climate, every student should be encouraged to report instances or evidence of cyberbullying to a teacher, counselor, or any other staff member. Students must be made aware of the proper channels through which to report inappropriate behaviors of all kinds. Also, an anonymous reporting system should be set up so that youth can inform school officials of a problem without fear of repercussion. The last thing a target of harassment wants to be seen doing is walking through the doors of the principal's office. Some schools have forms or email addresses on their websites where students can report anonymously (see Figure 6.1). Other schools have given secretaries or counselors cell phones and made the numbers available to students for calls or texts of concerns. The more responsive you are to these reports, the more comfortable students will feel coming to you with their problems.

**Prevention Point:** Create anonymous ways for students to report concerns they have. No student wants to be seen going into or coming out of the principal's office.

Retaliation or reprisal against any student who anonymously or publicly reports an act of cyberbullying must be expressly forbidden. Students who do retaliate should be subject to disciplinary and remedial action. Of course, any student who intentionally makes false accusations of cyberbullying or other behaviors must also experience consequences. You should take time to investigate any reports received and not respond until it is clear what happened and exactly who was involved.

**Figure 6.1**

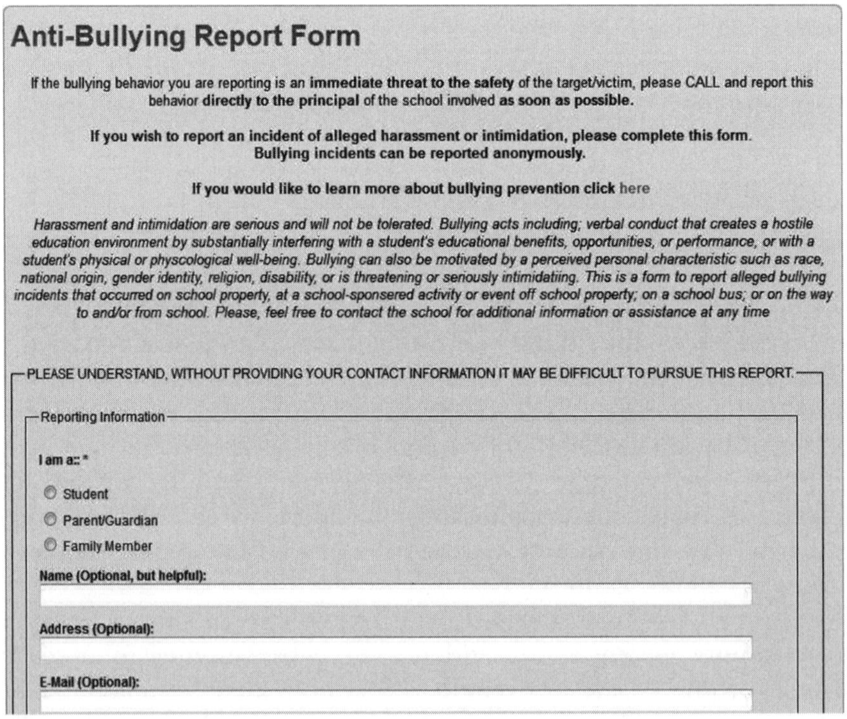

## Anti-Bullying Report Form

If the bullying behavior you are reporting is an **immediate threat to the safety** of the target/victim, please CALL and report this behavior **directly to the principal** of the school involved **as soon as possible.**

If you wish to report an incident of alleged harassment or intimidation, please complete this form. **Bullying incidents can be reported anonymously.**

If you would like to learn more about bullying prevention click here

*Harassment and intimidation are serious and will not be tolerated. Bullying acts including; verbal conduct that creates a hostile education environment by substantially interfering with a student's educational benefits, opportunities, or performance, or with a student's physical or physcological well-being. Bullying can also be motivated by a perceived personal characteristic such as race, national origin, gender identity, religion, disability, or is threatening or seriously intimidatiing. This is a form to report alleged bullying incidents that occurred on school property, at a school-sponsored activity or event off school property; on a school bus; or on the way to and/or from school. Please, feel free to contact the school for additional information or assistance at any time*

PLEASE UNDERSTAND, WITHOUT PROVIDING YOUR CONTACT INFORMATION IT MAY BE DIFFICULT TO PURSUE THIS REPORT.

Reporting Information

I am a:: *

○ Student
○ Parent/Guardian
○ Family Member

Name (Optional, but helpful):

Address (Optional):

E-Mail (Optional):

Source: Community Unit School District 300[11], Carpentersville, IL

# CULTIVATE HOPE

If the climate at school is positive, it will foster and convey a general sense of hope: hope that the student has a bright future if he or she works hard, hope that help is available for the student if trouble arises, and hope that the difficulties of adolescence can be eased with the help of adults at school. Schools with a good climate, for example, assist students who are transitioning into the school or certain classes or clubs; promote more involvement with the family and community; and provide students access to specialized services and organizations when necessary to deal with emotional, psychological, or behavioral issues. When new classes of students arrive at the beginning of the year, we recommend that you provide an intentional orientation not just to the physical layout of the school but also to the school's accepted values and shared beliefs about acceptance, respect, and a genuine interest in seeing everyone succeed. Get those students to understand that there is hope for the future in your school and its classrooms.

Toward that end, administrators and teachers must convey an optimistic attitude, which hopefully will be contagious throughout the school. Without a doubt there are some days when we are frustrated and tired and pushed to the point of breaking. But we cannot reveal these emotions to students (or worse yet, take our troubles out on them). As adults, we are generally better equipped than students to handle the trials that life can bring on. We just need to do our best to serve as a beacon of hope to the students who look up to us. No matter what difficulty they might be experiencing at the time (and most students will face many challenges throughout adolescence), they should and must remain hopeful when in your school and around you.

# THE IMPORTANT ROLE OF SCHOOL COUNSELORS

School counselors are well positioned to play a leadership role in affecting the climate of the school and community.[12] Their insights and services can identify students who are troubled or involved in bullying, and counselors can help these students before the situation becomes more serious or severe. Moreover, their specific knowledge of counseling, classroom guidance, coordination services, and consultation positions them to be effective catalysts and advocates for systemic change within the school. This means that they can reach not only those who come to their office for advice and support but also the rest of the student body through messaging, information sharing, and a guidance curriculum.[13] This can help those students to think hard about and understand concepts like harm, respect, conflict resolution, and inclusion/exclusion.

Some schools have well-developed counseling programs in place, while others simply assign a counselor to do whatever is needed on an

## School Counselors Can Help

School counselors play a vital role within the school building. They are responsible for conducting individual and group counseling; presenting seminars to larger groups to address academic, personal/social, and career needs; and, overall, implementing a comprehensive guidance program that is developmental in nature and age appropriate. It makes sense that they take an active role in helping to establish a positive school climate. A school's climate doesn't only include the interactions among students but also the interactions among faculty, staff, and administrators. A school that frowns upon cyberbullying, and all that it is comprised of, including social media safety and sexting, is a school that creates a positive and safe climate within the building.

The role of a counselor is to provide the foundational skills for safe Internet use so cyberbullying doesn't occur. These skills could range from learning about unsafe Facebook use to overall being conscious of what they leave online for the future . . . their digital footprint. It is up to the student to take this information and actually implement it. It is the job of the counselor, in collaboration with faculty and staff, to ensure Internet use at school is safe. We all hope that students take this knowledge home.

Now how does staying safe online directly relate to school climate? If students understand the lasting effects of both bullying and cyberbullying, they may in turn think before they act negatively when an opportunity to harass someone else arises. Being proactive instead of reactive will ensure a positive and safe climate within a school. Being proactive includes teaching what bullying and cyberbullying actually are, presenting scenarios in which students can see the types of bullying that can occur in person and online, as well as having students work together to brainstorm ideas and have discussions about how to eliminate bullying and cyberbullying at school. Student awareness is just as important as faculty and staff awareness. This knowledge will create an environment where students respect, encourage, and support one another.

It's this collaboration among teachers, counselors, and other school staff that makes prevention possible. It's not simply the sole job of the counselor to stop bullying within in a school. . . . It's the group response of adults that builds this culture of awareness and prevention. When the whole building works together, change can happen. When teachers welcome counselors into their classrooms, it already creates a positive relationship between them. These positive relationships are a model of how positive interactions occur within the school building. In this way, we become our students' role models for building positive relationships and an overall positive school climate where students can grow and learn as individuals, reach their maximum potential, and continue on to be productive members of their community and society.

—Lauren D. Russell, school counselor
Tahanto Regional Middle/High School, Boylston, Massachusetts

ad hoc basis. We highly recommend a more comprehensive approach, as research indicates that all-inclusive school-counseling programs (consisting of a formal evaluation of services provided, personnel supervision, and measurement of student mastery of guidance competencies) impact school climate[14] and are a necessary component of any effort directed at school safety.[15] For example, one study found that students in schools with more fully implemented school-counseling programs (such as those in which counselors provide classroom and large-group presentations, curriculum activities, advising, support during emergency situations, and community outreach, among other program elements) had a more positive experience, believed that the school more adequately prepared them, felt their peers behaved better in school, and experienced a stronger sense of belonging and safety.[16]

On a more general level, counselors can bring attention to the quality of teacher and student interactions and how these affect students on a psychological and social level.[17] Furthermore, they can cultivate and promote excellence in academic achievement, as that specific aspect of climate has been found to decrease bullying.[18] Finally, they can spearhead initiatives to assess and reassess climate through measurement of student perceptions of their school (see Chapter 8).[19] Regular appraisal of school climate is essential so that only the most relevant and advantageous programs and policies are implemented to most optimally prevent and respond to problems. Cumulatively, counselors on campus seem uniquely placed as the hub around which positive connections can be made between students themselves, students and teachers, and students and the educational process—thereby making counselors ideal people to effect change in this area. As one 18-year-old student from Kentucky told us: "When I was younger, I was bullied. They made my life a living hell. Because of them, I hated everything, including myself. If it wasn't for my school counselor, I don't know if I'd be here."

## INFORM AND INVOLVE THE COMMUNITY

You could have a number of amazing initiatives going on at your school, but they will be less successful than they could be if you don't enlighten and involve parents and the community. For example, it would be ideal if you could hold a PTA (or equivalent) meeting at each school to demonstrate to parents that the school is on top of issues related to use and abuse of technology by students. Here, you may make the rules (and consequences) very clear and pass out materials that parents and students should go through together. You can petition parents for their conscientious help in identifying, preventing, and responding to cyberbullying, sexting, and other high-tech misbehaviors and try to enlist not just their minds but also their hearts. It can sometimes be difficult to induce parental participation and support at these events, especially at public schools, but it is truly important so that they learn how to do their part. Perhaps extra credit can be given to students whose parents show up, or raffled prizes, food, and other incentives could be offered. To be sure, caring about this topic shouldn't require such tangible bribes or rewards. However, when one considers how busy everyone seems to be, one realizes that such rewards may be necessary. Many parents don't want to pay attention to a problem until it affects their own son or daughter; of course, the damage is already done by that point—damage that might have been prevented.

> **Prevention Point:** Educators shouldn't have to deal with cyberbullying and sexting alone. Enlist the help of parents, law enforcement officers, and other community leaders to educate students about being safe and responsible online.

## CONTINUE TO LAY THE GROUNDWORK

The school should also have a comprehensive plan in place that continues to enhance the climate through curriculum enhancements, assemblies, signage, the modeling of appropriate interactions by adults and student leaders, and the commendation and reward of positive student behavior. It is essential to spend much more time pointing out and exalting proper behavior than dealing with improper behavior. At the classroom level, we need to understand that youth may not naturally know the right ways to use technology, nor will they always consider the implications (short- or long-term) of their actions. We must also come to terms with the fact that some of their parents are falling short with regard to their responsibility to be involved in their adolescents' online lives and activities and to teach them what to do and what not to do. In the classroom—regardless of the subject matter taught—subtle and overt messages must be communicated that promote wisdom and discretion on the Internet and via electronic devices. There are always ways to introduce the topic, and it will always be relevant to the teens in front of you. Even if they haven't been paying attention as you discuss Shakespeare or the topography of the ocean floor, broach the topic of positive and negative technology use, and they will lock in to what you are saying as they process your words through the lenses of their own experiences. Please note that some of these messages will have to be direct—otherwise, students may not pick up on the gravity and conviction with which the school and its educators desire to approach and tackle this issue.

### Use Resources Available to You

School personnel can use this book as the anchor of a cyberbullying and sexting prevention and intervention campaign. Our goal is (and has always

### What YOU Can Do to Spark Climate Change in Your School

1. *Identify and act on warning signs.* Teachers who ignore or fail to recognize warning signs from students such as a sudden drop in educational performance, absenteeism, withdrawal and isolation, and other obvious indicators cannot help those who need it. Educators must be keyed into the psycho-emotional health of all students and especially those in their classes. You know when students are acting unusual—trust your gut and investigate. The student may not want to talk with you about what is going on, but if you persist, maybe eventually the student will open up. Plus you are sending a message to that student, and others, that you care.

2. *Get involved.* When an instance of teen technology abuse is discovered, teachers may be unwilling to get involved and/or report the incident. They may not appreciate the seriousness of the problem, fear retaliation, be uncertain of the legal implications, be indifferent, or be just plain busy. None of these are valid excuses; all instances must be looked into. Deal with them now or pay the price later.

3. *Supervise.* Students using computers or other devices in school often have access to the Internet and social networking sites despite efforts to restrict them through filters and firewalls. Teachers who do not properly supervise their students' usage of on-campus computers and personal cell phones allow them to potentially engage in cyberbullying or fall victim to it while on school grounds. Actively monitor the online activities of students and set the tone that students who use technology in a distracting or harassing manner will be disciplined.

4. *Take it seriously.* An ambivalence toward the seriousness of teen technology abuse sets a negative tone for students, who may see this attitude as a basis for forming a similar perspective. If a student confides in you about a cyberbullying incident or some other online problem, it has reached a pretty serious level. Most students do not share these experiences with adults, so you should be honored that an adolescent trusts you to help him. Don't let that student down. Do what you need to do to help him, even if you don't fully understand why it is such a big deal.

5. *Avoid sarcasm and degradation.* Making light of a student being victimized online reinforces to the bully that what she is doing is either funny or, at the very least, trivial and insignificant. It also demonstrates to the target and other potential targets that something must be wrong with him since he can't laugh or shrug it off. It also perpetuates the idea that public humiliation of another person is acceptable. Stop all forms of public humiliation no matter how minor they seem. Explain to students that humor can be used to show someone that you care about him or her, but it must not be taken too far—and that everyone has different limits.

6. *Educate yourself.* Not being "in the know" or current on the newest technologies puts teachers at a disadvantage. Failing to understand the technology and various media through which cyberbullying, sexting, and other high-tech misbehaviors occur prevents teachers from knowing what to do and how to do it. Also, one teacher's improper or uneducated response could cast the rest of the adults at school in a bad

*(Continued)*

(Continued)

light. This then discourages youth from approaching any adult. Continually ask teens about their online activities and new devices so that you can keep up with what is popular and the potential problems created by the latest trends.

7. *Know the law.* It is sometimes difficult to interpret whether certain comments online are bullying or protected free speech. Some educators are also unsure of the extent to which schools can discipline students for their online behaviors. Therefore, you must educate yourself on how the law applies to your school and to online behaviors. Chapter 9 of this book will help to clarify some of these issues for you. Some of the best lawyers in the country don't fully understand these issues, so don't be frustrated by a lack of clarity. Just respond in a thoughtful, caring, and reasonable way, and you will be just fine.

8. *Avoid trash talking and complaining.* It's no secret that adults in the workplace sometimes do not get along. Faculty or staff who talk badly about their colleagues in the presence of students send a message that it's okay to publically make fun of or degrade a peer. Model appropriate behaviors and talk with your students about more effective ways of handling disagreements with others.

9. *Don't be biased.* When an educator intervenes to resolve a bullying incident, he or she must be careful not to allow a favorable opinion (or unfavorable opinion) of one student to prevent the pursuit of a resolution that is fair to all involved. A biased mediation by a teacher may deter victims from seeking help in the future.

10. *Consistently enforce school policy.* Almost every school has some type of policy in place against harassment and bullying, and most schools have updated their wording to include cyberbullying. However, it is not only useless but extremely detrimental to have policies on the books but lack enforcement. Often, students will perceive certain administrators to be "pushovers" and will take advantage of the situation. Consistent enforcement doesn't have to be synonymous with harsh or serious discipline. Research suggests that the certainty of punishment is a much more powerful deterrent than the seriousness of punishment.

*Adapted from Kay Burke's "Dirty Dozen" Teacher Behaviors That Can Erode the Classroom Climate.*[20]

been) to meaningfully equip those on the front lines with practical strategies they can immediately implement in schools and homes. For example, you might be able to assign this very book, chapter by chapter, to a "task force" at your school, which can then have conversations about the reading. Next, you could create an email list to facilitate dialogue between and among administrators on the discussion questions at the end of each chapter. You could also create a website/blog/group where each administrator could respond to the "quiz" questions that are on this book's companion website (www.schoolclimate20.com). They will be able to learn from each other, and this will contribute to a team-effort mentality across the district. Additionally, you can require each school to designate a "Cyberbullying Trustee"—someone specifically trained to handle incidents of online aggression who understands youth culture and immersion in technology. Then you can create a master list of Trustees to be posted on the Web and made known throughout the school so that everyone there knows the primary point of contact for technology-related matters.

**Prevention Point:** Visit www.schoolclimate20.com for free resources to help you learn and teach about cyberbullying and sexting!

There are also a number of free resources available on our Cyberbullying Research Center website (www.cyberbullying.us). For example, you can fill out our "Cyberbullying Report Card for Schools" to see where you stand on prevention/response initiatives at your school and a "Notes" section to indicate a plan of action (and timeline) for correcting deficiencies. You can download numerous cyberbullying-related scenarios to share with students and stimulate dialogue about the issues. These discussions will also demonstrate that school personnel recognize the gravity of the problem and want to do whatever they can to help. You can quickly get up to speed on the identification and prevention of these online problems and how to respond when they do occur through downloadable fact sheets, top-ten safety tips, online quizzes, and our frequently updated blog.

## SUMMARY

In this chapter we offered specific strategies for what we feel to be the most promising approach to prevent cyberbullying, sexting, and other online misbehaviors. We heartily believe that students who take some measure of ownership over their school and feel as though they are safe, secure, and respected will refrain from engaging in behaviors (whether online or off) that might damage the positive relationship they have with others at school. Even though the research connecting school climate to student behaviors online is still emerging, numerous studies have already demonstrated beneficial outcomes. Implementing some of the strategies outlined above will without question lead to fewer disciplinary problems at school, as well as fewer issues online. And your school will become a better place in which to learn and work.

In the next chapter, we discuss another key strategy to foster and maintain a positive climate: the utilization of social-norming messages that remind students that most of their classmates do use technology responsibly. Once students feel like they are an important part of the school community, they will more frequently want to behave in concert with the expected and understood norms. Continually clarifying that bullying, cyberbullying, and other problems just don't happen at your school—or that if they do occur, they are immediately and effectively handled—is an important mechanism to get students (as well as staff, parents, and other adults in the community) fully committed to being coproducers of a school climate marked by respect, honesty, and integrity.

## DISCUSSION QUESTIONS

1. What are the aspects of the top-down approach to improving school climate? What comprises each level of the approach, and why is each level important to school climate as a whole? Do you see this working at your school?

2. Why is it important for teachers and school personnel to know each student individually? What benefits do students and school personnel receive from having a more personal connection with each other? What can you do to improve your ability to learn the names and unique characteristics of your students?

3. What is the importance of having a smaller teacher-to-student ratio? What can educators do if the size of their classroom is larger than optimal?

4. How does the formal policy in place reflect a school's attitude toward bullying behaviors? What are the benefits of having students' voices heard when considering and revising your policy? How do you incorporate student perspectives and voices in the governance of your school?

5. Which of the climate initiatives discussed above would work best at your school? What other ideas do you have that would contribute to a positive environment?

## REFERENCES

1. H. Ginott, *Teacher and Child: A Book for Parents and Teachers* (New York: Macmillan, 1975), 13.

2. e-Lead, "Creating a Learning-Centered School Culture & Climate," accessed June 9, 2009, http://www.e-lead.org/resources/resources.asp?ResourceID=25

3. D. Curtis, "10 Tips for Creating a Caring School," Edutopia, March 13, 2003, reprinted at http://www.njbullying.org/documents/10TipsforCreatingaCaringSchool.doc

4. K. Cotton, *School Size, School Climate, and Student Performance* (School Improvement Research Series, Close-Up #20), May 1996, http://upstate.colgate.edu/pdf/Abt_merger/Cotton_1996_Size_Climate_Performance.pdf

5. K. Burke, ed., *Mentoring Guidebook Level 1: Starting the Journey*, 2nd ed. (Thousand Oaks, CA: Corwin, 2002).

6. K. Burke, ed., *Mentoring Guidebook Level 1: Starting the Journey*, 2nd ed. (Thousand Oaks, CA: Corwin, 2002).

7. K. Burke, ed., *Mentoring Guidebook Level 1: Starting the Journey*, 2nd ed. (Thousand Oaks, CA: Corwin, 2002).

8. K. Burke, ed., *Mentoring Guidebook Level 1: Starting the Journey*, 2nd ed. (Thousand Oaks, CA: Corwin, 2002).

9. K. Burke, ed., *Mentoring Guidebook Level 1: Starting the Journey*, 2nd ed. (Thousand Oaks, CA: Corwin, 2002).

10. K. Burke, ed., *Mentoring Guidebook Level 1: Starting the Journey*, 2nd ed. (Thousand Oaks, CA: Corwin, 2002).

11. Community Unit School District 300, "Bully Prevention Report Form," accessed October 5, 2011, http://www.d300.org/form/20756/

12. N. J. Cunningham and D. S. Sandhu, "A Comprehensive Approach to School-Community Violence Prevention," *Professional School Counseling* 4 (2007): 126–133.

13. R. E. Leone, M. J. Mayer, K. Malmgren, and S. M. Meisel, "School Violence and Disruption: Rhetoric, Reality, and Reasonable Balance," *Focus on Exceptional Children* 33 (2000): 1–20.

14. N. Gysbers, K. Hughey, M. Starr, and R. Lapan, "Improving School Guidance Programs: A Framework for Program, Personnel, and Results Evaluation, *Journal of Counseling and Development* 70, no. 5 (1992): 565–570.

15. D. R. Nims, "Violence in Our Schools: A National Crisis," in *Violence in American Schools: A Practical Guide for Counselors*, ed. D. S. Sandhu and C. B. Aspy (Alexandria, VA: American Counseling Association, 2000), 3–20.

16. R. T. Lapan, N. C. Gysbers, and Y. Sun, "The Impact of More Fully Implemented Guidance Programs on the School Experiences of High School Students: A Statewide Evaluation Study, *Journal of Counseling and Development* 75, no. 4 (1997): 292–302.

17. B. Tableman (with A. Herron), "School Climate and Learning," *Best Practice Briefs*, no. 31 (December 2004), http://outreach.msu.edu/bpbriefs/issues/brief31.pdf

18. X. Ma, "Bullying and Being Bullied: To What Extent Are Bullies Also Victims? *American Educational Research Journal* 38, no. 2 (2001): 351–370.

19. C. L. Emmons, "School Development in an Inner City: An Analysis of Factors Selected From Comer's Program Using Latent Variable Structural Equations Modeling, *Dissertation Abstracts International* 54, no. 4-A (1993): 1287.

20. K. Burke, ed., *Mentoring Guidebook Level 1: Starting the Journey,* 2nd ed. (Thousand Oaks, CA: Corwin, 2002).

# 7

## *It Takes a Village*

### *Social Norms, Bystanders, and Peer Mentoring*

*The most important point is that MOST KIDS DON'T BULLY. It's a small % of youth who do that. The "norm" is to treat each other respectfully. And since kids want to be "normal," they should emulate what most of their peers do and not be jerks.*

—Larry Magid, technology journalist and
Internet safety advocate

You now have in your quiver a number of social and behavioral "arrows" that can be used to point and direct teens in the right behavioral direction with their online activities. In the previous chapter, the onus of responsibility for the success of the climate-related strategies we presented rested largely on the shoulders of educators. In the current chapter, we would like to expand our focus to include how teens themselves can share the load and even spearhead their own successful climate-related initiatives. To be sure, they will require some initial guidance and some periodic check-ins by adults. However, we are proposing promising ideas that motivated youth leaders at school can take on, make their own, and really run with. These include social norming, bystander intervention, and peer mentoring.

## SOCIAL NORMING

When a particular behavior is perceived as typical and is widely accepted by a peer group, individuals will naturally participate in it. This is often the case even if that perception may be inaccurate. For example, many people assume that *everyone* speeds on the highways, drinks alcohol underage, engages in premarital sex, or engages in any number of other relatively minor infractions of the law. These misperceptions—created and perpetuated by the social group, popular media, and culture—tend to normalize the behavior or action and attract more participants, eventually leading to the behavior taking on a life of its own. Indeed, most of us have a tendency to conform to these norms simply because we look to others for guidance on how to act—because we either don't know what is the best move in a situation or what is culturally expected.[1] Sometimes this is a positive and welcome trend, such as behavior that the majority of society would prefer everyone adopt (e.g., seat belt use). Other times, however, the behavior is deemed (and perhaps even proven to be) detrimental to individuals, the reference group, or even society as a whole (e.g., drinking and driving). In those cases, society wishes it would stop and does what it can to reduce the behavior's frequency.

> **Prevention Point:** There is often a disconnect between what is perceived to be happening among youth and what is actually happening.

There is often a disconnect between what is perceived to be happening among youth and what is actually happening. For example, at a recent presentation that included approximately 100 educators and students, we asked the audience for estimates of how many students graduate from high school having had sex. One student, sitting in the front row, threw his hand in the air and enthusiastically and confidently exclaimed: "One hundred percent!" We first commented that now everyone in the room knew what *he* was doing, but then corrected him by saying the number is actually much less than that—46 percent, according to recent statistics.[2] In our cyberbullying assemblies, we regularly ask students to estimate the number of youth who cyberbully others. Students commonly report numbers in the 70 to 90 percent range, and the vast majority estimates the proportion to be greater than 50 percent. They are shocked to learn that only about 20 percent of students have ever engaged in cyberbullying.[3] Conventional wisdom would have us believe that *all* adolescents are irresponsible and may be inclined to use technology as a weapon to hurt their peers, even though research shows that relatively few teens actually do. It is important to stress this so that teens who behave appropriately realize that they are in the majority. The social norms theory approach seeks to redefine what is perceived as typical behavior among a collective by focusing attention on (and lauding) the majority who are engaged in positive attitudes and behaviors.

## AN OVERVIEW OF SOCIAL NORMS THEORY

As we've alluded, teenagers tend to do what others are doing—largely in order to fit in—as they try to figure out who they are and what they stand for. As they survey the landscape of trends in behaviors and attitudes, they pick up on what is seemingly accepted, endorsed, and done among their peer group. This influences them consciously or subconsciously, and they then naturally tend to jump "on board" and adopt similar thoughts, words, and actions. For example, if a high school freshman is told by his parents that he can't hang out with friends after Friday night football games because that's when "everyone" parties and gets drunk, he might begin to view that behavior as commonplace and therefore acceptable (or perhaps even mandatory in order to fit in). Though misguided, he may attempt to conform to that behavior since he believes that it is "normal." If an eighth-grade girl is told that a lot of her peers at school eat what they want but then self-induce vomiting so that they can stay thin, she might begin to do the same. This would be unfortunate since such behavior occurs among a small minority of young girls, but even incorrect perceptions of what peers are doing are often strong enough to encourage others to participate.[4]

Social-norming campaigns focus on modifying the social environment so that appropriate behaviors not only are encouraged but are perceived widely to be commonplace. This occurs by identifying a particular activity among a population, assessing how widespread it actually is, and then using well-devised strategies to communicate what most individuals are actually doing.[5] Since "overestimations of problem behavior will increase these problem behaviors while underestimations of healthy behaviors will discourage individuals from engaging in them,"[6] the goal is to publicize the positive behaviors in which the majority of individuals are participating and creatively induce the minority to join their ranks. It is interesting to note that the role of social norms and peer perceptions in guiding behaviors has been found to be much stronger than the influence of cultural messages, familial pressures, and personality traits.[7]

Social norming has demonstrated much value in the area of alcohol abuse, and interventions are increasingly used with young adults who belong to small groups, such as members of fraternities and sororities, athletes, and college and vocational students.[8] Some of this programming presents group members with actual and perceived social norms for their group and encourages members to consider why erroneous beliefs exist. For example, several hundred students at Washington State University participated in a pioneering small-group norms intervention that focused on alcohol use and abuse.[9] In this early study, researchers first administered questionnaires to the entire university student body regarding perceived and actual social norms of alcohol use. Then, researchers surveyed individuals at required meetings of small groups on campus regarding their own drinking attitudes and behaviors and the students' perceptions about the attitudes and behaviors of others.

Several weeks later, trained peer facilitators conducted 45-minute discussions at subsequent meetings of these same groups. The discussions began with the topic of perceptions toward being drunk and also covered drinking norms and expectations among university students. Facilitators informed the group members of the tendency for college students nationwide to exaggerate the extent of alcohol use among other students, and they showed five informative posters illustrating perceived and actual social norms based on the data of the student-body and small-group questionnaires. The facilitator then led a final discussion within the group about the significance of the results and subsequently administered a shortened version of the previous questionnaire. Results from the study indicate that this intervention was the most effective in bringing about a desired perception change and that a reduction in actual drinking behavior was seen after four months.

> *One student, when asked what he had learned said, "I learned that what my friends tell me they think and what they really think are two different things." I thought that summed it up better than I ever could.*
>
> —Gary McDaniel, MSW, clinical social worker,
> Morgan County Schools

Along similar lines, the National Institute on Alcoholism and Alcohol Abuse reports that several universities and colleges that continually displayed and communicated accurate social norms experienced reductions of up to 20 percent in dangerous drinking over a relatively short period of time.[10] In another project, researchers conducted a similar experiment in which 60 participants were randomly assigned to three intervention groups: an Alcohol 101 class (which shared national drinking rates and attitudes), a presentation on campus drinking norms, or a control group.[11] Results indicated that both of the experimental groups modified students' misperceptions regarding peer alcohol use, supporting the hypothesis that providing accurate information about the nature and extent of alcohol consumption among students reframes their perceptions and, in turn, their actual behaviors. This finding was mirrored in other research involving 306 randomly selected students attending one university in which survey results indicated that many had an exaggerated perception of the amount of alcohol that others drank at every social event (bars, athletic events, fraternity and sorority socials, and off-campus and on-campus parties).[12] Correcting misperceptions of the prevalence of peer drinking has led to reductions in alcohol abuse among young adults in Switzerland, France, and Germany as well—complementing the findings of many studies involving American young adults.[13]

It is important to note that social-norming strategies have also proven effective among younger populations. A discussion with high school youth in one study found that students estimated that 75 to 95 percent of their peers drink, while a corresponding anonymous survey revealed that 70 percent *do not* drink.[14] The participants were shocked when they learned of the survey results, and those who did not prefer to drink expressed relief when they realized they were in the majority. Another study involving middle school students in 21 South Dakota schools found that students overestimated alcohol use among their peers by 9.5 percent and marijuana use by 8 percent.[15] Tobacco use has also been positively changed through social norms, as illustrated by a study that targeted several Illinois high schools from 2001 to 2005. Baseline data collected from 2,010 students in 2001 found that 83 percent did not smoke, even though the perception was that only 15 percent did not smoke. Similarly, 53 percent did not drink, while the perception was that only 8 percent did not drink. Over 16 months, high school students (the primary audience) and parents, community members, and middle schoolers (the secondary audience) were targeted with normative messages via posters, flyers, mailers, community presentations, advertising, and promotional items. A few examples of these kinds of messages are provided in Figures 7.1–7.3 and in the following list:[16]

- North students: 8 out of 10 don't smoke cigarettes.
- Most Lincoln students choose not to drink alcohol.
- Most (8 out of 10) Falcons choose not to smoke cigarettes.
- 7 out of 10 East students drink non-alcoholic drinks when they hang out with friends.

Anecdotal and quantitative findings after the first two years were very encouraging. For instance, staff and parents reported more accurate perceptions of the norms of non-use among students, and students' perceptions of their peers' use consistently declined. Moreover, cigarette use in the last 30 days dropped from 16 percent to 12 percent, while alcohol use in the last 30 days dropped from 46 percent to 41 percent.[20] Overall, it is clear that perceptions of what friends and peers are doing with regard to cigarette, alcohol, and tobacco use meaningfully affect an individual's own participation within and across the adolescent years.[21]

Social norming has also been used to counter other unhealthy, dysfunctional, or deviant behaviors among young adults. Specifically, the approach has also been applied to body weight and image norms, dating violence, at-risk sexual behavior, drinking and driving, and digital piracy.[22] In each case, the paradigm was successfully applied to a group of individuals to increase positive behavior by correcting perceived norms and focusing on actual behaviors and beliefs. Much of the research in this area consistently shows that individuals overestimate how permissive peers are with regard to negative attitudes and behaviors and, conse-

**Figure 7.1**

Source: Hobart and William Smith Colleges[17]

**Figure 7.2**

Source: Hobart and William Smith Colleges[18]

**Figure 7.3**

Source: Hobart and William Smith Colleges[19]

quently, think that positive attitudes and behaviors are *not* the peer norm (even if they actually are). These incorrect perceptions may result from

> "(a) attribution error where behavior occasionally observed in others is thought to be typical of them when only incomplete or superficial information about peers is available, (b) social conversation among youth about the most extreme behavior in their midst getting disproportionate attention, thus creating a sense that the extreme behavior is common, and (c) entertainment and news media further amplifying misperceptions by focusing almost entirely on images and stories of the risky or problem behavior."[23]

## SOCIAL NORMS THEORY AND TRADITIONAL BULLYING

Efforts have also been undertaken to utilize social-norming strategies to educate youth about interpersonal violence and schoolyard bullying to promote appropriate behaviors and interactions among peers. Just as with the behaviors described above, there appears to be a difference between how much bullying teens think is occurring and how much is actually happening.[24]

In one public junior high school, a social-norms marketing campaign proved successful in reducing gossip and rumor spreading using the Montana Model of Social Norms Marketing.[25] Data were first collected from 122 students via a web-based survey to gauge individual perceptions of the frequency with which peers engaged in rumor spreading.

Participants were then exposed to normative classroom messages by school faculty over the course of two years. This messaging strategy concentrated attention on the fact that the vast majority of students do not spread rumors. Prior to the intervention, about 13 percent of the surveyed students reported they had spread rumors once a week or more, while 77 percent believed that other students spread rumors once a week or more. Two years later, 20 percent of the surveyed students reported they spread rumors once a week or more, while fewer than 63 percent believed that other students spread rumors once a week or more. Obviously, the decrease in *perceived* rumor spreading by others is in keeping with social norms theory. It highlights the value of the campaign and its intended goal of correcting misperceptions of the frequency of problematic peer misbehavior. However, the increase in self-reported rumor spreading is counterintuitive. It may be due to the effect of the social-norming campaign in increasing students' awareness, recognition, and "labeling" of their own problem behavior (i.e., rumor spreading) or because the students were two years older and more likely to spread rumors at that age. This finding stresses the importance of including control groups (students who don't receive norming messages) to see if changes observed can be attributed more clearly to the intervention.

Similarly, a massive social-norming campaign—involving both traditional community-wide media (billboards, television ads, radio announcements) and localized efforts (posters, banners, stickers, T-shirts, screen savers, video announcements)—was recently used to reduce dating violence among adolescents.[26] This effort, titled "Choose Respect" and developed by the US Centers for Disease Control and Prevention (CDC), was first implemented in May 2006 in ten major US cities. The goal of the initiative was to motivate young adolescents (11–14 years old) to challenge harmful beliefs about dating abuse and take steps to form healthy, respectful relationships and prevent dating abuse before it begins. A great deal of material and information related to this program is available on the CDC's dating-violence website, but no formal evaluation has occurred to chart its implementation among populations of youth or to measure its effectiveness.

Another similar effort involved an antiviolence campaign that targeted adolescents from rural communities in five states: Kentucky, Louisiana, Illinois, Idaho, and California.[27] In this program, high school students served as role models to middle schoolers and communicated the unacceptability of using bullying and other violence to resolve conflict. This message was conveyed through a variety of media (including print, radio, and television), with respect for diversity of individuals, conflict resolution, and bullying prevention being the main issues highlighted. Presentations were also made to younger students in classrooms, assemblies, and community events over the course of a year. While mixed results were found across the towns in a randomized trial, students who received the messages reported decreased physically violent aggression and decreased verbal victimization after a few months as compared to students in a control group.

Most recently, social norms were used to reduce the prevalence of bullying across five middle schools in New Jersey.[28] In this study, data were first collected about the incidence of bullying among the student body, which were then compared to data on student perceptions of that rate. The researchers then used posters to display the rates of actual behaviors and pro-bullying attitudes in the school to show students that their perceptions of the norm differed markedly from reality. After this intervention, data were collected again, and researchers found that perceptions of peer bullying, pro-bullying attitudes, offending, and victimization were all reduced, while reporting of bullying to school personnel and family members increased.

## USING SOCIAL NORMING TO PREVENT CYBERBULLYING AND SEXTING

In light of the findings described above, it can be argued that the social norms approach holds much promise in preventing cyberbullying and other inappropriate online behaviors. Successful efforts began by collecting valid and reliable data on the frequency and scope of actual misbehavior among the population, as well as perceptions of how often it occurred among each respondent's peer group.[29] Then, a campaign was constructed to strategically convey the actual extent of the misbehavior (which was no doubt much less than most teens thought) to everyone involved. The program included multimedia, consistent messaging, thought-provoking activities, and other educational endeavors that promoted a reconceptualization and reframing of the issue. Finally, new data were collected following each intervention to assess its effectiveness in correcting inaccurate perceptions and consequently bringing about a change in behavior.

**Prevention Point:** Before you can reshape the norms in your school, you need to find out what your students believe is happening.

Creating a successful campaign among students involves several essential steps. As mentioned, the school should first collect data to find out if youth overestimate their peers' involvement in cyberbullying or sexting. This can be done through anonymous web-based (e.g., SurveyMonkey) or paper-based survey methods, complemented by feedback received through focus group interviews with a select but representative group of students (see Chapter 8 for details about how to do this). Subsequently, the results can be shared through morning announcements, student assemblies, mass emails, letters home to parents, YouTube videos, table tents in the cafeteria, the school marquee, the school newspaper, brochures, or hallway posters to change prevailing attitudes of the acceptability and prevalence of cyberbullying and sexting while focusing attention on how most youth are "doing the right thing." Furthermore, the messaging strategy can be used to promote healthy and productive use of the Internet and cell phones in more general terms. Finally, the campaign should be evaluated via follow-up research to measure its value in reducing the misperceptions and negative behavior of the target audience.

Social-norming initiatives can be spearheaded by a school official or a public community figure who is relatable and well respected among the student body, or it can be led by (older) peers under adult supervision, in keeping with the structure of traditional peer-mentoring programs (more on this below). Over time and as needed, additional formal and informal lessons—as well as continued interaction between the mentors and mentees—can occur. Cumulatively, these efforts can drastically affect the quality of the school environment by shaping its culture and atmosphere, as well as the prevailing attitudes of those who learn and work there. In the following text, we provide several specific ideas you can put into action to reshape student beliefs about inappropriate online behaviors.

## Coordinate a Student Play

One idea that has worked very well in some communities is the creation and performance of a school play with social-norming messages interwoven in the fabric of its storyline. It can include one or several different skits to deliver the actual social norms message of positive online behavior to students in a creative, relatable, and hard-hitting manner. This production can travel to classrooms within the school, be presented to the entire student body or community, or be shown as part of afterschool and/or extracurricular youth programming.

A skit might include one character who is sexting a boy she has a crush on while another character, who is her friend, explains that the behavior is not "cool." The mere mention that other students do not sext may be sufficient motivation to refrain from the behavior. Additionally, the play can be made interactive as the actors can solicit suggestions from the audience and then improvise on these to convey the appropriate social-norming message. The skits should be fun and interesting to watch, but they should also be direct and to the point and focus mostly on positive uses of technology among the student body. It is up to the creative talent of the drama department to determine how best to present it with props, acting, and a script. If done well, a theatrical production involving fellow students has the potential to have a positive and lasting impact on the entire student body.

### Using Stage Productions to Enhance School Climate

Taproot Theatre has been touring social-issue plays to schools in the Northwest for over 25 years, and the Taproot Road Company serves over 90,000 students in the Northwest each year. We began with drug and alcohol prevention plays in the 1980s, and our hope is to be relevant to whatever issues students are facing.

One reason we feel cyberbullying has become such an important topic is that students are now unable to escape bullying when they go home from school. Students can be bullied via text messaging and social media sites 24 hours of every day. Telling students not to visit certain sites isn't working—wouldn't you want to know what's being said about you? As we've interviewed school administrators, they've expressed the recurring theme that a growing number of school violence incidents begin online and culminate when the students see each other on campus.

In an effort to change the culture of schools, Taproot Theatre premiered the show *New Girl* in 2008. It was a five-character drama in which Rachel, a new student at Clements High School, is pressured into participating in the cyberbullying of one of her classmates. The show dealt with harassment via text messaging, Facebook, and MySpace.

*New Girl* became one of the most popular secondary school shows in Taproot's history with over 210 performances from 2008 to 2011. As national tragedies involving cyberbullying took the spotlight in 2010, *New Girl* was featured on local news shows and in newspapers around the greater Seattle area. Typically, Road Company shows are retired after two years when new material is written, but in the case of *New Girl,* the production was brought back for a third year due to high demand. Following the success of *New Girl* and the response from schools, we commissioned *Don't Tell Jessica,* a play that specifically addresses student interactions via Facebook.

Our plays are designed to spark discussion at a schoolwide level and create a common frame of reference for members of the school community to talk about the problem. Our shows can empower students who are targeted by bullying to find an ally who can assist them in addressing the problem. Students who exhibit bullying behavior get the much-needed opportunity to see the face of the person getting bullied and can begin to empathize with that person's pain. We provide teachers with pre- and postshow discussion questions to help students continue to explore the themes of the plays and ask penetrating questions. These cumulatively contribute to the creation and maintenance of a positive climate at school, with the play serving as one of the major catalysts.

We're trying to help these students find hope. Specifically, it's the hope that we can all live and work together in a community and school environment where everyone is safe, respected, and valued.

—Nathan Jeffrey, director of outreach
Taproot Theatre Company, Seattle, Washington

## Role-Playing

Teachers, administrators, and support staff in schools and youth programs can also organize and facilitate role-playing activities that deliver similar social-norm messaging. An example of such an activity might be three scripts that are given to two students to act out in front of the class. Two of the scripts could focus on positive Internet or cell phone attitudes and behavior, and one script could focus on negative attitudes and behavior (being mindful to focus more strongly on the two involving positive usage, thereby correcting misperceptions about what behaviors are normal among the student body). The role-playing may be done in front of a small group so that a discussion can be held after the activity. Here, the adult facilitator (or older peer mentor) might ask questions and encourage dialogue to reinforce the right behaviors.

### Solidarity Walk or March

As another suggestion, a school could develop a day of awareness to focus on the actual social norms of cyberbullying. At the beginning of the awareness day, school staff can provide students with the perceived social norms across campus by anonymously surveying and then sharing attitudes toward cyberbullying, (mis)perceptions of its occurrence across the student body, and actual numbers related to its prevalence. Following the presentation of what should be an eye-opening disparity between perceived and actual frequency of the problem behavior, students and faculty who support positive online attitudes and actions might engage in a "walk" or "march"—perhaps around the perimeter of the campus or school track. This show of solidarity should provide an overwhelming visual of peers who are on board with "doing the right thing," which will hopefully induce the remainder (or the silent dissidents) to start thinking and acting in similar ways.

### Four Corners

Schools can also implement an in-class social-norms activity that requires active participation and kinetic learning from students. Before the activity begins, initial data once again should be collected. It most likely will indicate a difference between perceived and actual social norms among the youth in the classroom. Then the supervising adult can designate the four corners of the room to represent four different social norms (always acceptable, sometimes acceptable, rarely acceptable, and never acceptable). That adult can read aloud several social-norms statements to students regarding cyberbullying, sexting, and other negative online behaviors, such as, "One of my friends sent a naked photo of herself to the boy she likes because he asked her to," or "He doesn't get along with a girl in his class, so he made a fake screen name and instant messaged her pretending to be the boy she likes, and then he printed out the conversation and passed it around."

The students can stand in the middle of the room as a group as the teacher reads the statements. After each statement is read, students can walk to the corner of the room that they feel best represents their personal sentiments toward the statement. It would probably be best to encourage

**Canadian Initiatives: Students Making a Difference Against Bullying**

- In Nova Scotia, in 2007, a boy in Grade 9 showed up at school on his first day wearing a pink polo shirt. He was bullied incessantly for his choice of color, teased verbally as well as threatened physically. Two boys, David Shepherd and Travis Price, both in Grade 12, decided to take action to stand up for this boy. They went to a local discount store and bought 50 pink T-shirts and tank tops. They also messaged their classmates online, asking them to wear pink the next day. On that day, hundreds of students showed up wearing pink, conveying a very strong positive statement to the entire school community.

- In April 2011, two Nova Scotia students committed suicide after having been cyberbullied. As a result, students in a Grade 8 class decided to campaign against cyberbullying. Many of them pledged to boycott sites such as Formspring and even Facebook, where cyberbullying takes place on a regular basis. They signed forms pledging to stay away from sites where cyberbullying occurs anonymously. They created a video illustrating their campaign, decorated a wall in the school's main foyer with pledge stickers, and organized informational sessions in the evening for parents.

- In Mallorytown, Ontario, nine Grade 8 students began a movement called "Cyberbullying Needs To Stop" (CBN2S). They presented information to their own school, and the response was so positive, they now visit other schools in the district. They bring with them a PowerPoint presentation that highlights instances of cyberbullying and the importance of thinking before sending out an email or text message. They also provide instruction in how to adjust Facebook settings, as well as other practical tips for Internet safety.

- A group of teens from Churchill Secondary School and David Lloyd George Elementary School, both in Vancouver, British Columbia, organized a flash mob at a crowded mall one Thursday afternoon in January 2011. (A flash mob is a large group of people who suddenly break into synchronized song or choreographed dance—sometimes both—for unsuspecting pedestrians, passengers, or shoppers and then disperse when the performance is over as if nothing happened.) The group of 300 students wore pink T-shirts with the word "Acceptance" written across the front and danced to the Grammy award–winning Bruno Mars song "Just the Way You Are."

The above examples of student-led initiatives are a very encouraging sign. It shows that not only is the message getting to students—that cyberbullying is unacceptable, dangerous, and preventable—but that students are taking leadership roles to spread that message to others. We all know that peer pressure can be effective, so why not with social awareness as well as academics? As educators, we cannot be everywhere, nor can we clone ourselves in every school in order to spread this message. But with "ambassadors" such as the ones in these examples, the message *is* getting out to those in need of hearing it; this can greatly contribute to a positive school climate. When students feel safe, they perform well. When it comes to awareness of bullying in all forms, educators must get involved. However, it is the students who can effect change with their enthusiasm, their initiative, and the added bonus of being integral members of the very demographic in need of these ideas and strategies. Leaders in the student body, enlisting the help of others, are the ones best positioned to truly revolutionize the climate at their schools.

—Lissa Albert, MS (Ed Tech), Montreal School Board member and cyberbullying awareness educator students to use blindfolds or to close their eyes (be sure to move desks out of the way!) so they are not influenced by the choices of their classmates. They can open their eyes when arriving in their respective corners and discuss why they chose the way they did. This activity can also be done with live-polling technology using clickers or cell phones so that youth can anonymously select an answer to a question and see how their answer rates among those of their peers. The overarching goal of the activity is for students to visualize and understand that the majority of youth do not support the negative attitudes and behaviors of cyberbullying.

As this section has demonstrated, the social norms theory approach seeks to change prevailing mentalities regarding what is perceived as "normal" by focusing on the positive attitudes held and the positive behaviors engaged in by the majority. Various studies have proven that social norms programs are very useful in dispelling myths that youth tend to hold about their peers' thoughts and actions. As such, interventions and programming grounded in social norming show much promise when extended to the prevention of cyberbullying and sexting.

## PLEDGES

We've been seeing a lot of "cyberbullying pledges" surfacing in recent months. For example, the "Megan Pledge" was launched in honor of 13-year-old Megan Meier, who committed suicide in 2006 after being cyberbullied (by an adult) on MySpace. Obviously, the intention is good—to enlist and rally the support of youth who belong to a school to tackle the problem of peer harassment. That said, it is important for us to take the time to think through how best to address the problem at hand. Setting up a pledge campaign is fairly simple and inexpensive, which is probably why so many adults think that they are a good idea to demonstrate that "something" is being done in the way of cyberbullying prevention. But what about its utility? We should never implement programming because it is easy to do or because we want to check off an item on our list of efforts to combat a problem.

We aren't aware of any research that has attempted to evaluate the effectiveness of cyberbullying or sexting pledges, but studies have reviewed other types of pledges. For example, research on "virginity" pledges based on data from the National Longitudinal Study of Adolescent Health in the mid-1990s and on drug/alcohol abstinence pledges in high schools (such as in the DARE program) has shown that those who truly believe in what they are pledging for/against do hold fast to that commitment as time goes on.[30] This makes sense because pledging to do something provides adherence to a group identity, and let's face it, we all want to belong to a cultural or countercultural group. This is of course even more relevant for most adolescents in the throes of identity development and exploration. It seems, then, that a teen making a meaningful choice to refrain from engaging in an attractive but inappropriate behavior (such as cyberbullying or sexting) should make that choice *outside* of the influence of peers and group dynamics that may shape that choice.

However, it must be mentioned that pledges may be most useful when used in contexts where there are some—but not too many—individuals who pledge. This might seem to fly in the face of the point of social norming, but it deserves comment. You can't try to get every student in a school to pledge to do something, because every student will then generally do so in name only—just to fit in—which doesn't necessarily result in any change in attitudes or behaviors. This caveat should not dissuade you from creating a pledge campaign; we simply want you to be aware of this potential pitfall as you set your big-picture goals. Our colleague Stan Davis (whose extensive work on bullying and bystanders[31] we greatly respect) believes that dialoguing about cyberbullying and its impact with students can help them internalize the harm that is experienced and the negative outcomes that can result, and—more importantly—can help them envision and then realize their potential for *positive* outcomes. This involves reflecting on the good deeds they have done while interacting online and the good deeds that others have done online toward them.

He also suggests that young people write and sign a letter to *themselves* outlining their own plans for keeping themselves and others safe in the digital world. The best way to go about this would be to divide the letter into two parts: "what I will NOT do, and why" and "what I WILL do, and why." These letters should not be read by adults (and the young people should know that the letters will not be read), because when it is known that adults will read the letters, young people are likely to write what they think adults want to hear rather than what they really plan to do. The sealed letters should then be returned to the teens sometime in the future to reinforce their resolve. Accordingly, pledges can prove beneficial if done correctly and if linked to a broader, more comprehensive approach to safety and responsibility.

## STOP STANDING BY AND START STANDING UP!

*The only thing necessary for the triumph of evil is for good men to do nothing.*

—Edmund Burke

As technology has allowed bullies to expand the reach and scope of their torment to an ever broader audience, it has also allowed for increasing numbers of others to see and potentially respond. Cruel posts on Facebook or humiliating pictures sent via cell phone can be viewed by countless individuals, and the question becomes, what does a teen do when he or she sees such examples? In our research, we have found that 42 percent of students had witnessed other people being cyberbullied. We suspect this number is a bit lower than expected due to the wording of the question, which suggests we were interested in experiences that were synchronous: they saw the cyberbullying *as it was happening.* In assemblies at schools, we regularly ask students to indicate by a show of hands if they "have seen cyberbullying." Usually most of the hands go up.

At this point, the question remains: What should teens do if they see technology being used in a harmful way? Well, that depends on a lot of factors, including the nature of the incident, the relationships involved, their expectation of future harassment or violence, and their interpersonal skills. No doubt many teens are more than capable of intervening on behalf of the victimized—by helping the target, redirecting the bully, or informing an adult who can respond. The problem is that most students don't tell adults about their experiences or those of other students. Researchers Stan Davis and Charisse Nixon found that less than 20 percent of students who "saw or heard rumor-spreading, exclusion, harassment based on religion, gender, race and sexual orientation or who witnessed kicking or other physically aggressive acts"[32] told an adult about the experience. Our own research similarly has found that teens are reluctant to tell adults about their experiences with cyberbullying. And whose fault is that? If we are honest with ourselves, we know it is primarily ours. If adults consistently, appropriately, and effectively responded to bullying, cyberbullying, or any other adolescent problem behavior, youth would feel more comfortable coming to us with their concerns (this is discussed in detail in Chapter 9).

**Prevention Point:** Teens are reluctant to tell adults about their experiences with cyberbullying. Think about why that is and then work to gain their trust.

That said, encouraging students to stand up for one another can help tremendously and complement our own prevention and response efforts to create a positive climate at school for a number of reasons. First, it reinforces the mind-set among students that they are all members of the same community where everyone is looking out for one another. How can a school claim to have a positive climate if incidents of harassment are ignored, dismissed, or trivialized by students? Second, there is a greater chance that school personnel will adequately address inappropriate behaviors if students who witness such behaviors are emboldened to take action. If students know that any participation in cyberbullying or sexting is likely to be met with disapproval from classmates and, ultimately, potential consequences from school administrators or parents (see Chapter 9 for more information about when and how to respond), they will hopefully reconsider their involvement in these behaviors.

Since adults cannot be everywhere to witness every adolescent problem, we should equip youth with the tools necessary to take some action. Indeed, it is likely that students will see or hear about these problems before adults. We certainly do not want to put more youth at risk by pressuring them to actively intervene in situations that might not be safe (e.g., standing up to a physically aggressive bully), but we should give students guidance about what they can do. For example, it would be helpful for bystanders to carefully document what happened and then take the details to an adult they trust will respond appropriately. A bystander might simply take the target aside to tell her that what happened was not cool and he is there and available to help make the problem go away. A student could also organize her friends to make a statement about the behavior without doing anything directly. As discussed above ("The Canadian Initiative: Students Making a Difference Against Bullying"), students who disapproved of the way some were bullying a classmate for wearing a pink shirt to school responded by encouraging many others in the student body to wear pink. The one or two students who were involved in the bullying were no match for the couple hundred proudly decked out in pink the next day, and this very effective response required neither physical altercation nor adult intervention.

We shouldn't assume that all students will have the skills necessary to move from "standing by" to "standing up." Instead, we should provide them with opportunities to learn what to do in specific situations. Educators can use role-playing to help students develop strategies. Take the following example: *Connor is receiving nasty comments on his Facebook page from two students at school. He deletes them immediately, but they keep coming nonstop.* Ask students what they would do if they saw these messages. Would they step up and do something? Whom would they tell, and what would they say? Would they say anything to Connor? Several scenarios like this would make for a lively classroom discussion, and if something similar does actually manifest online, hopefully someone (or many students) will take action to respond based on what he or she learned and how he or she was encouraged.

When we speak with teen cyberbullying victims, they frequently let us know that they don't necessarily want the students doing the bullying to be punished. Rather, they just want the problem to go away. One way this can happen is to empower the bystanders to take action to get hurtful content deleted. We should encourage teens who see cyberbullying on Facebook, for example, to report it to Facebook. This can be done anonymously, and the bully will never know who reported it. Facebook also has a "social reporting" feature that allows users to report

**Minnesota Twins**

Last year, our twin boys, Maverick and Tyler, started 7th grade in a school that included 7th- through 12th-grade kids. We expected some bumps along the way but Tyler was getting quieter and pulling into himself. We also were concerned about the friends he had chosen to hang around in school.

At first Tyler didn't want to talk about it. Finally, after hours of talking to him about being available to support him with problems or getting into trouble, he started to cry.

He said, "You just don't understand. They will put me in the hospital. They will slit my throat." My son went on to explain how they were growing marijuana, selling it to younger kids, and how they had connections that could make his life miserable. He had cut himself because the pressure had just gotten to be too much. He didn't know who to turn to. He was too scared to come to us or tell anybody. We immediately filed a police report and went to the school administration with our concerns.

The school response was not nearly enough. The older kids were given a short suspension, then returned to school and, just as my son feared, cornered both of the boys while alone in the bathroom and again threatened physical harm.

The situation began to affect the boys' grades, their ability to make friends, and their personal safety. They felt failed by the school, their friends, and the system. We did everything we could. We continued to meet with the school and offer suggestions for keeping them safe and protecting them. We got them involved in individual counseling, and they started taking medication to help with the depression and anxiety issues.

Then one day, a senior named Emily found them at their lockers and said that she was worried about what the older kids were saying to them. She wanted them to know that she didn't support her peers acting like that and she wanted the boys to know that they were not alone. The next evening they came home with a note from Emily that said, "I want you to know I am serious. I am here for you anytime and you can talk to me. Keep your chin up." She gave her home phone, cell phone, and email address if they needed to talk to her. It changed the boys' outlook immediately. Tyler stated, "Maybe there is hope, Mom. Maybe I am not all alone. She is pretty popular, you know."

I had sat in therapy sessions with my sons for months and listened to how one had written suicide plans and neither one of them knew how to get out from under the pressure. With one act of kindness and bravery, Emily made them think there was hope. She had seen Tyler hunkered down in the corner of a hallway and decided she had to do something. She continues to check in with them daily and make sure that they know she is around. The school needs to have a better response and take some responsibility for what happens on school grounds. But Emily has shown that even one person can make a huge difference. And for my twin sons, that was key to what they needed to begin to change their lives.

—mom from Minnesota[33]

offensive or threatening content to the site and to a "trusted friend." Facebook then forwards the content to the friend so he or she can help. Hopefully, as the reader of this book, you are the friend whom youth feel comfortable confiding in, and you can take the steps necessary to end the victimization.

**Prevention Point:** Encourage bystanders to report inappropriate content or behavior to the relevant website, Internet service provider, or cell phone service provider. In this way, they will be doing their part to help their peers and make cyberspace a friendlier place.

Sometimes it can be difficult for students to stand up to a bully, especially if the person doing the bullying is a friend. One way to address this concern is to encourage students who are put in this situation to respond in a way that is supportive of their friend but not of the behavior. So if someone is laughing about an embarrassing picture or mean-spirited video, students can subtly express their disapproval by not laughing along. A concerned student could also try to change the subject or encourage the friend who is participating in the hurtful behavior to do something else (like download a new app to their phone or explore a new website that is becoming popular). Bringing students together in small groups to brainstorm and talk about these and other appropriate response techniques for a variety of situations, before they arise, can help empower students to do the right thing when the time comes. You can also take advantage of the skills, experiences, and knowledge of older students to educate the younger ones about these issues.

## PEER MENTORING

We know that peers are a very powerful influence on the attitudes, beliefs, and behaviors of adolescents at this stage of their developmental trajectory. The concept of mentoring within this social group generally involves student leaders advising and counseling other students about issues affecting them. Peer mentoring has been effective in reducing traditional bullying and interpersonal conflict within schools and, as such, should be considered in a comprehensive approach to preventing cyberbullying, sexting, and other online behavioral problems as well.[34] Through its use, for example, newer cohorts of students can learn from the wisdom of other adolescents who have already experienced online aggression and have figured out effective ways to deal with it. This wisdom may sink in more quickly and deeply when it comes from peers rather than adults, as kids have the tendency to tune out adults when being taught certain life lessons (can you relate to that, or were you tuning *us* out?). As one mother in California told us: "Parents and teachers can get up and preach, but if they hear it from another kid, they will remember it." This effect may be especially pronounced when older students work with younger students, since the latter often desire to emulate and become like the former. Overall, these efforts can significantly and positively affect the social climate within the school community, benefiting youth and their families, teachers and staff, and the community as a whole. As Mike Tully, a noted school law attorney points out: "Never overlook the possibility of using students themselves as agents of change."[35]

Again, the basic purpose of peer mentoring is to employ students to change the way other students think about the harassment or mistreatment of others in certain situations. Remember from our discussion of social norming at the beginning of the chapter that many teens have a distorted view of what their peers are doing and thinking. Mentors can be used as a reality check for youth who think that the reports of cyberbullying or sexting they see on the news mean these behaviors are commonplace and even normative. Mentors can also be utilized to help students appreciate the responsibility and risks associated with the use of computers, cell phones, and the Internet. To illustrate, one student mentor stated,

> I have started to talk to other children who have had a similar experience and try and help them because they are going through the same thing that I went through and it helps to talk to people who understand. I tell them to be brave and not to worry because everything will be okay.[36]

Ultimately, a primary goal is to encourage teens to take some responsibility for the problems that affect their schools and to work together (and with adults) to come up with a solution. Another goal is to foster respect and acceptance of others—no matter what—and get kids to see how their actions affect others and how they can purposefully choose behaviors that promote positive peer relations. This, then, can drastically affect the quality of the school environment by modifying and enhancing the climate there.

**Prevention Point:** Take advantage of the power of peer approval and use teens to educate other students about how to use technology safely and responsibly.

Peer mentoring can be incorporated into your broader initiatives in a number of ways. For example, high school leaders could talk formally or informally to other students in the cafeteria during lunch about these issues. A few high school students could also organize a presentation for small, classroom–sized (20+) groups. One-on-one sessions might even be held in which a trained student meets with a cyberbullying victim to offer support and help. Finally, skits can be presented in auditoriums or cafeterias by high school students for assemblies comprised of their peers or of younger students in nearby middle or elementary schools. All of these interactions can include one or more activities.

Schools can thereby enlist and utilize students to convey a number of important messages on Internet safety and responsibility, including the following:

- Reiterating that they are not alone in experiencing victimization and the resultant pain, rejection, humiliation, and loneliness
- Encouraging them to speak up and not remain silent when confronted with cyberbullying
- Sharing one or more highly relatable vignettes or stories about cyberbullying
- Explaining the "language" of cyberbullying, including the relevant terms and technology
- Discussing the consequences (legal, social, and professional) of sending or posting sexually explicit images online
- Describing positive ways in which conflict between peers can be de-escalated or resolved
- Getting students to think about the various ways to address a cyberbullying situation
- Providing an opportunity to discuss and answer any questions, clarify any confusion, and reinforce how to deal with online problems and issues

Over time, additional formal and informal lessons—as well as continued interaction between the mentors and mentees—can occur. And eventually the mentee can become the mentor and pass his or her valuable information on to the next generation. The more students who become involved in mentoring, the more effective it may be at shaping the climate at school—which will possibly translate into adults having to do less toward that very end.

## SUMMARY

By now you are hopefully convinced of the value of creating a climate in which peer respect, the "Golden Rule," and courteous interaction with others both at school and online is "what we do around here" and "just how it is at our school." One major way this can happen is by focusing attention on the majority of youth who utilize computers and cell phones in acceptable and positive ways. If research shows that fewer than one in five teenagers cyberbullies others, a social-norming approach would not emphasize this fact. Rather, it would be reframed so that cool and relevant messaging strategies emphasize that the vast majority of students (over 80 percent) are using online technology with integrity, discretion, and wisdom. Ideally, the remainder would desire to fit in and be like everyone else and would feel an informal compulsion to stop cyberbullying others and "get on board." Spending too much time painting cyberbullying in alarmist colors may very well encourage more youth to act in similar ways, since those youth will perceive that the behavior is "normal" and "everyone is doing it."

Also evident is the critical role that bystanders can serve in encouraging appropriate speech and behavior across the student body. They can model appropriate behaviors and intervene or tell others when they see or hear something that is not acceptable. Additionally, peer mentoring holds great promise in contributing to your climate goals by mobilizing student leaders to act as agents of change and influence the way other youth think about technology use and misuse. Mentoring also helps to promote a greater appreciation of the responsibilities and risks associated with computers, cell phones, and the Internet and enables teens to see how their individual and group actions affect the emotions and lives of others. We need to continually come alongside and encourage youth to take responsibility for these problems and work together to develop a climate where positive behavior is the norm—and problematic behaviors (wherever they occur) are immediately condemned by adolescents and adults alike.

## DISCUSSION QUESTIONS

1. What is the importance of a social-norming campaign? How might you determine the existing normative beliefs at your school?

2. What are some ways to accomplish social norming in your school or community? How can you determine which techniques would work best with your student population?

3. What are the benefits of involving all stakeholders (students, teachers, administrators, parents, and others) in social-norming campaigns? What specific role can each play?

4. What is the role of the bystander in contributing to a positive school climate? How can individuals be taught to stop standing by and start standing up, and how can this belief gain traction across an entire student body?

5. Why is peer mentoring important for students and a school as a whole? What obstacles might you encounter when attempting to set up a peer-mentoring system, and what can be done to overcome them?

6. How do social norms, active bystanders, and peer mentoring fit into an overall program to achieve a positive school climate? Do you feel one is more useful than others, either in general or specifically

in your school? Do you feel one is more easily implemented than others?

## REFERENCES

1. S. E. Asch, "Studies of Independence and Conformity: A Minority of One Against a Unanimous Majority," *Psychological Monographs* 70, no. 9 (1956): 1–70; M. Sherif, *The Psychology of Social Norms* (New York: Harper, 1936).

2. Centers for Disease Control and Prevention, "Sexual Risk Behavior: HIV, STD, & Teen Pregnancy Prevention," updated July 12, 2011, http://www.cdc.gov/HealthyYouth/sexualbehaviors/index.htm

3. J. W. Patchin and S. Hinduja, *Cyberbullying Prevention and Response: Expert Perspectives* (New York: Routledge, 2012).

4. S. B. Austin, N. J. Ziyadeh, S. Forman, L. A. Prokop, A. Keliher, and D. Jacobs, "Screening High School Students for Eating Disorders: Results of a National Initiative," *Preventing Chronic Disease* 5, no. 4 (2008): A114.

5. H. W. Perkins, ed., *The Social Norms Approach to Preventing School and College Age Substance Abuse* (San Francisco: Jossey-Bass, 2003).

6. A. D. Berkowitz, "The Social Norms Approach: Theory, Research, and Annotated Bibliography," revised August 2004, p. 6, http://www.alanberkowitz.com/articles/social_norms.pdf

7. A. D. Berkowitz and H. W. Perkins, "Resident Advisors as Role Models: A Comparison of Drinking Patterns of Resident Advisors and Their Peers," *Journal of College Student Personnel* 27 (1986): 146–153; B. Borsari and K. B. Carey, "Peer Influences on College Drinking: A Review of the Research," *Journal of Substance Abuse* 13 (2001): 391–424; D. B. Kandel, "On Processes of Peer Influences in Adolescent Drug Use: A Developmental Perspective," *Advances in Alcohol and Substance Use* 4 (1985): 139–163.

8. Perkins, *The Social Norms Approach*.

9. L. Barnett, J. M. Far, A. L. Moss, and J. A. Miller, "Changing Perceptions of Peer Norms as a Drinking Reduction Program for College Students," *Journal of Alcohol and Drug Education* 41 (1996): 39–62.

10. Berkowitz, "The Social Norms Approach."

11. B. Hagman, P. Clifford, and N. Noel, "Social Norms Theory–Based Interventions: Testing the Feasibility of Purported Mechanism of Action," *Journal of American College Health* 56, no. 3 (2007): 293–298.

12. W. Miley and M. Frank, "Binge and Non-binge College Students' Perceptions of Other Students' Drinking Habits," *College Student Journal* 40, no. 2 (2006): 259–262.

13. Perkins, *The Social Norms Approach*; L. R. Franca, B. Dautzenberg, and M. Reynaud, "Heavy Episodic Drinking and Alcohol Consumption in French Colleges: The Role of Perceived Social Norms," *Alcoholism: Clinical and Experimental Research* 34, no. 1 (2010): 164–174; N. Bertholet, J. Gaume, M. Faouzi, J. Daeppen, and G. Gmel, "Perception of the Amount of Drinking by Others in a Sample of 20-Year-Old Men: The More I Think You Drink, the More I Drink," *Alcohol and Alcoholism* 46, no. 1 (2011): 83–87; S. U. Haug, M. Hanke, C. Meyer, and U. John, "Overestimation of Drinking Norms and Its Association With Alcohol Consumption in Apprentices," *Alcohol and Alcoholism* 46, no. 2 (2011): 204–209.

14. A. Gordon, "The Truth About Teen Alcohol Use 101: A Social Norms Approach," *School Library Journal* 48 (2002): 60.

15. J. Juvonen, S. C. Martino, P. L. Ellickson, and D. Longshore, "'But Others Do It!' Do Misperceptions of Schoolmate Alcohol and Marijuana Use Predict Subsequent Drug Use Among Young Adolescents?" *Journal of Applied Social Psychology* 37, no. 4 (2007): 740–758.

16. Social Norms Consultation, "Case Studies—Evanston High School (ETHS) Strength in Numbers," accessed February 14, 2012, http:// socialnormsconsultation.com/case_studies/evanston_hs.html

17. Hobart and William Smith Colleges, Alcohol Education Project, Youth Health & Safety Project, "Catalog of Secondary School Project Posters," accessed February 14, 2012, http://alcohol.hws .edu/posters/posterschools.htm

18. Hobart and William Smith Colleges, "Catalog of Secondary School Project Posters."

19. Hobart and William Smith Colleges, Youth Health & Safety Project, "Catalog of Social Norms Middle School and Junior High School Bullying Project Posters," accessed February 14, 2012, http://www.youthhealthsafety.org/Bullyposters.htm

20. D. J. Hanson, "Social Norms Marketing Reduces High School Drinking," *Alcohol Problems and Solutions*, 2003, http://www .potsdam.edu/hansondj/youthissues/1093545307.html; National

Social Norms Institute at the University of Virginia, "Evanston Township High School (ETHS): Strength in Numbers," 2003, http://www.socialnorms.org/CaseStudies/evanston.php

21. L. Duan, C. Chou, V. Andreeva, and M. Pentz, "Trajectories of Peer Social Influences as Long-term Predictors of Drug Use From Early Through Late Adolescence," *Journal of Youth and Adolescence* 38, no. 3 (2009): 454–465; R. S. Olds, D. L. Thombs, and J. R. Tomasek, "Relations Between Normative Beliefs and Initiation Intentions Toward Cigarette, Alcohol and Marijuana," *Journal of Adolescent Health* 37, no. 1 (2005): 75.

22. J. M. Perkins, H. W. Perkins, and D. W. Craig, "Peer Weight Norm Misperception as a Risk Factor for Being Over- and Underweight Among UK Secondary School Students," *European Journal of Clinical Nutrition* 64, no. 9 (2010): 965–971; R. Bergstrom and C. Neighbors, "Body Norms Behavior and the Social Norms Approach: An Integrative Review of the Literature," *Journal of Social and Clinical Psychology* 25, no. 9 (2006): 975–1000; J. A. Mutterperl and C. A. Sanderson, "Mind Over Matter: Internalization of the Thinness Norm as a Moderator of Responsiveness to Norm Misperception Information," *Health Psychology* 21 (2002): 519–523; J. G. Silverman, A. Raj, L. A. Mucci, and J. E. Hathaway, "Dating Violence Against Adolescent Girls and Associated Substance Use, Unhealthy Weight Control, Sexual Risk Behavior, Pregnancy, and Suicidality," *Journal of the American Medical Association* 286, no. 5 (2001): 572–579; M. P. Martens, J. C. Page, E. S. Mowry, K. M. Damann, K. K. Taylor, and M. D. Cimini, "Differences Between Actual and Perceived Student Norms: An Examination of Alcohol Use, Drug Use, and Sexual Behavior," *Journal of American College Health* 54, no. 5 (2006): 295–300; H. W. Perkins, J. W. Linkenbach, M. A. Lewis, and C. Neighbors, "Effectiveness of Social Norms Media Marketing in Reducing Drinking and Driving: A Statewide Campaign," *Addictive Behaviors* 35, no. 10 (2010): 866–874; X. Wang and S. R. McClung, "Toward a Detailed Understanding of Illegal Digital Downloading Intentions: An Extended Theory of Planned Behavior Approach," *New Media & Society* 13, no. 4 (2011): 663–677.

23. H. W. Perkins, D. W. Craig, and J. M. Perkins, "Using Social Norms to Reduce Bullying: A Research Intervention Among Adolescents in Five Middle Schools," *Group Processes & Intergroup Relations* 14, no. 5 (2011): 705–706.

24. See, for example, M. J. Bigsby, "Seeing Eye to Eye? Comparing Students' and Parents' Perceptions of Bullying Behavior," *School of Social Work Journal* 27, no. 1 (2002): 37–57; C. Salmivalli, K. Lagerspetz, K. Bjorkqvist, K. Osterman, and A. Kaukiainen,

"Bullying as a Group Process: Participant Roles in Their Relations to Social Status Within the Group," *Aggressive Behavior* 22, no. 1 (1996): 1–15; D. W. Craig and H. W. Perkins, "Assessing Bullying in New Jersey Secondary Schools: Applying the Social Norms Model to Adolescent Violence" (paper presented at National Conference on the Social Norms Approach, San Francisco, CA, 2008).

25. J. E. Cross and W. Peisner, "RECOGNIZE: A Social Norms Campaign to Rumor Spreading in a Junior High School," *Professional School Counseling* 12, no. 5 (2009): 365.

26. Cross and Peisner, "RECOGNIZE."

27. R. C. Swaim and K. Kelly, "Efficacy of a Randomized Trial of a Community and School-Based Anti-violence Media Intervention Among Small-Town Middle School Youth," *Prevention Science* 9 (2008): 202–214.

28. Perkins, Craig, and Perkins, "Using Social Norms to Reduce Bullying."

29. P. Fabiano, "Learning Lessons and Asking Questions About College Social Norms Campaigns" (paper presented at The National Conference on the Social Norms Model: Science-Based Prevention, Big Sky, MT, July 29, 1999).

30. P. S. Bearman and H. Bruckner, "Promising the Future: Virginity Pledges and First Intercourse," *American Journal of Sociology* 106, no. 4 (2001): 859–912.

31. S. Davis and J. Davis, *Schools Where Everyone Belongs: Practical Strategies for Reducing Bullying* (Champaign, IL: Research Press, 2007); S. Davis and J. Davis, *Empowering Bystanders in Bullying Prevention* (Champaign, IL: Research Press, 2007).

32. S. Davis and C. Nixon, "Empowering Bystanders," in *Cyberbullying Prevention and Response: Expert Perspectives*, ed. J. W. Patchin and S. Hinduja (New York: Routledge, 2012), 98.

33. National Sexual Violence Resource Center, "In Bullying Prevention, the Homecoming Queen Reigns Anew!" accessed November 16, 2010, http://www.nsvrc.org/blog/bystander/3235/

34. J. Mahdavi and P. K. Smith, "The Operation of a Bully Court and Perceptions of Its Success: A Case Study," *School Psychology International* 23 (2002): 327–341; D. Pepler, W. Craig, S. Ziegler, and A. Charach, eds., *A School-Based Anti-bullying Intervention: Preliminary Evaluation* (Oxford, UK: Heinemann, 1993).

35. J. M. Tully, "The Outer Limits: Disciplining Students Without Getting Sued," 2007, p. 6, http://ebookbrowse.com/the-outer-limits-disciplining-cyber-mischief-without-getting-sued-pdf-d81366963

36. J. O'Connell, "The Bullied Girl," *The Guardian*, October 8, 2003, http://www.guardian.co.uk/uk/2003/oct/09/children.politics/

# 8

## *Prevention Through Assessment*

### *Taking the Pulse of Your School and Students*

*You really need to conduct research among your students to figure out exactly what is going on. You can't just make assumptions. Climate is largely a social thing, and intangible, and therefore not easily observable. However, it is measurable—and it needs to be assessed so that you can specifically figure out how students feel about their school and the interactions and relationships therein. Only then can you wisely and effectively implement programming to increase academic, emotional, psychological, social, and behavioral well-being there.*

—Nancy Willard, director, Center for Safe and
Responsible Internet Use

One of the first steps in tackling a problem is to identify the nature and extent of that problem. Otherwise, you don't really know what you are dealing with. For example, you might suspect that you have a significant problem with cyberbullying at your school based on a number of "clues." These can include students telling you what happened to them, other teachers letting you know of their suspicions and observations, or parents alerting you to problems involving their children. To be sure, all of these incidents should be addressed; it is unacceptable for even one child to be cyberbullied. That said, without a concerted effort to understand your climate and the extent of negative behaviors that may be going on "under the radar," you really do not know the complete picture. You might be seeing just the tip of the iceberg. Moreover, identifying problems *before* they get out of hand is essential so that you can remedy them prior to any long-term consequences for students, staff, or the climate of your school.

## SURVEY YOUR STUDENTS

One way to take the pulse of your school and to learn about problems that may be simmering just under the surface is to collect data from students, staff, and even parents. Obtaining good data is essential for a number of reasons. It demonstrates mindfulness of the potential issues associated with the misuse of online technologies (or other threats to your positive climate), and it demonstrates a willingness to assess the extent to which it affects students (or the work environment for staff members). In addition, it helps justify the use of increasingly scarce financial resources (e.g., to pay for Internet safety training or materials) and can be used to legitimize and support your requests for grant funding from public or private organizations. It can also be used to evaluate a particular programmatic or policy initiative to determine whether your efforts are having the desired effects (through pre- and posttesting). Note that formal assessments are also encouraged or even mandated in some states (e.g., Connecticut) in order to be compliant with the antibullying laws in place.

All of this is done so that you and others in the school community can obtain a baseline understanding of the extent of online behavior problems that could negatively affect your school—such as cyberbullying and sexting. As we have demonstrated throughout this book, these issues have the potential to significantly disrupt your school's learning environment and destroy the positive climate you've worked so hard to develop. A simple assessment will also allow for a deeper and more detailed understanding of how adolescents use and abuse technology. And since these behaviors may be hard to see and because targets of all forms of bullying are often reluctant to come forward, conducting a survey is one of the best ways to gather information about exactly what is going on and what might be done about it.

> **Talking Points: How to Conduct Research Among Your Students**
>
> - Clearly measure the prevalence, frequency, and scope of cyberbullying, sexting, or any other adolescent issue among students.
> - Identify the demographic, personal, familial, social, and school factors that may be contributing to problems.
> - Add credibility and legitimacy to funding/resource requests to deal with problems.
> - Provide up-to-date data on how technology is being used and misused at school and away from school.
> - Determine the extent to which the misuse of technology is negatively affecting the school climate and students' ability to learn.
> - Shed light on the underlying causes of the problem behaviors; data can then be used to guide programming efforts.
> - Demonstrate to students, staff, and parents that your district is motivated to measure and understand the ways students are using and misusing technology.
> - Continue to promote your district's image as a leader in this area.
> - Contribute to compliance with Children's Internet Protection Act (CIPA) and Broadband Data Improvement Act (BDIA) requirements.

A comprehensive survey of your students will allow you to learn more about what they are doing, experiencing, and seeing. Here are some issues that we believe are worth exploring:

1. How much cyberbullying and sexting is occurring among students at your school?
2. Are the characteristics of cyberbullying victims different from those of traditional victims?
3. What social, emotional, or even physical effects does cyberbullying have on the victim?
4. How do youth cope with cyberbullying?
5. Do youth who engage in cyberbullying also engage in traditional forms of schoolyard violence?
6. Do targets of cyberbullying miss more school than other students? What are some emotional, psychological, and social buffers that serve to preempt or attenuate offending or victimization?
7. What proportion of your students are on Facebook or Google+ or other social networking sites? What are some examples of student harassment or general misuse that you are seeing on these sites?
8. How comfortable are students with talking to adults at school about what is going on online?

Being proactive about identifying concerns through questions like these will allow you to confront problems more comprehensively instead of being forced to put out proverbial fires with substandard extinguishers. Finally, such research contributes important information to the existing knowledge base on bullying, cyberbullying, and other online behavioral problems and their relationship to school climate. Other schools then can use this information as a learning tool and model to emulate in their own research, evaluation, policy, and programming efforts.

> **Prevention Point:** Don't be afraid of research. Collect information from your students to guide your efforts in a more informed and meaningful way.

Now that you understand the value of research and data, how do you go about doing it? A comprehensive research project can be time-consuming and expensive and require a set of skills that you may not possess. Even a simple survey of your school community, however, can be very instructive, and you can get most of the information and resources you need for little or no cost. This chapter will break down the most important considerations to keep in mind if you want to obtain an accurate measurement of the experiences of members of your school community. In the following text, we take you from "start" to "finish"—choosing a group of students of whom you'll ask questions, making sure that group represents the larger population whose behaviors you want to know about, developing appropriate questions, administering the survey, and then learning from the results. If you didn't take a research methods or statistics course in college, don't worry—we have written this summary in a way that should be accessible and easy to understand.

## Sampling

In a perfect world, schools interested in learning more about their student bodies would survey all youth to understand their individual and collective experiences and perceptions. In smaller districts, this might not be a problem, but in large districts with tens of thousands of students, it can be downright impossible. The good news is that schools do not need to survey *every* student to be able to make generalizations about the population as a whole. Schools can identify a smaller *sample* of students to survey, and as long as that sample is representative of the larger population, conclusions can be drawn. The key word here is *representative*. The Gallup Organization states that "the fundamental goal of a survey is to come up with the same results that would have been obtained had every single member of a population been interviewed."[1] For example, if a principal decides that she is going to survey a sample of her high school but simply targets only those who are on the student council, the survey respondents will not necessarily be representative of all students in the school (because the attitudes and actions of a typical student council member don't really mirror those of an average student). Even if she decides to approach the first 25 students that show up for school on a particular day, there is a good chance they too will be different from the overall student body (e.g., possibly more responsible).

Another mistake would be to post a survey on the school's website inviting students to respond to questions about cyberbullying. These types of "opt-in" surveys are likely to generate responses predominantly from those who have had experiences with the behavior in question (in this case, those who have been cyberbullied). We also know that not all youth spend the same amount of time online and on the school website, nor are all equally inclined to take the time to participate in an online survey or be equally candid when it comes to revealing personal stories or sharing sensitive experiences with others. Thinking about all of these factors may make your head hurt, but all of them will affect whose data you collect—and, most importantly, whether the information collected mirrors the makeup of the student body whose behavior you want to better understand.

The easiest way to ensure that your sample is representative of your school is to select students randomly. Many database programs such as Microsoft Excel include easy methods for selecting cases in this manner. Simply enter all student names into the database and have the program automatically select the specific students to be surveyed. Another option for larger districts is to randomly select homeroom teachers or first-hour classes. Assuming that every student has an equal chance of being included in those classes, your sample should approximate the population if large enough (more on that below).

Given that some students will be unavailable for surveying, will only partially complete a survey, or will decline participation altogether (see the "Confidentiality, Consent, and Ethical Issues" section below), it is important to ensure that the final complete sample is relatively representative of the broader school population by comparing them on certain demographic characteristics such as age, gender, and race. If 20 percent of your sample is African American but 45 percent of your school is African American, you've got a problem. If done correctly, randomly selecting students should result in a sample that is quite similar to the population as a whole.

How big your sample size should be really depends on a lot of factors (e.g., size and diversity of your school or district, number of questions you intend to ask). There are some complicated statistical formulas that can assist in providing a precise number based on how comfortable you want to be with the results, but generally speaking, the larger the sample the better. You certainly wouldn't want to draw conclusions about a school district of 10,000 students after speaking to only 10 of them. Overall, a 15 to 25 percent sampling rate should provide you with enough responses to work with. This means that you should specifically survey around 1,500–2,500 students within a district of 10,000. Smaller populations should sample more than 15 to 25 percent, since extraordinary experiences can strongly affect small samples but are less problematic with a large sample size.

**Prevention Point:** You don't need to ask every student at your school about experiences with, and perceptions of, cyberbullying and sexting to understand the problems at your school. Query a smaller but randomly selected sample, and you will get all of the information you need.

You also need to be aware that some of the most at-risk students are more likely to be absent on any given day, so efforts should be made to include those who are absent on the day of surveying. Also, be sure to develop language-specific surveys for students who do not speak English as their native tongue. If your sampling list of students includes some with any other special needs, do your best to accommodate them (give them more time or a quiet place to take the survey, etc.). In short, once you have your randomly generated list of students, every effort should be made to include them in your research.

### Use Data to Guide Your Climate Improvement Efforts

The US Department of Education and our Center have strongly urged schools that are considering embarking on a school climate improvement process to do a couple of things. First, it is important to research different organizations' school climate improvement models and implementation strategies. Too often someone's school climate improvement model is to have a 14-session class or curriculum about positive school climate or social/emotional learning. That will never transform school communities. Second, we strongly recommend that schools use psychometrically sound, reliable, and valid school climate surveys. There are a number of those out there. And ideally, schools are using surveys that recognize not only student voice, parent/guardian voice, and school personnel voice but also the voice of community members, because school climate as an assessment is an incredibly simple, powerful engagement strategy. Everybody says, "Oh yeah, I know I need to include parents, Oh yeah, I know I need to include the community." It never happens. And when I ask about that, principals and superintendents say "I don't know what to do." Well, this is a concrete engagement strategy that uses data in a very thoughtful way.

—Jonathan Cohen, cofounder and president
National School Climate Center

## SURVEY DEVELOPMENT

The next step in the research process is to develop a set of questions that you would like to ask students. Chapter 2 included questions that can be used to assess the quality of your climate. We have also provided you with a selection of our cyberbullying and sexting survey questions to get you started (see the appendix at the end of this chapter). When coming up with questions, it is important to create ones that are clear, precise, and understandable for the intended audience. Different questions will probably be necessary for elementary students than for high school students. We recently surveyed fourth graders who were puzzled by words such as *ineffective* and *seldom*, so we switched them out for *not helpful* and *rarely*, which they more naturally understood. It is also imperative that questions are worded in a way that will give you the information you are looking for. Describe behaviors and their timeline specifically. Here are some examples:

> **Bad:** "Has anyone ever said anything mean to you online?"

> **Good:** "Has someone from your school created a hurtful Facebook page about you in the past 30 days?"

Just about everyone has had something mean said about them online. You want to distinguish this from actual *cyberbullying*. Even the question "Have you ever received an upsetting email from someone you didn't know?" is problematic since spam (unsolicited email) is widespread these days and can be very upsetting when it clutters one's inbox. Take the time to clearly and carefully define important concepts or terms within the survey. We discussed at length the differences in definitions of *cyberbullying* (Chapter 3) and *sexting* (Chapter 4). Given the definitional variations that exist, it is crucial that you clearly explain to students what you mean by these terms. Don't just assume that "they know what it is." That might be true, but again, many people seem to have different views on these concepts. For example, we formally define *cyberbullying* as "willful and repeated harm inflicted through the use of computers, cell phones, and other electronic devices." But when we present it to youth and ask them about their experiences, we define it in this way: "Cyberbullying is when someone repeatedly harasses, mistreats, or makes fun of another person online or while using cell phones or other electronic devices." The first definition isn't too vague or confusing, but the second one just makes everything clearer. When in doubt, your rule of thumb should be to keep it simple.

In addition, avoid "double-barreled" questions that ask two (or more) questions at once. For example, consider the following question:

> **Bad**: "Have you ever been robbed, sexually assaulted, shot, or bullied?"

This question essentially asks about four very different experiences. It is much more likely that a student has been bullied than shot, yet these two experiences are treated as equal in this question.

> **Bad**: "Do you think that parents, teachers, and police officers should take cyberbullying incidents more seriously?"

Similarly, this question also really asks multiple questions. Perhaps the respondent feels that teachers are doing a good job but the police need to do more. How should he respond? Try to keep survey questions relatively short, because long questions can be confusing or inadvertently include multiple embedded questions.

Also refrain from including "double negatives":

**Bad**: "Do you think that cyberbullying isn't a problem that will never go away?"

**Good**: "Do you think cyberbullying is a problem?"

**Good**: "Do you think we can stop cyberbullying?"

**Bad**: "Teachers lecturing to us about not being on our phones so often couldn't be more unhelpful in keeping us safe."

**Good**: "Teachers lecturing to us about how we need to stop using our phones so much doesn't help us to stay safe."

In addition, avoid including "loaded" or "leading" questions that direct the respondent to answer in a certain way.

**Bad**: "Don't you think that everyone experiences cyberbullying?"

**Good**: "How many of the students at your school do you think have been cyberbullied?"

**Bad**: "Do you think cyberbullies have problems at home that lead them to act out against others in a mean way?"

**Good**: "Why do you think cyberbullies are mean to others?"

Here's another point to consider: if you are designing a closed-ended survey question (you provide a list of answers that a student selects from), make sure the possible responses are mutually exclusive and exhaustive. A respondent should find one and only one answer that expresses her views.

**Bad**: "What is your favorite social networking website?"

    A. Google+
    B. Facebook
    C. YouTube

This question is clearly not exhaustive. What if the student's favorite site is Twitter? Often it is best to include "Other" and a field in which respondents can report an option that is not on the list.

**Bad**: "How old are you?"

    A. 10–12
    B. 12–15
    C. 15–20

This question is neither exhaustive nor mutually exclusive. Which response would I select if I was 9 years old? How about if I was 12? It's also not a good idea to group responses without considering the implications. In the above example, why should we group 10-, 11-, and 12-year-old students but then group together everyone who is between 15 and 20? This latter category is especially problematic since in many states the age of legal adulthood is 17 or 18. Grouping those who are legally considered juveniles with adults can lead to problems when analyzing the responses later.

**Good:** "What grade are you in?"

    A.  5th or lower
    B.  6th
    C.  7th
    D.  8th
    E.  9th or higher

This is a good response set for a survey that is targeted to middle schoolers. While it is highly unlikely that elementary or high school students are responding if you deliberately target the middle school students at your school, you never know for sure. Plus, if a middle school student does select *A* or *E* in this example, you know that there is something wrong with that student's data. This is a good way to determine whether respondents are being truthful or simply going through the survey quickly by selecting a certain letter (or a random letter) every time. Flag those students who respond in a way that is inconsistent with your sample and investigate further.

As you can see from these examples, creating a survey the right way can be fun and intellectually stimulating. If you feel overwhelmed, don't be. Feel free to adapt the questions we have provided at the end of this chapter for your needs. But you also need to consider the unique characteristics of your school as well as other possible behaviors, perceptions, or attitudes you are interested in. And don't be afraid to get help from others: other schools, local university faculty, or us! We regularly assist schools with assessment initiatives and would be happy to do what we can to help you.

## SURVEY ADMINISTRATION

Now that you have a great survey ready to administer to students, how do you get them to participate? The most common way to conduct surveys in schools is to hand out a paper copy of the survey to students and have them answer the questions during class time. Students can simply circle their answer or write responses directly on the questionnaire, or they can mark their responses on a separate answer sheet (e.g., a Scantron or bubble sheet). Both of these methods will require some time for someone to digitize or enter the responses into an electronic database. Another option would be develop your survey with an online survey program such as SurveyMonkey or Qualtrics. To ensure that only the students selected in the random sampling process participate, you could escort groups of students to the school's computer lab to complete the survey. Whatever you do, be sure to give students some privacy as they are responding so they do not fear embarrassment, shame, retaliation, or punishment for what they are sharing.

### Assessment Leads to Better Understanding

I orchestrated the administration of a survey of our students through the principals of our middle and high school in order to gain a better understanding of how they perceive issues related to digital citizenship (e.g., cyberbullying, sexting, online reputation, etc.). The survey provided us with a way of deepening our insight into the perspectives of our primary stakeholders: our students.

The initial impact of the data was to convince us that our students had a more sophisticated understanding of digital citizenship and safety than we anticipated. Our principals, school counselors, superintendent, parents, and everyone else we showed the data to were proud of how unexpectedly "savvy" our students are. We all get dosed repeatedly with so many fear-based, doom-and-gloom messages about our kids that we grow to expect bleak results from them, but when we looked at the actual data, we felt proud of our students and impressed by their decency. The overwhelmingly positive and appropriate responses from our students created a lot of buy-in from the adults in our school and community; everyone likes to back a winner, right?

Positive momentum started to build on those positive student responses. We subsequently scheduled a bullying-prevention summit for our students to show community stakeholders all the things that were being doing to prevent bullying in our schools. Our high school principal invited me to start a bullying-prevention task force at the high school, and our middle school principal invited me to do training for his entire faculty.

The adult buy-in has been wonderful, but the best part is seeing how the students have responded to their own data. When I put the graph up on the screen in a classroom and say, "Ninety-seven percent of our students said there's no way they would send a nude picture to someone who requested it. That's outstanding! This student

*(Continued)*

(Continued)

body is so smart. Someone tell me why that is such a great answer?" almost every hand in the room goes up, and students are proud to tell me why it's so important not to send nude photos. I know that they're not really telling me so much as they are each other. Their attention and enthusiasm for the subject was high, they were energized by being told how smart they are, and they were reinforcing to themselves and each other a critically important social norm. When I ask them about some of the problems or potential consequences with sending these kinds of pictures, they say things like "Because if I send that picture to someone I'm in a relationship with and then we break up, they might send that picture to other people . . . my parents might see it . . . I don't want a nude picture of myself on the Internet forever. What if I accidentally hit the 'send all' button instead of the send button?" The cool thing is, most of these kids really do know this stuff. It's only a few who don't, and showing them how the majority of their friends think and feel is so much more powerful than telling them what I think they should think and feel.

When we analyze the open-ended responses by creating a "word cloud," the single word that shows up over and over again as the number one reason for students making the choices they make is *friend*. This single word choice reinforces to me what we have always known about teenagers, even if we haven't wanted to admit it: they are influenced by each other, not us. Does the word *principal* ever show up in their explanations for why they make the choices they make? No. Does the word *teacher*? No. How about *social worker*? No. *Parent*? Occasionally. *Friend*? Always. Having access to good data helped us to remember this point and allows us to tailor our messages in a way that has proven very effective.

—Gary McDaniel, MS, clinical social worker
Morgan County Schools

# DON'T FORGET ABOUT THE ADULTS!

*If, as the research literature tells us, school culture is an important determinant of achievement, then it follows that the place to start in assessing the culture of a school's staff, and making any desired change in it, is to examine the perceptions of the instructional staff with respect to the school, its students, and their place in it.*

—Don Morris, research analyst, Miami-Dade Schools[2]

The vast majority of cyberbullying and sexting research is done by asking students about their experiences with the behaviors. While this is a very important perspective to obtain, schools should also consider surveying staff and parents about what they are seeing and hearing. If 20 percent of the student body reports experience with cyberbullying but only 5 percent of parents believe that their child has been a victim, then there is a disconnect between what the parents know and what teens are experiencing. If 80 percent of students report that cyberbullying is a significant problem in the school but only 10 percent of staff believe that to be true, the school has some work to do. You can encourage school staff to more consciously make note of incidents that they hear about and then report them to one person, or you can formally survey adults in the school to obtain a more systematic perspective. The best approach is to assess student experiences, staff observations, and parent perceptions so that you can "triangulate" your results to gain a more complete picture of what is going on.

## FOCUS GROUPS

Focus groups are another great way for you to learn about the experiences of students in your schools. Focus groups, a qualitative research method, involve interviewing and fostering dialogue among a small number of participants (usually 6 to 12) in a collective setting in order to generate data.[3] Rather than the researcher individually asking questions of one subject in isolation or multiple subjects in sequence, the researcher poses questions to a group and seeks to promote interactions among everyone who is there so that views, comments, thoughts, and other responses can build upon, clarify, expand, and augment each other. Indeed, this discussion is essential in order to "produce data and insights that would be less accessible without the interaction found in a group."[4] Generally, focus groups allow exploratory research to be conducted in a cost-effective way. These groups help generate large amounts of raw verbatim data (statements and feelings and perspectives and experiences!) from participants and often result in new understandings as participants jointly make sense of shared ideas and considerations.[5]

A significant advantage of focus groups is that they allow for follow-up questions to gather more information about a particular issue. They also allow the facilitator to clarify questions should some be unclear or if they are subject to interpretation. We have all taken a survey where we wondered about the intent or meaning of a specific question. In these situations, we probably just went with our gut in answering it. But this might have not been the way the question was intended, which means that the response it elicited was useless for the purpose of the study. Having a person on hand to clarify questions or terms is especially useful for younger students who might need more explanation of concepts.

If you are interested in convening one or more focus groups, it is probably a good idea to recruit someone from outside the school to facilitate the group. A certain amount of skill is needed to moderate a group in a way that yields the most and best information. Moreover, utilizing a teacher or counselor from the school may inhibit student responses. You want the students to feel comfortable openly talking about what they are experiencing and seeing at school, and they may be reluctant to discuss these issues with a staff member they regularly interact with.

---

### Sample Focus Group Questions

**Introduction**

- What is your first name? Age? The grade you are in?
- Also, tell us one thing that you enjoy doing outside of school.

**Main Questions**

- How often do you go online?
- What kinds of things do you do?
- Where do you hang out most when you are online?
- Where do you access the Internet from most often?
- How many of you have a computer in your bedroom?
- What are some of the bad things that happen when kids use the computer?

*If cyberbullying isn't listed:* Cyberbullying is another bad thing associated with the Internet—do you know what cyberbullying is? *(Have them explain/clarify their definition).*

- What is the worst instance of bullying you or someone you know have/has experienced?
- What is the worst instance of cyberbullying you or someone you know have/has experienced?
- How does it make you feel—emotionally, psychologically?
- How does it affect different areas of your life?
- What do you think are the underlying/root causes?
- How do you deal with it? How should kids deal with it?
- Why do you think kids would talk to an adult about cyberbullying? Why do you think they wouldn't?
- What can kids do to influence their friends that cyberbullying is NOT COOL? Is there anything?
- Would you stick up for someone you know online if they were being cyberbullied?
  - O Would you defend them, or would you not want to get involved for fear that you'd be the bully's next victim?
- People who see cyberbullying take place are called bystanders, and we really think it's important that bystanders go talk to an adult about the problem if the victim cannot. Do you agree?
  - O How can we encourage bystanders to stand up more and do the right thing, rather than doing nothing and staying quiet?

Following are other considerations when organizing a focus group:

- Pretest your questions among a select group of students to make sure they are clear and generate discussion.
- Select a private room with no distractions.
- Limit the discussion to less than 90 minutes.
- Record the discussion so that you can go back later to transcribe responses.
- Try to avoid including known bullying victims with their bullies, as this may create a power dynamic not conducive to openly sharing information.

## CONFIDENTIALITY, CONSENT, AND ETHICAL ISSUES

Any time you are surveying others, especially minors (individuals who are under the age of consent in your state), you need to be aware of the ethical issues involved. First and foremost, you want to protect the safety of your subjects by ensuring that their responses will remain confidential to the maximum extent allowable by law. Generally it is best to conduct anonymous surveys by not collecting any identifying information from respondents so that it is largely impossible to link particular answers to specific individuals. How would you respond if you collected a survey that included the student's name and that student reported numerous experiences with cyberbullying others or talked about regularly cheating at school? You might feel compelled to respond or even subconsciously treat this student differently.

You should be aware, however, that surveys can sometimes be linked to individuals even without identifying information, especially if you ask questions about certain demographic characteristics of small groups in your school. For example, if you ask students to report their gender, grade, and race, and there are only a handful of Hispanic seventh-grade boys in your school, their responses are not as anonymous as would be preferred. Ensuring confidentiality is especially important when asking about certain beliefs or behaviors that are potentially unpopular, deviant, or even criminal. Respondents are unlikely to be truthful when reporting about behaviors that could get them in trouble if they think their responses could be linked back to them. You should remind students both orally and in writing that their answers are anonymous and will not be linked back to them to alleviate any fears they might have. It may not ease all of their concerns, but it will help.

**Prevention Point:** If you are going to survey your students, be sure their parents are fully informed about the purpose and goals of the project.

In addition to maintaining confidentiality, the ethics of social science research dictate that respondents participate voluntarily and be informed in advance of the nature of the questions that will be asked. This means that respondents should agree to participate by signing an informational document that outlines the purposes of the study along with any known risks. Students who are younger than 18 likely require a parent's or guardian's *consent* (formal permission obtained, usually indicated via that signed form) to participate in the study, in addition to a student's *assent* (or "agreement," either oral or written depending on the student's age) to participate. States and individual school districts can have different requirements for consent and assent, so educators looking to survey students should contact their local legal counsel for clarification. You may also want to partner with a university researcher who can assist you with survey development and consent procedures. The bottom line is that you want individuals who participate in your study to be informed about what you are doing and how the data will be used.

## SUMMARY

Assessment is already an important aspect of what you do. Educators regularly assess student learning through tests or other assignments. Measuring their experiences with cyberbullying, sexting, or other online problems will help you to better understand what they are dealing with on a day-to-day basis and allow you to be proactive in doing something about it. Online behaviors may not be visible to adults who don't fully understand technology, so asking students to report what they are seeing and experiencing can be very useful. This chapter has provided you with all of the tools you need to gather data about the behaviors, perceptions, and attitudes of members of your school community. Creating and maintaining a positive school climate requires that you stay ahead of any major technology issues that may eventually disrupt the learning environment at your school, and conducting a formal assessment through surveys and focus groups is a very valuable way to help do that.

## DISCUSSION QUESTIONS

1. Why is obtaining data from students, parents, and staff beneficial in determining what problem behaviors might be affecting the climate of your school? How can you go about doing this?

2. Why is obtaining a representative sample important when surveying students? How might an unrepresentative sample affect your findings?

3. How can one develop a set of survey questions that are concise and specific? Why is it important to put in the time to properly develop questions within your survey?

4. What are some key points to consider when administering surveys?

5. What are the benefits of surveying educators and parents as well?

6. Why is it important to address issues such as confidentiality, consent, and ethics when surveying students?

## REFERENCES

1. Gallup, "How Are Polls Conducted?" 2010, p. 1, http://www.gallup.com/poll/File/125927/How%20Are%20Polls%20Conducted%20FINAL.pdf

2. D. Morris, "Achievement Gains and Staff Perception of School Climate," Miami-Dade County Public Schools *Research Brief* (May 2008), http://drs.dadeschools.net/ResearchBriefs/RB0707.pdf

3. R. K. Merton, M. Fiske, and P. L. Kendall, *The Focused Interview: A Manual of Problems and Procedures* (Glencoe, IL: The Free Press, 1956).

4. D. L. Morgan, *Focus Groups as Qualitative Research* (Newbury Park, CA: Sage, 1988), 12.

5. D. W. Stewart and P. M. Shamdasani, *Focus Groups: Theory and Practice* (Newbury Park, CA: Sage, 1990).

# Appendix A

## Our Survey Questions

Below you will find the questions that we include in our surveys, along with the technical details (see Appendix B) that researchers can use to evaluate reliability and validity. Feel free to adapt these questions for your needs. Please do let us know if you use them, as we want to keep track of the samples on which our instrument has been applied.

---

### Cyberbullying and Online Aggression Survey Instrument
*2010 version*
Sameer Hinduja, PhD, and Justin W. Patchin, PhD

#### Cyberbullying Victimization

Cyberbullying is when someone *repeatedly* harasses, mistreats, or makes fun of another person online or while using cell phones or other electronic devices.

Response set for all of the questions below: 0 = Never; 1 = Once; 2 = A few times; 3 = Many times; 4 = Every day

- ☐ I have seen other people being cyberbullied.
- ☐ In my lifetime, I have been cyberbullied.
- ☐ In the last 30 days, I have been cyberbullied.

In the last 30 days, I have been cyberbullied in these ways . . .

- ☐ Someone posted mean or hurtful comments about me online.
- ☐ Someone posted a mean or hurtful picture online of me.
- ☐ Someone posted a mean or hurtful video online of me.
- ☐ Someone created a mean or hurtful web page about me.
- ☐ Someone spread rumors about me online.
- ☐ Someone threatened to hurt me through a cell phone text message.

☐ Someone threatened to hurt me online.

☐ Someone pretended to be me online and acted in a way that was mean or hurtful to me.

In the last 30 days, I have been cyberbullied in these online environments . . .

☐ In a chat room
☐ Through email
☐ Through computer instant messages
☐ Through cell phone text messages
☐ Through cell phone
☐ PictureMail or VideoMail
☐ On MySpace
☐ On Facebook
☐ On a different social networking website (other than MySpace or Facebook)
☐ On Twitter
☐ On YouTube
☐ In virtual worlds such as Second Life, Gaia, or Habbo Hotel
☐ While playing a massive multiplayer online game such as World of Warcraft, Everquest, Guild Wars, or Runescape
☐ While playing online with Xbox, Playstation, Wii, PSP, or similar device

### Cyberbullying Offending

Cyberbullying is when someone *repeatedly* harasses, mistreats, or makes fun of another person online or while using cell phones or other electronic devices.

Response set for all of the questions below: 0 = Never; 1 = Once; 2 = A few times; 3 = Many times; 4 = Every day

☐ In my lifetime, I have cyberbullied others.
☐ In the last 30 days, I have cyberbullied others.

In the last 30 days, I have cyberbullied others in these ways . . .

☐ I posted mean or hurtful comments about someone online.
☐ I posted a mean or hurtful picture online of someone.
☐ I posted a mean or hurtful video online of someone.
☐ I spread rumors about someone online.
☐ I threatened to hurt someone online.
☐ I threatened to hurt someone through a cell phone text message.
☐ I created a mean or hurtful web page about someone.
☐ I pretended to be someone else online and acted in a way that was mean or hurtful to them.

In the last 30 days, I have cyberbullied others in these online environments . . .

☐ In a chat room
☐ Through email
☐ Through computer instant messages
☐ Through cell phone text messages
☐ Through cell phone
☐ PictureMail or VideoMail
☐ On MySpace
☐ On Facebook
☐ On a different social networking website (other than MySpace or Facebook)
☐ On Twitter
☐ On YouTube
☐ In virtual worlds such as Second Life, Gaia, or Habbo Hotel
☐ While playing a massive multiplayer online game such as World of Warcraft, Everquest, Guild Wars, or Runescape
☐ While playing online with Xbox, Playstation, Wii, PSP, or similar device

## Sexting

Sexting is the sending or receiving of sexually explicit or sexually suggestive nude or seminude images or video.

Response set for all of the questions below: 0 = Never; 1 = Once; 2 = A few times; 3 = Many times; 4 = Every day

How often in the last 30 days have you experienced the following while using a computer?

☐ Someone sent you a message using email, Facebook, or some other website asking for a naked or semi-naked picture or video of you.

☐ Someone sent you a naked or semi-naked picture or video of someone else that you know through email, Facebook, or some other website.

How often in the last 30 days have you experienced the following while using a cell phone?

☐ Someone text messaged you and asked questions about sex or said sexual things that made you uncomfortable.

☐ Someone text messaged you asking you to send them a naked or semi-naked picture or video of yourself.

☐ Someone text messaged you with a naked or semi-naked picture or video of someone from your school.

☐ Someone text messaged you with a naked or semi-naked picture or video of someone else that you know (not from your school).

How often in the last 30 days have you done the following on the computer?

☐ Sent someone a naked or semi-naked picture or video of yourself (using email, Facebook, or another website).

☐ Sent someone a naked or semi-naked picture or video of someone else from your school (using email, Facebook, or another website).

☐ Emailed someone asking that person to send you a naked or semi-naked picture or video of him- or herself.

☐ Posted a naked or semi-naked picture or video of someone else that you know online.

☐ Posted a naked or semi-naked picture or video of yourself online.

How often in the last 30 days have you done the following on your cell phone?

☐ Text messaged someone with a naked or semi-naked picture or video of yourself.

☐ Text messaged someone with a naked or semi-naked picture or video of someone from your school.

☐ Text messaged someone with a naked or semi-naked picture or video of someone else that you know (not from your school).

☐ Text messaged someone asking that person to send you a naked or semi-naked picture or video of him- or herself.

☐ Text messaged someone asking that person to send you a naked or semi-naked picture or video they have of someone else.

# *Appendix B*

## *Psychometric Properties for Cyberbullying Scale*

*(Utilized in four different studies (2007–2010) of 12,000 11- to 18-year-old youth over 90 schools. Coefficients represent range across the four studies.)*

**Scale Construction**

*Cyberbullying Victimization Scale*
*Variety scale:* Recode to dichotomy (never = 0; once or twice, a few times, many times, every day = 1); range = 0–9.
*Summary scale:* never = 0; once or twice = 1; a few times = 2; many times = 3; every day = 4. Sum responses with higher values representing more involvement in cyberbullying; range = 0–36.

*Cyberbullying Offending Scale*
*Variety scale:* Recode to dichotomy (never = 0; once or twice, a few times, many times, every day = 1); range = 0–5.
*Summary scale:* never = 0; once or twice = 1; a few times = 2; many times = 3; every day = 4. Sum responses with higher values representing more involvement in cyberbullying; range = 0–20.

**Internal Reliability**

*Cyberbullying Victimization Scale—previous 30 days (Cronbach's alpha range 0.926–0.935)*

- ☐ I have been cyberbullied.
- ☐ Someone posted mean or hurtful comments about me online.
- ☐ Someone posted a mean or hurtful picture online of me online.
- ☐ Someone posted a mean or hurtful video online of me online.
- ☐ Someone created a mean or hurtful web page about me.

☐    Someone spread rumors about me online.
☐    Someone threatened to hurt me through a cell phone text message.
☐    Someone threatened to hurt me online.
☐    Someone pretended to be me online and acted in a way that was mean or hurtful.

*Cyberbullying Offending Scale—previous 30 days (Cronbach's alpha range 0.956–0.969)*

☐    I cyberbullied others.
☐    I posted mean or hurtful comments about someone online.
☐    I posted a mean or hurtful picture online of someone.
☐    I posted a mean or hurtful video online of someone.
☐    I spread rumors about someone online.
☐    I threatened to hurt someone online.
☐    I threatened to hurt someone through a cell phone text message.
☐    I created a mean or hurtful web page about someone.
☐    I pretended to be someone else online and acted in a way that was mean or hurtful to them.

## Factor Analysis

| Cyberbullying Victimization Scale | Loadings |
| --- | --- |
| I have been cyberbullied. | .686–.706 |
| Someone posted mean or hurtful comments about me online. | .770–.804 |
| Someone posted a mean or hurtful picture online of me online. | .880–.861 |
| Someone posted a mean or hurtful video online of me online. | .888–.900 |
| Someone created a mean or hurtful web page about me. | .889–.910 |
| Someone spread rumors about me online. | .771–.789 |
| Someone threatened to hurt me through a cell phone text message. | .808–.855 |
| Someone threatened to hurt me online. | .850–.870 |
| Someone pretended to be me online and acted in a way that was mean or hurtful. | .838–.866 |

All loaded onto 1 component; eigenvalue range 6.07–6.40 (67.53%–71.52% of variance).

| Cyberbullying Offending Scale | Loadings |
| --- | --- |
| I cyberbullied others. | .727–.762 |
| I posted mean or hurtful comments about someone online. | .838–.857 |
| I posted a mean or hurtful picture online of someone. | .940–.949 |

| Cyberbullying Offending Scale | Loadings |
|---|---|
| I posted a mean or hurtful video online of someone. | .941–.949 |
| I spread rumors about someone online. | .890–.916 |
| I threatened to hurt someone online. | .914–.923 |
| I threatened to hurt someone through a cell phone text message. | .910–.924 |
| I created a mean or hurtful web page about someone. | .933–.942 |
| I pretended to be someone else online and acted in a way that was mean or hurtful to them. | .917–.933 |

All loaded onto 1 component; eigenvalue range 7.21–7.34 (80.11%–81.57% of variance).

## Inter-Item Correlations

| Cyberbullying Victimization Scale | 1 | 2 | 3 | 4 | 5 | 6 | 7 | 8 |
|---|---|---|---|---|---|---|---|---|
| 1. I have been cyberbullied | | | | | | | | |
| 2. Someone posted mean or hurtful comments about me online | .43–.57 | | | | | | | |
| 3. Someone posted a mean or hurtful picture online of me online | .36–.57 | .62–.67 | | | | | | |
| 4. Someone posted a mean or hurtful video online of me online | .30–.58 | .56–.67 | .80–.89 | | | | | |
| 5. Someone created a mean or hurtful web page about me | .37–.59 | .59–.62 | .80–.87 | .83–.92 | | | | |
| 6. Someone spread rumors about me online | .35–.51 | .67–.72 | .55–.63 | .53–.62 | .60–.69 | | | |
| 7. Someone threatened to hurt me through a cell phone text message | .37–.54 | .62–.68 | .60–.69 | .60–.72 | .62–.73 | .65–.70 | | |
| 8. Someone threatened to hurt me online | .50–.60 | .64–.70 | .63–.71 | .62–.73 | .67–.75 | .61–.66 | .75–.80 | |
| 9. Someone pretended to be me online and acted in a way that was mean or hurtful | .35–.55 | .62–.64 | .59–.77 | .56–.77 | .60–.78 | .56–.66 | .6.–.70 | .69–.73 |

| *Cyberbullying Victimization Scale* | *1* | *2* | *3* | *4* | *5* | *6* | *7* | *8* |
|---|---|---|---|---|---|---|---|---|
| 1. I cyberbullied others | | | | | | | | |
| 2. I posted mean or hurtful comments about someone online | .52–.68 | | | | | | | |
| 3. I posted a mean or hurtful picture online of someone | .45–.70 | .72–.83 | | | | | | |
| 4. I posted a mean or hurtful video online of someone | .53–.67 | .71–.75 | .90–.94 | | | | | |
| 5. I spread rumors about someone online | .49–.63 | .72–.78 | .82–.83 | .82–.86 | | | | |
| 6. I threatened to hurt someone online | .51–.66 | .67–.78 | .78–.83 | .83–.85 | .80–.84 | | | |
| 7. I threatened to hurt someone through a cell phone text message | .48–.64 | .63–.75 | .79–.84 | .77–.84 | .71–.83 | .82–.88 | | |
| 8. I created a mean or hurtful web page about someone | .51–.66 | .69–.72 | .86–.92 | .88–.94 | .82–.82 | .79–.83 | .84–.85 | |
| 9. I pretended to be someone else online and acted in a way that was mean or hurtful to them | .46–.64 | .65–.74 | .85–.86 | .86–.89 | .79–.85 | .78–.82 | .82–.85 | .88–.89 |

# 9

## *Effective Prevention Requires Effective Response*

*Whenever one of my teachers says, "just ignore them," it annoys me so much. I can't ignore it. It will always be stuck in my mind. Why can't I ever stop thinking about what the bully did? It makes me depressed, angry, sad, and upset when I hear that expression.*

—Fifth-grade student from Ohio[1]

Even though the focus of this book is on *preventing* problematic online behaviors before they start (or get too out of control), responding decisively and effectively to incidents when they do arise is essential to maintain the viability and stability of your positive climate. Failing to respond, or responding in a counterproductive way, sends a message to your students that the policies you have on paper don't really matter. Indeed, students and staff who agree to participate in the school community inherently buy into a "social contract" that must be enforced or it may be considered superficial and meaningless. This chapter will provide a broad overview of considerations to keep in mind when responding to instances of cyberbullying, sexting, or other online issues.

As will become clear, the emphasis should be on informal responses that keep the best interests of the students at the forefront. Harsh or erratic discipline does little to stop further inappropriate behaviors, and much research demonstrates the inability of threats of serious punishment to deter adolescents. Instead, you should think creatively about how to resolve the situation without bestowing additional negative attention on the target.

If you've followed the model outlined in this book, the students in your school should already know that cyberbullying is unacceptable and that the behavior will result in consequences. Once the offending student has been identified, develop a response that is appropriate given the harm done and the disruption experienced. Always take the time to address all misbehaviors, no matter how small you think they are. For instance, you can pull the aggressor aside and explain the hurtfulness of his behaviors, while also providing support and encouragement to the target. For more serious behaviors, you may want to involve your school liaison officer or other member of law enforcement to assist with thoroughly investigating the incident as needed, especially if you believe it to be criminal in nature (e.g., involving stalking, physical threats, sexually explicit pictures or videos of minors). But every effort should be made to address underlying peer conflict issues or online misbehaviors before they get to the point where formal (especially criminal) response is warranted. These small steps are indispensable in creating and maintaining a bully-free atmosphere at your school.

## CAN SCHOOLS RESPOND TO BEHAVIORS THAT OCCUR AWAY FROM CAMPUS?

Though a comprehensive discussion of legal issues is outside the scope of this book, one of the most common questions we get from educators and parents is whether schools can intervene in student behaviors that occur away from school. Before going any farther, we should point out that our perspective is limited to laws and court rulings in the United States and that some of the brightest legal minds in this country often disagree on these issues. As such, it is important to consult with your local attorney before taking any formal actions that may result in long-term consequences to students or staff.

**Prevention Point:** Schools can and should respond to student behaviors that occur away from school if they substantially disrupt the learning environment at school.

The short answer to the question of whether schools can intervene is that they *can* respond to cyberbullying, sexting, or other problematic

online behaviors that originate off-campus *under certain circumstances.*
Courts typically support students' First Amendment and free expression rights, but courts in several cases have upheld the actions of school
administrators in disciplining students for off-campus misbehaviors
involving the Internet, cell phones, or other electronic devices. In these
instances, it is imperative that the school demonstrate that the student's
actions substantially or materially disrupted learning, interfered with
the educational mission or discipline at school, utilized school-owned
technology to harass, or threatened or infringed on the rights of other
students.[2]

In general, school officials can place educationally based restrictions
on student speech as is necessary to *maintain an appropriate school climate.*[3]
These could include detention, suspension, change of placement, or loss
of extracurricular privileges, to name a few. While formal disciplinary
action may be warranted, the best tack to take may very well involve an
informal (but comprehensive) response. As such, schools can implement a
variety of practical strategies to stop problematic online behaviors among
students. Several of these are presented below.

One perennial problem in bullying and cyberbullying response strategies is convincing the targets (or others) to come forward with their experiences. As we discussed in Chapter 7, the majority of those who are bullied
simply do not tell adults about what is going on. That is primarily because
they are concerned that whatever the adult does will do more harm than
good. If we want to encourage more students to come forward with their
problems, we as adults need to do a better job of responding in an effective
manner. Educators need to remember that *the number one goal is to get the
inappropriate behaviors to stop.* This alone is primarily what targets of bullying demand: that the bullying ends. They often don't even want the bully
to get in trouble—they just want their life back. If we can accomplish this
goal, then everything else will fall into place.

If, on the other hand, targets come forward to report cyberbullying
and an administrator simply dismisses the experiences, telling students
to "suck it up" or "just ignore it," the climate at school will suffer. While
readers of this book will no doubt disagree, some adults continue to view
bullying as "a rite of passage" or something that everyone just has to
deal with at some point in their lives. For example, a judge in California
recently ruled against a school that disciplined a student for bullying,
saying that "the court cannot uphold school discipline of student speech
simply because young persons are unpredictable or immature, or because,
in general, teenagers are emotionally fragile and may often fight over hurtful comments."[4] It is this mentality that needs to change. If adults do not
take bullying seriously, students won't either. We know that *you* take it
seriously, which is why you are reading this book. So now that you know
that you can get involved, let's move on to what you can actually do to
*effectively* respond.

# JUST SAY NO TO "ZERO TOLERANCE": UTILIZE INFORMAL RESPONSES WHEN APPROPRIATE

Zero tolerance became very popular in school policy in the 1980s and 1990s in an effort to crack down on drugs and guns.[5] During this time, approximately 90 percent of schools had zero-tolerance policies for alcohol, drugs, and weapons.[6] Commonly, these policies require the automatic suspension (or expulsion) of a student who is found to be in possession of any weapon or any amount of illicit substances at school. Don't get us wrong—these policies are a fine idea *in theory*. Educators want to clearly communicate that they have zero tolerance for drugs or weapons at their school and that violators will be severely punished. The problem is that these policies, by definition, do not allow educators to use their discretion to handle situations outside the letter of the law. Over the years, there has been no shortage of misapplications of zero-tolerance policies:

- A South Carolina high school freshman was expelled in 2007 for bringing a butter knife to school. A spokesperson for the school remarked: "Despite the fact that the student was an exceptional student, this has nothing to do with how good she was in the classroom. She was in possession of a knife."[7]
- A kindergarten student from Nevada was suspended for bringing a nail file to school, which violated the school's recently passed policy prohibiting "items that resemble weapons."[8]
- A nine-year-old from Virginia was suspended for ten days and recommended for expulsion for bringing a plastic toy gun to school.[9] He did not threaten anyone with it and told school officials that he put the gun in his school bag to keep it away from his sisters.
- A 13-year-old eighth-grade student from Virginia was suspended for ten days for being in possession of a knife at school.[10] The student had acquired the knife from a friend who had confided in him that she contemplated suicide. He was able to get the knife from her but didn't immediately inform anyone at school. When an assistant principal found out about the knife at lunchtime, she acknowledged that the student was acting in the other student's best interest but suspended him nonetheless.

> **Prevention Point:** Zero-tolerance policies force you to take a specific action that might not be the best option given the unique circumstances of the particular incident.

Bullying, cyberbullying, sexting, and most other adolescent problems are essentially relationship problems. Every student and every relationship is different, so forcing educators to adopt a standard response to all bullying incidents is, in our view, counterproductive. If there is one thing we have learned, it is that no single response strategy will work with every case. Educators should use their intimate knowledge of the students (and relationships) to handle the incident in the most appropriate way given all of the factors involved. Of course this should be done within the legal and policy framework established by the state and school (e.g., avoiding corporal punishment). Oftentimes skilled counselors or principals can address a bullying incident "under the radar"—stopping the bullying without directing unnecessary attention to the target.

## NATURAL AND LOGICAL CONSEQUENCES

As we all know, there are consequences for every behavior—both positive and negative—and teens need to understand the negative repercussions that go hand in hand with the misuse of technology. In parenting circles, there has been a lot of discussion recently about "natural and logical consequences." A natural consequence is something that naturally or automatically occurs as a result of a behavior (without human intervention). For example, if a child puts his hand on a hot stove, he will get burned. If a student does not study, she will get poor grades. These can be very powerful learning experiences.

However, some natural consequences are so significant that we can't simply allow teens to learn for themselves. For example, a youth who drives drunk may get in an accident and end up killing someone. For these kinds of behaviors, it is better to preempt the *natural* consequence by utilizing a *logical* consequence—one that is directly related to the potential risk involved. We don't want our children to drink and drive, and so if they exhibit risky behaviors associated with alcohol, we might need to take the car away for a while or have them visit car accident victims in the hospital. For maximum effect, the logical consequence should occur as soon as possible after the behavior (since natural consequences are often immediate and the brain then connects them directly to the behavior). It is essential that your students are able to clearly link the problematic behavior to the punishment.

The same approach can be used when disciplining our children for inappropriate online behaviors. If they are making hurtful comments about others on Facebook, force them to take a break from Facebook for a few days. If they are sending nasty or racy text messages, then they should lose their cell phone privileges for a while. Be sure to explain why the behaviors are inappropriate and demonstrate what some of the natural consequences could be (harm to the target, permanently damaged online reputation, etc.).

Just as we wouldn't sentence all minor law violators to capital punishment, there should be a continuum of consequences commensurate with the harm (or potential harm) caused. It doesn't make sense to completely ban all technology for an indefinite period for anything but the most egregious infraction. Adults have to realize that just one weekend without use of a cell phone is like corporal punishment for most teens. Therefore, the consequences should be reasonable and dependent on the circumstances. And be sure to stick with it. If students do not learn from their mistakes and continue the problematic behavior, the consequences may need to be ratcheted up.

---

**What Schools Should Do When Made Aware of a Cyberbullying Incident**

- Assess the immediate threat.
- Ensure the safety of the target.
- Demonstrate compassion and empathy toward the target.
- Restrain the bully if necessary (separate from target; closely monitor).
- Contact parents.
- Investigate and gather evidence.
- Contact the service providers so that offending content can be removed.
- Contact the police when physical threats are involved.
- Enforce disciplinary policy.
- Be creative in your sanctions when possible.

---

## WHEN CAN EDUCATORS SEARCH THE CONTENTS OF STUDENT CELL PHONES?

The second most commonly asked question we receive has to do with whether educators have the authority to search the contents of student cell phones. Here, too, the answer depends on a number of interrelated factors. The key issue in this analysis is the standard of "reasonableness." According to *New Jersey v. T. L. O,* students are protected by the Fourth Amendment, which protects citizens against unreasonable searches and seizures.[11] In *T. L. O.,* the Supreme Court stated that the standard that law enforcement officers must reach to conduct a search (probable cause that a crime has been committed) is not required of educators. Rather, the standard applied to school officials is whether the search is "justified at its inception and reasonable in scope." Of course there is a bit of subjectivity to this standard, and what appears to be reasonable for one person may not be for another. In *T. L. O.,* the Court ruled that for a search of student property to be justified, there must exist "reasonable grounds for believing that the search will turn up evidence that the student has violated or is violating either the law or the rules of the school." This seems to be the standard by which schools should determine whether a search of a student cell phone is permissible.[12]

A couple of recent cases shed some light on how this particular standard can apply to the search of student cell phones. The case most often cited is *Klump v. Nazareth Area School District*.[13] In this case, a teacher confiscated a student's cell phone because it was visible in class, which was in violation of school policy (it accidentally fell out of the student's pocket). The teacher and assistant principal then searched the cell phone's number directory and attempted to call nine other Nazareth students to determine if they too were in violation of the policy. They also accessed text and voice mail messages and communicated with the student's brother without indicating to him that they were school staff.

The court agreed that the school was justified in seizing the phone but stipulated that staff should not have used the phone to "catch other students' violations." In summary, the US district court in *Klump* concluded, "Although the meaning of 'unreasonable searches and seizures' is different in the school context than elsewhere, it is nonetheless evident that there must be some basis for initiating a search. A reasonable person could not believe otherwise."[14]

In another case from November 2010, a Mississippi federal court identified no Fourth Amendment violation when a teacher seized, and administrators reviewed, photos and text messages in a cell phone confiscated from a boy (J. W.) who used it in violation of a schoolwide ban.[15] As discussed above, the seizure was allowed because the school had a policy prohibiting the possession or use of cell phones at school. The issue in this case was the legitimacy of the search of the phone's contents, which included incriminating pictures of the student wearing what appeared to be gang clothing.

The court ruled that the school was justified in searching the cell phone:

> Upon witnessing a student improperly using a cell phone at school, it strikes this court as being reasonable for a school official to seek to determine to what end the student was improperly using that phone. For example, it may well be the case that the student was engaged in some form of cheating, such as by viewing information improperly stored in the cell phone. It is also true that a student using his cell phone at school may reasonably be suspected of communicating with another student who would also be subject to disciplinary action for improper cell phone usage.[16]

Our reading of the available case law in this area leads us to conclude that the Mississippi court got this case wrong. Searching the student's phone will not yield any additional evidence that he is in violation of the school's policy prohibiting possession of the phone at school. Seeing the phone at school already sufficiently established that point. The court argues that "a student's decision to violate school rules by bringing contraband on campus and using that contraband within view of teachers appropriately results in a diminished privacy expectation in that contraband."[17] The court in *Klump* did not follow this reasoning as the court sided with the student. And while the Supreme Court established a different search and seizure standard for educators in *New Jersey v. T. L. O.*, it did not suggest that any policy violation whatsoever negated the expectation of privacy a student previously held.[18]

The Mississippi court did attempt to distinguish the facts of *J. W.* from *Klump* by saying that J. W. *intentionally* violated school policy whereas Klump *accidentally* violated the policy. The court in *J. W.* seems to suggest that if a student chooses to deliberately violate a school policy, that student should also be willing to shed any other constitutional protections with respect to the contraband. We're unconvinced that this should be a relevant factor.

In short, at both ends of the continuum of circumstances, the law is fairly clear: if a reputable student advises a staff member that another student has the answers to the math exam on his mobile device, this would almost certainly allow for a limited search by an administrator. At the other extreme, conducting a search of a cell phone that was confiscated because it was ringing in a student's backpack would likely not be allowed. Of course, there is quite a bit of gray area in between.

With all of this said, schools would be wise to include a specific statement in their policies that regulate student-owned devices brought to school. The policy should advise everyone that students who bring their own devices on campus are subject to a "reasonable search" if suspicion arises that the device contains evidence of a violation of school policy or the law. Students, staff, parents, and law enforcement officers working in the schools need to be aware of this policy so that no one is surprised if and when certain actions are taken.

## SPECIAL CONSIDERATIONS WHEN RESPONDING TO SEXTING INCIDENTS

Teen sexting can be a complicated issue for adults to address. As a result, many find themselves ill-equipped and confused about how to respond. It is important that any adult who is made aware of sexually explicit or suggestive nude or seminude images of minors acts quickly to limit the extent of harm that may result. If a teacher is made aware of a sexting incident, she should inform her supervisor immediately and avoid discussing the incident with other teachers. Administrators should work with their school liaison officers or other law enforcement partners to collect any evidence and investigate the incident to determine its nature and extent. We want to make very clear that administrators and educators should avoid forwarding, copying, transmitting, downloading, placing on a USB thumb drive, or showing any non–law enforcement personnel any evidence collected from a cell phone, computer, or other electronic device after the initial discovery of sexual content or at any other time during the investigation. This could lead to felony criminal child pornography charges against the educator, even if the action was taken in the best interests of the student(s) involved.[19] To avoid legal liability in instances of sexting, it is highly recommended that school administrators only confiscate the device and let law enforcement search its contents.

It is important to identify all of the students involved and to contact their parents. With regard to the child who is featured in the pictures, the situation must be addressed in a delicate manner since emotional and psychological harm most likely has occurred (especially if the incident has come to the school's attention). The student (and perhaps even the parents) should be encouraged to meet (separately or together) with a counselor or another mental health professional to deal with the trauma and stress of the incident.

---

**Prevention Point:** Take extreme care when dealing with sexually explicit images of minors. Avoid unnecessarily showing other staff these images.

---

When dealing with student(s) who disseminated the image(s), contacting parents is mandated in some school districts prior to the onset of an investigation. Then, it is critical to identify the motivations behind the behavior. For some students, the picture or video was sent without forethought and betrays an immature developmental level and belief that such a practice is harmless, normative adolescent behavior or somehow necessary to gain attention and validation from another student (or peer group). For others, the images were distributed in order to intentionally humiliate or otherwise inflict harm on another person—and can be considered cyberbullying, sexual harassment, blackmail, extortion, stalking, or the dissemination of child pornography.[20] Informing parents may motivate them to speak with and discipline their child in the way they see fit. It should also induce them to pay closer attention to what their child is doing with his cell phone and may lead to restrictions placed on texting, picture messaging, Web access, or other online connectivity. Parents who are informed can then continue to educate their children about the consequences of such behavior.

One of the most critical tasks to tackle when addressing sexting is to minimize the distribution of the problematic images. After checking the call and text logs, law enforcement can inform school administrators as to who else may have sent or received the images. This should prompt one-on-one meetings with those students to determine the extent of image dissemination. Confidentiality should be promised, and warnings (or discipline) should be given when necessary to deter further broadcast of these pictures (and use of cell phones on campus, if prohibited by school policy). In addition, efforts must be made to keep the incident from being covered by the local news. Such attention only increases the notoriety of the target and problem behavior and often leads to further embarrassment, emotional harm, and victimization.

After all evidence is collected, educators should work with law enforcement and parents to determine the most appropriate response per school policy and existing law. As discussed above, every sexting incident is different and therefore should be handled in a way that ensures the safety of all students involved and that also encourages students to refrain from inappropriate behaviors in the future. Educators also want to do what they can to control the sensationalism of what happened to ensure that it is not glamorized but disdained, and strongly deter anyone else who might do it in the future.

---

**What Schools Should Do When Made Aware of a Sexting Incident**

- Identify the target and provide emotional support.
- Identify the students involved and immediately determine the extent of distribution.
- Minimize further dissemination by speaking with all who possess the image(s) or video(s).
- Contact service providers to remove content if it is online and publicly accessible.
- Contain the incident and resultant fallout to prevent media attention from further victimizing the target.
- Discipline the students involved and other direct aggressors as appropriate.
- Counsel indirect participants (possessors).
- Contact parents of both the target and bully.
- Contact police to collect evidence.
- Investigate the back story to determine if sexting was experimental or aggravated (see Chapter 4 for distinction).
- Assess whether threats, blackmail, extortion, or other misbehaviors followed the sexting incident.

---

## POLICY ISSUES

Some school districts do not yet have formal policies concerning electronic devices at school. This is unfortunate because experience shows us that when formal policies and procedures don't keep pace with the rapid changes in technology and its use, school administrators struggle to capably address wrongful behavior. Some schools have attempted to prevent inappropriate technology use at school by simply prohibiting students from bringing their devices to school. Short of strip searching students as they come through the front door, it is practically impossible to enforce a complete ban like this. Most administrators have largely conceded this point and therefore have enacted policies that say something to the effect of "If I see it, you lose it." A colleague of ours recently quipped that schools should approach cell phones the same way they do underwear: "We know you have them—we just don't want to see them in class." To be sure, this book discusses many of the challenges facing educators when it comes to teens and technology. But remember, the first chapter of this book detailed many examples of positive ways teens can use technology, both inside and outside of the classroom. With that in mind, increasing numbers of schools are loosening their overly restrictive cell phone policies. This is certainly a positive development, in our view, that if done appropriately can benefit both students and teachers alike.

While we clearly need to recognize the potential problems that may accompany the positives when students "bring their own devices" to school, it is important to stress again, as we did in Chapter 1, that the problem isn't cell phones or other particular devices. The problem is how these devices are being (mis)used by some. Most schools already have a bullying/harassment policy. These documents should be reviewed to make sure they explicitly cover cyberbullying. Students, staff, parents, and others need to understand that inappropriate behaviors will not be tolerated and are subject to discipline. And be specific: talk about harassment and cheating and disrupting the class environment by texting or Facebooking, and talk about threats and explicit pictures and pornography laws and police intervention. Clearly outline the consequences for prohibited behaviors. Get students and parents in on this discussion. Schools will have problems as the school community gets used to these changes, but hopefully the problems will be few and far between and will get better with time. Students will learn appropriate behaviors and these should—in time—become the norm if a positive school climate is prioritized and established. For example, ten years ago, cell phones were much more of a problem in our college classrooms than they are now. University students, at least in our experience as professors, have gotten better at cell phone etiquette and are not letting the devices distract from learning. Sure, a phone occasionally will go off in class, but usually the student is apologetic and immediately acknowledges the faux pas. Of course middle and high school students are different from those in a university, but we are optimistic that we can work through the same challenges at the secondary school level.

After a policy is created or revised, the school community needs to be educated about it. Students should be informed about the circumstances under which their personal portable electronic devices can be confiscated and searched. They should also be reminded that anything they do on a school-owned device is subject to review and appropriate discipline. This should be explained to students and parents, possibly through assemblies, community meetings, and messaging strategies (voice mails, memorandums, etc.). In addition, schools may hold an inservice workshop for others in the school community—including school board members, the superintendent, key administrators, local law enforcement, and school district attorneys—to educate and then discuss different scenarios that might arise and warrant formal response.

> *I think it's a good idea that all schools include in their handbook definitions of the types of bullying and sexting as well as the consequences and/or disciplinary actions, but then perhaps kids should be quizzed on this every school year. Call me an airhead, but I never read the school's student handbook until my family moved to Florida my junior year of high school. I remember I got in trouble the first day of school because I clearly did not read the dress code part of the student handbook. My old school handed out agendas and handbooks at the beginning of the school year, but no one ever read them. Those things would just get stuffed at the bottom of our lockers. If all schools enforced something as simple as reading the student handbook and made sure students understand what they're reading, then I think they would be a step closer to educating kids that they can get help if they're being bullied.*
>
> —anonymous student from Florida

### Cyberbullying

We believe cyberbullying should be an explicit element of the school's harassment, intimidation, and bullying policies. It shouldn't be assumed that "bullying is bullying" no matter how it is carried out. While the behaviors can be similar, it is important, even if only symbolically, to clearly denote cyberbullying as a subset of bullying that is subject to school regulation. Currently at least 48 states have laws that require schools to have a bullying policy.[21] Thirty-eight of those include specific language related to electronic forms of harassment.

The procedures for investigating and responding to cyberbullying might not vary significantly from the way schools have always handled peer harassment issues. It is a matter of getting to the bottom of what happened, why it happened, and what needs to be done to make sure that it doesn't happen again. From a policy standpoint, the only significant update will be the provision that even those behaviors that occur away from school (i.e., online) are potentially subject to discipline (as outlined above). Even though court rulings in the United States have permitted schools to discipline students for their off-campus behaviors for decades, this issue was significantly amplified when technology became widely available. The challenge is to develop a policy that is comprehensive and unambiguous, yet flexible enough to allow for changing manifestations of harassment (such as those involving new sites and devices). It is also crucial that the policy adequately serves your needs. You can test it by searching the news for cyberbullying headlines and attempting to apply your policy to those behaviors if they occurred at your school. Does your policy sufficiently guide your procedures and specify appropriate disciplinary actions?

---

### Elements of a School Cyberbullying Policy

- Specifically define *cyberbullying* as a form of bullying that uses computers, cell phones, or other electronic devices to harass, humiliate, threaten, or otherwise harm a student. (The policy can include reference to school staff, but the term *bullying* is generally reserved for behaviors as they occur among school-aged youth.)
- Outline procedures for investigating cyberbullying incidents. Who should receive reports, and how should they be processed?
- Include language that all instances of cyberbullying will be subject to reasonable discipline, even those that occur away from school or at a school-sponsored event, if such behaviors substantially and materially disrupt the learning environment at school or interfere with the ability of other students to learn or feel safe at school.
- Detail procedures for preventing cyberbullying. How will students and staff learn about cyberbullying and the penalties for policy violation?
- List out graduated consequences and remedial actions. Include a range of disciplinary responses and note that the response will be commensurate with the potential or actual harm or disruption caused.

NOTE: *Remember that we are not attorneys, and educators should always consult with their legal counsel when developing or revising policies.*

---

## Sexting

It is similarly critical that schools have policies and procedures in place that define what sexting is, how it will be investigated, who will be involved, and what will happen to those who participate (including the person being depicted in, the person who receives, and the person who distributes the images). Just as with cyberbullying, zero-tolerance approaches to sexting are generally unwise given the varying nature of sexting incidents, which may involve many aggravating or mitigating factors. Sometimes only those involved know about it, and sometimes the entire school has seen, distributed, and commented on the pictures. Sometimes there are no visible consequences, and sometimes it leads to physical bullying and violence. Sometimes it involves a spontaneous mistake, and sometimes it involves well-planned, deceitful exploitation and even profit making. Policies need to be written in a way that allows educators to use their professional judgment and knowledge of the relationships of the students involved to handle the situation in the most appropriate way, keeping in mind the best interests of the youth.

In order for schools to act in accordance with state law, the administration should take note of and acknowledge students' rights (e.g., right to privacy and freedom of speech) and ensure that response action plans do not overstep those personal rights. School administrators will have to clearly identify how the current policies handle the possibility of sexting and the various associated issues—the possession and/or use of cell phones, search and seizure issues, disciplinary options, child pornography statutes, and so forth. Once this review is complete, the school board will need to revise the policies with insight from educational technology personnel, law enforcement, and legal counsel to cover all necessary groundwork and comply with the law and the students' civil protections.

---

### Elements of a School Sexting Policy

- Specifically define that *sexting* primarily involves the sending and receiving of sexually explicit or suggestive naked or semi-naked photos or videos via cell phone.
- Highlight that such images and videos of students often constitute child pornography and that creating them, possessing them, or transmitting them is a serious offense potentially subject to criminal prosecution. Students who send a sexually suggestive naked or semi-naked picture of themselves to others are subject to formal punishment. In addition, students who disseminate sexually suggestive naked or semi-naked images of other students are also subject to formal punishment. Finally, students who receive a sexually suggestive naked or semi-naked image of another student need to report the incident to a counselor or principal immediately.
- Detail who will be involved in the investigation and response (e.g., administrators, law enforcement, school counselor, psychologist, nurse, the parents of all students involved). Be clear about the responsibilities of each person. Remember that teachers who unnecessarily show other teachers sexting images could be prosecuted for distributing child pornography.
- State that in many cases, the contents of student cell phones can be searched by administrators if they have reasonable suspicion that a student has been involved in the behavior or in any other suspected school policy violation directly related to the use or contents of the device.
- Articulate a range of disciplinary responses that will result for those who engage in sexting. The punishment should be commensurate with the behavior. Were the images voluntarily distributed, or was coercion involved? Were images distributed without knowledge of the person pictured?
- Assert increased penalties for any bullying, blackmail, extortion, or threats that stem from, or are related to, sexting incidents.
- Include a clause that provides discretion to administrators and school law enforcement who deal with these cases, especially since sexting appears to occur along a continuum ranging from "stupid teen behavior," to problematic girlfriend/boyfriend relationships, to intentional exploitation, to intentional self-exploitation (youth who brazenly and willingly flaunt and advertise themselves online in a sexual manner).

*NOTE: Remember that we are not attorneys, and educators should always consult with their legal counsel when developing or revising policies.*

# WHEN TO GET LAW ENFORCEMENT INVOLVED

Law enforcement officers, especially those assigned to a school, do have a role in preventing and responding to cyberbullying, sexting, and other online misbehaviors. They need to be aware of ever-evolving state and local laws related to technology abuse and equip themselves with the skills and knowledge to intervene as necessary. In a recent survey of school resource officers, we found that almost one-quarter did not know if their state had a cyberbullying law.[22] This is surprising since their most visible responsibility involves responding to actions that are in violation of law (e.g., harassment, threats, stalking). Even if the behavior doesn't immediately appear to rise to the level of a crime, officers should use their discretion to handle the situation in a way that is appropriate for the circumstances. For example, a simple discussion of the legal issues involved in cyberbullying or sexting may be enough to deter some youth from future misbehavior. Officers might also talk to parents about their child's misconduct and express to them the seriousness of these behaviors.

> **Prevention Point:** Involve local law enforcement officers in educating your students about the legal issues associated with cyberbullying and sexting.

In addition, officers can play an essential role in preventing cyberbullying from occurring or getting out of hand in the first place. They can speak to students in classrooms about cyberbullying and online safety issues more broadly in an attempt to discourage them from engaging in risky or unacceptable actions and interactions. They might also speak to parents so that they are informed and can properly respond if their child is involved in an incident. Officers who take on this instructive role should first educate themselves about cyberbullying and sexting and the most effective ways to discuss these issues with teens. Threatening students with harsh punishment or coming across with a fear-based message, for example, is unlikely to work—and will likely lead to youth rebelling and doing what we don't want them to do. Law enforcement officers who demonstrate their knowledge about, and appreciation for, the devices and sites teens are using will make great headway in conveying important safety and responsibility strategies. It is critical that police officers, or any adult who works with students, develop a rapport so that teens feel comfortable coming to them when they encounter a problem. That will hopefully create many more opportunities for adults to stay informed and to intervene before the situation gets out of hand.

## EDUCATE STUDENTS ABOUT THE CONSEQUENCES BEFORE THE BEHAVIOR

Quite often when you investigate a cyberbullying or sexting incident, you will come to learn that the "offending" parties didn't fully understand the consequences of their actions or how what they did could have ever resulted in the problems that were created. As such, an educational response may be the best option. For example, you could have the student write a paper on the effects of harassment or provide her with a video camera and help her create a public service announcement about cyberbullying that can be used to educate the rest of the student body. Of course, you want to be careful not to bring undue negative attention to the students involved in the incident. For example, requiring students who were involved in a sexting incident to create a schoolwide program about the topic might not be the best option (although it could be done anonymously). Once again, your knowledge of the incident, the students involved, and the extent of awareness by the broader school population will help you to determine the best course of action.

Even though the vast majority of these incidents can and should be handled informally (e.g., by calling parents, counseling the bully and target, or expressing condemnation of the behavior), there may be occasions when a formal response from the school is warranted. This is particularly the case in incidents involving serious threats toward another student, if the target no longer feels safe coming to school, or if cyberbullying behaviors continue after informal attempts to stop it have failed. In these cases, detention, suspension, changes of placement, or even expulsion may be necessary. If these extreme measures are warranted, it is important that you clearly demonstrate the negative effect of the incident on the school or student(s) and present evidence that substantiates your disciplinary action.

---

**One School's Response to Social Networking Drama**

A rumor started circulating around one of the high schools that three senior girls were caught shoplifting from a local Wal-Mart. Interest in this incident grew because the alleged items stolen happened to be female undergarments. One of the boys in the girls' social circle began a Facebook posting stating that the girls were charged with a felony. Fourteen additional students then participated in a barrage of comments, which started off humorous but turned to "roasting" and eventually serious "trash-talking." The banter continued into the next week, and the postings continued with cruel, rude, nasty, and inappropriate comments. Finally, one of the 14 participants called to inform the girls of the postings. The girls were

*(Continued)*

(Continued)

humiliated and very embarrassed. This quickly escalated into anger, with threats being made both online and at school. The incident spread rapidly throughout the school, with many threatening text messages being sent back and forth between students. It was reported that a fight was going to break out. The administration then initiated an investigation, which involved the analysis of 6,400 comments on Facebook.

All students involved were suspended for the next day (Friday) in an effort to de-escalate the incident. Parents were notified, and it took a roundtable of administrators two days to sort through all the evidence. After everything was examined, parents were required to attend a formal meeting with their child. The principal, assistant principal, area superintendent, Safe Schools Team, and local detective attended. Each parent sat next to his or her child as a document camera scrolled down, highlighting the evolution of Facebook comments. The parents' disposition quickly changed from anger at the school district to tears of disappointment as they realized the extent of their child's participation. Some of the students seemed embarrassed in front of their parents, which was one of the outcomes we hoped to attain. Each school official had a message for the students. Then the students were escorted into the cafeteria while the principal, assistant principal, area superintendent, Safe Schools Team, and local detective met with parents. As a formal disciplinary measure, senior privileges were taken away due to the nature of the postings and the substantial disruption caused to the school environment, as well as the number of hours needed to prepare evidence. As a result of this session, students then attended a mandatory education session conducted by the district's Department of Safe Schools. After completing this session, students were allowed to walk for graduation.

The consequences were issued individually and confidentially to those students and parents involved. Thus it is difficult to determine if this specific response had an effect on the overall school climate. In order to prevent similar serious incidents from occurring, district officials crafted a bulletin asking principals to routinely reiterate messages about the proper use of technology with staff and students. This bulletin provided resources about the legal and ethical use of technology both in and out of school. Principals were also given scripts to remind students about the prohibition against cyberbullying and stalking and to skillfully address the issue of "sexting" with students in Grades 4–12, as well as in earlier grades if the need arose.

—educator from a school in the southern United States

## A CALL FOR EDUCATION AND OUTREACH

Based on our experience working with youth, and having been teenagers ourselves, we don't believe that formal law and policy is the "magic bullet"—because adolescents tend not to be deterred by rules and laws. Honestly, many adults are not deterred by rules and laws, either. This, though, does not mean that schools should not develop well-informed policies that include the elements described above. Policies are a necessary, but not sufficient, component of a comprehensive prevention and response plan. We don't want the presence of law and policy to take the place of purposed educational efforts to teach teens about the responsible use of technology. This sometimes happens when laws or policies are enacted as a way of quickly "dealing" with an issue without a thorough understanding of its fundamental causes.

Rather, schools must implement creative educational strategies to raise awareness among students about the consequences of online harassment or the shortsightedness and foolishness of sexting. Districts may partner with other community organizations or public offices to provide staff trainings on bullying, cyberbullying, sexting, and social networking safety. This can include in-school assemblies for students, professional development for staff, training for school board members, distribution of school rules and policies through student handbooks, newsletters/correspondence to the community, meetings with parent groups, and resources on the school web page and public forum. Any educational efforts around the issues of teen technology misuse should be aimed at the whole community when possible.[23]

Additionally, information and resources can be shared through take-home memorandums, student handbooks, newsletters/correspondence to the community, letters to the editor in local newspapers, town hall meetings, and automated phone calls to the families of students. Finally, the Web can be exploited via a Facebook Fan Page, a Twitter feed, or a page on the school website that covers cyberbullying and sexting identification, prevention, and response while detailing legal and policy issues relevant to students and parents—and that reminds them of the appropriate, ethical, and lawful use of technology. Parents in particular need to be instructed on the importance of paying strict attention to what their child is doing with technology. This may involve setting limits on texting, picture and video messaging, and web access. Cumulatively, these educational efforts seem absolutely essential in order to change prevailing mentalities among youth regarding what behaviors are acceptable and unacceptable.

## SUMMARY

As students communicate via various electronic devices, mistakes will be made—either intentionally or inadvertently. Cyberbullying and sexting, when it occurs, clearly leads to a variety of emotional, psychological, relational, physical, and behavioral issues that we want to try to prevent at all costs, especially since adolescence is hard enough to survive without all of these extra problems. While some responsibility to oversee and intervene must be shouldered by parents, other adults in supervisory roles are not exempt from doing their part. The blurring of boundaries and distinctions between online and offline interaction among an adolescent population underscores the need for educators and other youth-serving adults to pay attention to both venues with equal attention.

When you need to respond to online transgressions that affect your students and staff, we hope that this chapter has shown you what to do. More importantly, we hope that this book has shown you how building and sustaining a positive school climate can reduce the frequency with which you will have to respond. In these pages, we have covered a lot of material in as efficient a manner as possible, and we encourage you to give our suggested strategies a shot. They are working in schools across the nation, and we believe they can work in yours as well, no matter how unique your situation may seem. Climate is a fundamental issue. If you take care of the fundamentals, the rest should fall into place.

While you do your part, we invite you to keep in touch with us. We are completely committed and impassioned to help you create and maintain a positive school climate. Let us know (hinduja@cyberbullying.us or patchin@cyberbullying.us) if there is anything we can assist you with, and be sure to take advantage of the numerous free resources and constantly updated information available at our book site (www.schoolclimate20.com) and the Cyberbullying Research Center (www.cyberbullying.us). There, we will continue to share best practices, new climate initiatives, and so much more. This book has only begun the conversation, and it has hopefully stirred you to action. Now let's get back to work to make a meaningful difference—and be encouraged to know that we are doing it together!

## DISCUSSION QUESTIONS

1. How can schools react to online behaviors that do not originate or occur on school property? What must be considered when formally addressing to these behaviors?

2. Why are zero-tolerance policies sometimes problematic? What are the benefits of having discretion in situations involving bullying? What are the drawbacks?

3. What is a natural consequence versus a logical consequence when it comes to disciplining students? In what ways can both be used?

4. What steps should you take within your school when a cyberbullying incident comes to your attention?

5. What steps should you take within your school when a sexting incident comes to your attention?

6. What are the most important things to remember when searching student cell phones? What are the guidelines for doing this? What is your school's policy on searching cell phones?

## REFERENCES

1. S. Curtis, "Stop It! That's Not Nice!" *Educational Leadership* 68, no. 9 (2011), http://www.ascd.org/publications/educational-leadership/summer11/vol68/num09/Stop-It!-That%27s-Not-Nice!.aspx

2. S. Hinduja and J. W. Patchin, "Cyberbullying: A Review of the Legal Issues Facing Educators," *Preventing School Failure* 55, no. 2 (2010): 1–8.

3. S. Hinduja and J. W. Patchin, *Bullying Beyond the Schoolyard: Preventing and Responding to Cyberbullying* (Thousand Oaks, CA: Corwin, 2009).

4. *J. C. v. Beverly Hills Unified School District* (2010 WL 1914215 (C.D. Cal. 2010)).

5. R. Skiba and R. Patterson, "The Dark Side of Zero Tolerance: Can Punishment Lead to Safe Schools?" *Phi Delta Kappan* (January 1999), http://cranepsych.edublogs.org/files/2009/07/dark_zero_tolerance.pdf

6. D. Cauchon, "Zero-Tolerance Policies Lack Flexibility," *USA Today*, April 13, 1999, http://www.usatoday.com/educate/ednews3.htm

7. C. Francescani, "Expelled for Possession of a Butter Knife," *Cuomo on the Case*, ABC News, October 22, 2007, http://abcnews.go.com/TheLaw/story?id=3758286

8. "Kindergartner Suspended for Carrying a Nail File," *Deseret News*, February 2, 1997, http://www.deseretnews.com/article/541037/KINDERGARTNER-SUSPENDED-FOR-CARRYING-A-NAIL-FILE.html

9. D. Nakamura and J. Mathews, "School Gets Tough on Boy, His Toy Gun: 10-Day Suspension in Virginia Outrages 9-Year-Old's Parents," *Washington Post*, reprinted by the *San Francisco Chronicle (SFGate)*, October 14, 1998. http://www.sfgate.com/cgi-bin/article.cgi?f=/c/a/1998/10/14/MN105997.DTL

10. *Ratner v. Loudoun County Public Schools* (4th Cir 2001), http://pacer.ca4.uscourts.gov/opinion.pdf/002157.U.pdf

11. *New Jersey v. T. L. O.* (469 U.S. 325 (1985)), http://www.law.cornell.edu/supct/html/historics/USSC_CR_0469_0325_ZS.html

12. Hinduja and Patchin, "Cyberbullying: A Review of the Legal Issues."

13. *Klump v. Nazareth Area School District* (425 F. Supp. 2d 622 (E.D. Pa. 2006)), http://www.paed.uscourts.gov/documents/opinions/06d0400p.pdf

14. *Klump v. Nazareth Area School District.*

15. *J. W. v. Desoto County School District* (09-cv-00155-MPM-DAS (N.D. Miss.; Nov. 1, 2010)).

16. T.-Y. Oei, "My Students. My Cellphone. My Ordeal," *The Washington Post,* April 19, 2009, http://www.washingtonpost.com/wp-dyn/content/article/2009/04/17/AR2009041702663.html

17. *J. W. v. Desoto County School District.*

18. *New Jersey v. T. L. O.*

19. Oei, "My Students. My Cellphone. My Ordeal."

20. *Russell v. State* (74 S.W.3d 887 (Tex. Ct. App. 2002)).

21. S. Hinduja and J. W. Patchin, "Bullying and Cyberbullying Laws," February 2012, http://www.cyberbullying.us/Bullying_and_Cyberbullying_Laws.pdf

22. S. Hinduja and J. W. Patchin, "School Law Enforcement and Cyberbullying," in *Cyberbullying Prevention and Response: Expert Perspectives,* ed. J. W. Patchin and S. Hinduja (New York: Routledge, 2012).

23. K. McGrory, "Sexting 101: Miami-Dade Schools May Be First to Teach Danger," *Miami Herald,* reprinted at *Women's Care Center Education Division* [blog], July 30, 2009, http://wc2ed.blogspot.com/2009/07/sexting-101-miami-dade-schools-may-be.html

# *Index*

# CORWIN

A SAGE Company

The Corwin logo—a raven striding across an open book—represents the union of courage and learning. Corwin is committed to improving education for all learners by publishing books and other professional development resources for those serving the field of PreK–12 education. By providing practical, hands-on materials, Corwin continues to carry out the promise of its motto: **"Helping Educators Do Their Work Better."**